The Truth About Drugs

Dr Patrick Dixon

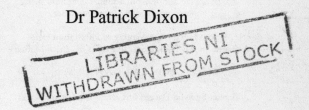

Hodder & Stoughton

LONDON   SYDNEY   AUCKLAND

British Library Cataloguing in Publication Data
A record for this book is available from the British Library

ISBN 0 340 66505 X

Typeset by Avon Dataset Ltd, Bidford-on-Avon, Warks

Printed and bound in Great Britain by
Clays Ltd, St Ives plc

Hodder and Stoughton Ltd
A Division of Hodder Headline PLC
338 Euston Road
London NW1 3BH

Contents

Acknowledgments

I am deeply grateful to David Partington at Yeldall Manor for help in locating sources and for other assistance. I am also indebted to all those staff and volunteers, far too numerous to mention, who over the last ten years have cared for those with drug-related health problems through the AIDS agency ACET (AIDS Care Education and Training). Your practical compassion in London, Dundee, Edinburgh, Glasgow, Dublin, as well as in nations such as Thailand, has been a profound inspiration to me as well as providing a great sense of urgency to do all we can to help prevent future tragedies caused by drug use. Thanks particularly to Peter Dorna and Gary Caruthers for comments and suggestions.

I am also very thankful to hundreds of others who at various times have shared with me what it has been like for them to be caught up in drug dependency, or to care for those affected directly or indirectly. Thanks are also due to Shirley Bray for help in research, proof-reading, indexing and organisation.

http://www.globalchange.com
patrickdixon@globalchange.com

Definitions

- Addiction – physical or psychological need to take a drug (same as dependency)
- Addict – someone with an addiction
- Dependency – physical or psychological need to take a drug (same as addiction)
- Substance abuse – taking drugs illegally or without medical supervision, or, in the case of alcohol, consuming enough to risk physical or mental health
- Drug user – someone who takes drug illegally or without medical supervision
- Drug injector – someone injecting a drug
- Drug – substance taken by the user for no medical purpose, in order to experience psychological or physical effects
- Psychoactive – altering the mental state of the user

Introduction

Jerry was a heroin injector in Edinburgh for a number of years. He used to sell vegetables in the market, until his life began to fall to pieces. After that he existed on benefits, with help from friends and whatever he could make from selling small quantities of cannabis, temazepam, heroin and anything else he could get.

Jerry hit a very bad patch, ran out of money and was too ill to steal. He was so desperate to get help that he overcame his fears of being identified and went to the local clinic to register as an addict. That meant he could turn up once a day for methadone.

The clinic used to hand him enough for a day but he was always trading it on the streets for the real thing. So they told him to drink it right there while they watched. Methadone lasts longer than heroin, but Jerry always craved the comfort that only the needle would bring.

A fellow addict called Dave came to see him, broke, in a terrible state, begging for help, anything, but refusing to go to the clinic, suspicious and hostile to anyone representing authority. His paranoia had got worse since taking a cocktail of other drugs. He could not and would not go. So Jerry made a decision. He went down to the clinic, got his methadone, swallowed it and left. Once outside he made himself vomit into a bag, and gave the vomit to Dave to drink. That is the power of addiction.

ADDICTION IS A SIGNIFICANT THREAT TO CIVILISATION

There has never been a time in human history when so many lives have been taken over by drugs. The scale of the problem is so vast that it almost defies human understanding.

Illegal drug trafficking is already *8 per cent of all international trade*, and has the power to wreck governments and economies as well as millions of individual lives. This is no ordinary social problem. Drug spending on this scale means that the illegal drugs industry is now larger than the entire global trade in cars, textiles, or steel.

Tens of billions of dollars a year are being spent by people whose lives are out of control, completely dominated by the daily compulsion to take another dose. Money wasted on drugs means less money spent on things such as health, education, or other activities. Drug taking has a direct, measurable impact on consumer spending – how else can it possibly account for nearly a tenth of all global trade? It affects everything in our society from homelessness, to divorce, mental illness, absenteeism, domestic violence, safety on the roads, school performance and crime rates.

And then there are the casualties, and deaths.

As a result of all this, the first decades of the third millennium will be increasingly dominated by an aggressive war against all kinds of drug misuse, including tobacco and alcohol. At the same time there will be calls for legalisation from those who say the war is lost.

I began this book largely convinced that cannabis laws should be relaxed, and that other drugs laws also needed softening. I have been forced to a very different view by new published research, and after seeing more of the brutal reality of addiction in places as varied as north-east India and Scotland.

We stand at the dawn of a new age, whose fashions, standards, consciousness and cultural norms will be very different from our own. The lesson of history is that the pendulum always swings – but which way will it swing on drug use? Will we see a new world order where mind-altering drugs are widely accepted and encouraged – or a new draconian Puritanism? The answer is that we will see both, depending on where we look.

Company managers, school teachers, factory workers, public service employees, doctors, nurses, other health care workers, parents, passengers, drivers, pedestrians, cyclists, police officers, judiciary, armed forces – all are now affected by the addictions of those they work with, whether they realise it or not.

MARKET FORCES WILL DRIVE ANTI-DRUGS MOVEMENT

Human misery and wretchedness alone will not be enough to cause a major change, but economic pressures will. Drug abuse is hitting productivity and profits. Market forces will provide the most powerful anti-drugs drive over the next twenty years, at a time when many communities are feeling more relaxed about the morality of drug use. Companies and communities which root out addiction will win orders and jobs from those that take no action. The process has already begun. Market forces will bring changes no government could ever achieve.

Today the drive to take drugs is out of control. As we will see, drug use among teenagers is sky-rocketing in many countries, despite huge health campaigns. Even smoking is becoming more widespread in the young of wealthy nations, after earlier falls in consumption. For millions of people, perhaps the majority in some countries, addiction is a part of every-day life. Those in emerging economies are spending their new wealth on tobacco, alcohol and other drugs.

USE NOT THE SAME AS ADDICTION

Of course, use is not the same as addiction, but use always precedes addiction. Use does not mean that a person is going to have health problems. Some drugs can have beneficial effects, for example, alcohol has a protective effect on the heart in small regular doses. But the same drugs can kill.

Drug users, addicts, pushers, alcoholics – all these words create images but the reality is often far removed from the stereotype. For example, you cannot tell just by looking who in your office, street, school or hospital ward is using heroin – or selling it. Even if the person is 'under the influence' it can be very hard for the inexperienced to tell exactly what is going on.

Many cocaine or heroin users are currently holding down executive posts in the City. A trained observer might notice the tell-tale line of old injection marks on a favourite vein of a colleague after a game of tennis, or the unmistakable pinpoint pupils of someone using opiates, but those might be the only outward signs.

'Once an addict, always an addict' is worse than a dangerous myth, it's a curse. And it's not even true. The fact is that most people who take potentially addictive illegal drugs are not taking them twenty years later, nor have they died of their addiction. As we will see, success rates are impressive in residential treatment programmes. They may be long and expensive but they work. However, while there are ways out of addiction, help is often hard to find and even harder to take.

Every government in the world is faced with the same issues: how to contain the drugs problem without wiping out other budgets in the process.

In Britain a new White Paper was launched in mid-1998 with new proposals which included:

- Better international co-operation
- More research
- Greater efforts to track down and destroy trafficking
- More face-to-face prevention in schools
- More seizures of profits from drug taking
- Better treatment facilities
- Switch of budget from treatment to prevention

INTRODUCTION

However, these proposals fall far short of what is urgently needed. A little more effort here and there will never deal with the roots of the drugs problem, and without any commitment to substantial extra funding, all that is being offered is for the same number of people to work even harder. As we will see, the proposals ignore fundamental issues and practical solutions, which together could completely transform the pattern of drug abuse in the nation.

More research is definitely needed. It is a shocking reflection of neglect by previous UK governments that most US figures in this book for drug-related issues have no parallel in Britain. The figures just don't exist, or where they do they are often soft estimates, based on hunch, intuition and educated guesswork. But how can you tackle a problem effectively that you have failed to measure in detail? First then, how serious *is* the drugs problem?

I

The Size of the Drugs Problem

A friend of mine found Tom sick in his council flat, lying on a bed covered in a dirty blanket. No furniture. No radio. No TV. No carpet. Just a bed and some clothes in a corner on the floor. Everything he had in the world apart from that had been taken and converted to heroin, temazepam, diconal – anything he could get. Swallow, snort, sniff, inject – whichever way, however he could. But Tom is now dead.

Tom is just an official statistic, merely one of hundreds in a big city among hundreds of cities, an ordinary kind of guy who made decisions that some years later led him to lose his life on the end of a needle. People like Tom are hidden away, an embarrassment to mothers and fathers, ignored by brothers and sisters, spurned by former partners, rejected by many health care professionals. In many people's lives, people like Tom don't exist. Tom could be your own neighbour, living in your street. Tom could be your own child or your best friend.

$400 BILLION MEGA INDUSTRY[1]

The international drug trade is a $400 billion mega industry. Drug taking used to be confined to small groups but is now a global obsession, almost beyond control in many countries. Despite three

6

decades of rapid growth it is disturbing that few governments have accurate figures for drug use. However, the international expertise drawn together by the United Nations Drugs Control Program (UNDCP) estimates that around 4 per cent of the world's adults use illegal drugs in a year. This is not an issue confined to wealthy nations. It's a pandemic, a plague.

- 140 million use cannabis (2.5 per cent)
- 8 million use heroin (0.14 per cent)
- 13 million use cocaine (0.23 per cent)
- 30 million use synthetic drugs e.g. amphetamines (0.5 per cent)

In most countries drug addicts inject heroin, cocaine and other drugs, and HIV has been transmitted as a result in more than eighty nations. Around *5 to 10 per cent of all HIV world-wide is drug-related*, that's 2–4 million extra AIDS deaths as a direct result, plus extending networks of sexual partners of drug injectors at risk, as well as babies in the womb. It's just the beginning, and the fight is getting harder.

Globalisation is making the flow of drugs easier, with non-existent border checks and unrestricted money flows between many nations. Armed conflicts around the world are also powering the drugs network, as arms are often traded direct for drugs.

SIZE OF THE US PROBLEM

The US has the *highest rate of illegal drug use in the industrialised world*. It's a major issue. That is why we are seeing such a huge shift towards fierce anti-drugs policies at every level of society, including American companies who can no longer afford to throw away profits by ignoring the problem. As we will see later, widespread drug misuse can make all the difference between staying in business or going bust.

These companies are operating in a climate which is worried about drugs, and of all those most concerned, parents of teenagers top the list. Around six out of ten American adults believe that drugs are the number one problem facing children today, followed by crime and family breakdown.[2] Around half of all adults know someone who is abusing drugs.

The huge US drugs problem is often used by pro-drugs campaigners to prove *not* that more should be done, but that 'the war is lost' and that control efforts should be *abandoned*, with cannabis legalised as a start. But the truth is rather different, and they are flying in the face of reality in the workplace and in schools. Other pro-drugs campaigners have pointed to recent falls in cocaine addiction to try to undermine those who want strict controls to continue. Their voices are confused.

The truth is that the drugs problem is far worse than many would like to admit, yet better than many others believe. The figures have been endlessly hyped up and down. Underplaying leads to complacency and so does overstating the case. Both distortions directly encourage drug addiction because they create uncertainty and scepticism about the real situation.

So what are the facts? Sales of alcohol or cigarettes are easy to measure because both are legal and regulated; however, hard figures on illegal drugs are scarce. Surveys on drug or alcohol abuse are notoriously unreliable. Some people exaggerate – especially as teenagers – while others deny all use. Official registers of, say, heroin addicts are always incomplete, and many people fear confessing to illegal activity. However, well designed research, gathering every source of information together, helps build a far more accurate picture. While we may be less certain about absolute numbers, the trends are very clear – and they *have* been *downwards* in the US.

Illegal drug taking is rapidly going out of fashion – or was. Numbers taking drugs within the last month have halved in the last twenty years: 25 million down to 12.8 million or 0.6 per cent of the population.[3] Sixty million Americans no longer take illegal substances. Fewer than 1 per cent are now using cocaine, inhalants or hallucinogens.[4] Despite these recent falls, more than a third of Americans over twelve have tried an illegal drug in the past, of which 90 per cent was cannabis. A third took cocaine or a prescription drug for non-medical purposes. A fifth took LSD. So then, even after recent falls, the epidemic remains very active.

But drug use is now *rising* once more, after a spell when public awareness and concern has fallen, with less profile on TV, radio or in the press. Drug use by teenagers has rocketed by 70 per cent since 1992.[5] And attitudes are softer this time round. Half of all 'baby-boomer' parents expect their own teenage children to try drugs and are fatalistic about it. Forty per cent believe that there is little they can say or do as parents to change things.[6] Nothing could be further from the truth, as we will see. Parents can have a huge positive influence on decisions their children take.

In America drug use is often associated with the underclass, black ghettos, the socially marginalised. Whilst it is true that poorest neighbourhoods are often where drug-related crime is most obvious, every stratum of society is affected.

Five hundred and thirty thousand Americans addicted to cocaine or crack[7]

Drug taking is one of the commonest leisure activities in America, and one of the most dangerous. Half a million people try cocaine for the first time every year, and although that may be only a third of the early 1980s figure, it's still a major problem. The total *number* using it each year has fallen 74 per cent from 5.7 million in 1985 to just 1.5 million. However, *consumption* is much the same, because most of the market is created by heavy users and those numbers are unchanged at 580,000, of which 250,000 use crack.[8]

Despite recent falls, one and a half million people in one country alone addicted to crack is a huge challenge. As we will see, crack changes people, changes schools, changes whole neighbourhoods. The intensity of the craving, the extremely short length of action, and the high cost all mean high levels of stealing, prostitution and violence.

Six hundred thousand Americans addicted to heroin[9]

The 1.5 million abusing cocaine or crack are serious enough, but a further 600,000 people in America are addicted to heroin, more than in the previous two decades.[10] The majority are older adults with long-term addiction, but growing numbers of teenagers and younger adults are trying it.[11] Most users inject low grade heroin, but snorting or smoking is becoming more common as heroin purity has risen. As a result, consumption per person has increased dramatically.[12]

These 600,000 people are spending $6–10 billion a year on heroin, just fighting withdrawal symptoms that threaten to over-whelm them every twelve hours of every day. And most of that money is probably raised from crime – from others around from whom they steal.

Thus heroin and cocaine together are consuming the lives of at least two million Americans, mostly young and in the prime of life, many still in High School. For every addict, there's another ten to twenty who are profoundly affected, whether as family members or work colleagues or neighbours or friends. That's more than twenty million people.

Ten million Americans smoke cannabis[13]

Then there is the growing use of cannabis. In 1995 an estimated 9.8 million Americans smoked marijuana, of which 5 million did so at least once a week on average, down from 8.4 million in 1984. However, while *regular use* has fallen, the number of *new users* a year has climbed steadily to reach 2.3 million in 1994.[14] In other words, more people than ever are trying it for a short time and then giving up. Cannabis use has become a phase of American adolescence and early adulthood. But cannabis brings other problems, as we will see.

Seven million Americans use other illegal drugs

What about other drugs? 4.7 million Americans have tried amphet-amine.[15] Other illegal drugs are used by a further 2.5 million of the population – for example, Rohypnol and other 'club drugs' such as ketamine, Quaaludes, xanax, MDMA and LSD.

Tobacco and alcohol are the big killers

Then there are the legalised addictions. One could argue that far too much attention is directed at heroin, cocaine and other illegal drugs while the greatest social impact is from alcohol and tobacco. It is true that in comparison to illegal drugs, tobacco and alcohol are the big American killers, and smoking is the worst. More than 400,000 people die from smoking every year in the US – more than from alcohol, crack, heroin, murder, suicide, car accidents and AIDS combined.[16] Sixty-one million Americans smoke, and first year students are smoking more cigarettes, not less.[17] Sixteen per cent now smoke regularly – almost double the figure for ten years ago.

PREVENTABLE DEATHS IN A YEAR[17]

- 39 per cent tobacco   (430,000)
- 9 per cent alcohol   (100,000)
- 2 per cent illegal drugs   (22,000)
- 3 per cent firearms   (33,000)

The smoking industry is wealthy and powerful, and so is the alcohol industry, which thrives on alcohol abuse. In 1995, $104 billion of alcohol was sold, of which 61 per cent was beer, 28 per cent spirits and 11 per cent wine. Beer sales have risen steadily from 1970 to 1995 at the expense of spirits, while wine drinking has remained relatively stable. Around $1 billion is spent every year on advertising alcoholic drinks, almost all of it on network and cable TV.[19]

So then, while there is far less drug taking in the US today than there was, there is still a major problem which is now growing again. The massive, overwhelming crack epidemic never did come, but levels of abuse remain high enough to affect day-to-day life for millions of people. Every year another rising generation is introduced to substances that will alter their minds, affect their bodies or kill them. Youth are the most vulnerable, and smoking is the biggest killer of them all.

It's obvious that the battle against drugs cannot be won without a serious rethink about tobacco and alcohol, both of which are major risk factors for illegal drug use.

Teenagers in the front line of addiction

Many teenagers are nicotine addicts before they arrive in High School, and smoking is often for them just the first step into a whole new world of illegal and dangerous experimentation. High school smoking prevention campaigns are often far too late. Pupils need to be targeted several years earlier.

The scandal of smoking[20]

Future generations will find it hard to understand how smoking was not comprehensively banned as a social evil in the closing years of the second millennium, after all the evidence of wide-scale fatalities and ill health. From our present day perspective such a suggestion is ludicrous and naïve. They will find it even more incomprehensible that tobacco companies were still allowed to advertise different brands in public places, without controls, in most of the world.

This is no adult habit: smoking is primarily a school-age addiction. Fifteen billion cigarettes are smoked every day world-wide — mostly by adults who became addicted as children.[21] In almost every case it's children, not adults, who make the critical decision to start smoking. The only reason we think of smoking as an adult addiction is because millions of adults are broken by the over-whelming power of a nicotine habit they first acquired as kids.

Not only is the drug extremely addictive physically, but it also takes over emotionally. Many smokers are double-minded. They think they *should* stop but they don't *want* to, because they like what a cigarette does for them. They are psychologically hooked, as well as physically dependent.

We are losing the smoking battle. As a direct consequence illegal drug taking will also rise even faster. Every day 3,000 children in America begin smoking cigarettes regularly, and as a result a third will have shortened lives.[22] Around 4.5 million children in the US smoke[23] – that's a third of high school seniors, with more than 20 per cent smoking daily, higher than at any time since the 1970s.[24] Almost half of all ninth–twelfth grade students smoked in 1996.

We are so desensitised to it all that even after three decades of health promotion it is still acceptable in many circles to own a shop which sells cigarettes, or to own shares in tobacco companies. Expect that to change.

Nicotine is one of the most addictive drugs in the world, yet it is pushed for free at children as young as eight by friends in the playground or outside school. Tens of thousands of small retailers regularly, illegally and irresponsibly, supply this killer drug to under-age children, and the tobacco industry for a generation has spent millions of dollars on high profile, glamorous sports sponsorship deals, likely to appeal to sports conscious teenagers.

Children who smoke are the 'bright' future of the tobacco industry. *If a single ten-year-old boy or girl in a school can be persuaded to start, the total extra sales will be up to $100,000 over seventy years.* Ten pupils are worth a million dollars. So the entire tobacco industry – from growers to cigarette manufacturers to wholesalers and corner shop retailers – is dominated by one fact alone: the number of new children who can be hooked on to nicotine.

Children are soft, highly lucrative targets, easy to tempt. Every instinct drives them to experiment as part of growing up, as an expression of independence or rebellion. Cigarette companies are aided by an enthusiastic, national volunteer sales force of millions of other child smokers. They need no organising, just regular supplying through a lax and irresponsible retail system.

So then, our kids are being allowed to grow up in a society where by the age of eighteen up to half of them are already addicted to a drug that some say is more difficult to break free from than heroin, more dangerous than all the combined hazards of cannabis, Ecstasy, amphetamines and LSD. What have we done? The answer is: not enough. Something has to change.

Four facts about smoking:

- 82 per cent of all those who try cigarettes do so before they are eighteen[25]
- 70 per cent of smokers say that they would not start if given the choice again[26]
- Adults make millions out of hooking kids on tobacco – every shareholder in a tobacco company, or in retail chains selling cigarettes, is benefiting from this childhood epidemic
- Smoking in the past is a major risk factor for future cannabis use – up to twenty times in one study[27]

Alcohol is also a teenage problem – linked to illegal drugs

We also need to look urgently at alcohol use and abuse, if we want to present a consistent message on addiction to teenagers.

Alcohol abuse is also a major teenage problem – often copied from parents. One in four tenth grade students and a third of twelfth graders reported having *at least five alcoholic drinks in the previous two weeks* in 1996.[28] The average age for a first drink has fallen from 17.4 in 1987 to 15.9 years.[29] Huge amounts of class room time have been given to illegal drugs or smoking, while basic facts about alcohol have been ignored. For example, 2.5 million American teenagers do not realise that a person can die from a severe alcoholic overdose such as a drinking challenge.[30]

The younger an individual starts drinking and the greater the frequency and amount, the greater the risk that the person will go on to smoke tobacco or use illegal drugs.[31] The same is true for child smokers or cannabis users: each of these increases the risk of trying other things. One experiment leads to another.

Exactly the same arguments go through a teenager's mind over whether to try dad's whisky bottle, mum's cigarettes, or a friend's joint. The only difference is that the first two are often copying behaviour and the third is usually rebellion. Some US children are starting to drink at ten, use prescription drugs at eleven, try hallucinogens at twelve, cocaine and crack at fifteen or sixteen.[32]

Illegal drugs in teenagers[33]

Exact numbers vary between studies, but the indications are that the numbers of teenagers using illegal drugs each month have doubled in five years. Eleven per cent of all teenagers between twelve and seventeen used illegal drugs in the past month in 1995,[34] up from 5 per cent in 1992, which was the low point from the 1979 peak of 16 per cent.[35]

A quarter of all senior high school students use illegal drugs at least once a month, while *7 per cent take drugs every day*.[36] In most cases the drug will be cannabis, a drug which we know accumulates in the body so that it is detectable for weeks after last use. Pupils taking drugs of any kind on a daily basis are likely to be affected mentally throughout every school lesson, to one degree or another. This will result either from the intoxicating action of the drug itself, or from the destabilising effects on emotions and concentration as the brain restores its own normal equilibrium between doses – for example, of amphetamines and barbiturates.

In twelfth grades, on average:[37, 38]

- 10 per cent take drugs every day
- 0.5 per cent use heroin at least once a month
- 1 per cent use heroin in a year

- 2 per cent use cocaine regularly
- 25 per cent drink alcohol every week
- 25 per cent use cannabis every month
- 50 per cent smoke cigarettes
- 10 per cent use uppers (e.g. amphetamines) in a year
- 12 per cent use hallucinogens in a year
- 3.5 per cent use heroin in a year

So then, on average, *one in ten older pupils are likely to be significantly affected almost every day by their daily intake of illegal drugs*. This is a major crisis in US education, and one of the greatest challenges in any school. Even if the damage is entirely limited just to those pupils, it's serious enough. But the knock-on effect is likely to be far wider across the rest of the peer group. This level of drug consumption undermines everything a school is trying to achieve. It robs teenagers of their future by wrecking their ability to achieve good grades. It adds to the underclass, to those who leave school virtually unemployable. It adds to the cost of welfare.

Average figures hide huge variations. In some classes of twenty there could be five or ten using illegal drugs most days, and other classes where drug use is almost unknown. A teacher could find that a single class of thirty contains a heroin injector, three who snort crack and fifteen who take speed, Ecstasy or LSD as well as cannabis. How can you operate normally in a class situation like that?

Most large schools will have heroin or crack addicts whether they know it or not. And that means pupils who may be injecting on site. If a user has run low he may be withdrawing as he walks into school. He can't wait.

And what happens when money is scarce? Everything hangs on goodwill from friends for a free shot, or making money fast some other way. That means a loan, or theft, selling to someone else (and maybe taking a risk with a bum deal, cut to the limit with rubbish), sex for a favour or worse.

Three hundred senior pupils and thirty of them drug taking daily adds up to a big 'drug-infected' group, many of whom will associate together, supply each other, teach each other and take drugs together, mainly out of school, at home, at a friend's or nearby. And of course, every user has a financial interest in seeing the other 270 become users too. Even if the existing users sell for the same price that they buy, the more users there are, the more they can buy at one time and the lower the price is for everyone.

A 10 per cent drug taking group is like a life-threatening cancer in a school. If not dealt with it is likely to spread, placing the other 90 per cent right in the firing line at the most vulnerable time in their lives. We are failing our children by shying away from tough measures. As we will see later, the primary aim should not be to throw drug users out but to encourage them to change, using similar methods to those being used in the workplace. But we do have to take firm action.

Despite all we have seen about the serious level of drug taking in school pupils, it is extraordinary that *fewer parents than ever are talking about these issues at home* – just 30 per cent in 1995–6 – ostriches with heads in the sand. Drugs should be a common topic of conversation in any home with teenagers – after all, it is at school, so why make it a 'no-go area' at home? We have to talk about these things, before they become issues and problems for our children.

Marijuana

And then there is teenage dope. Almost one in four high school seniors used marijuana within the last month in 1996 – only 10 per cent used any other drug as often.[39] From 1991 to 1996 the number of twelve- to seventeen-year-olds using marijuana *doubled*. The number of eighth graders trying it rose from 10 to 23 per cent. Since most cannabis users smoke it in tobacco, almost all the 25 per cent of high school seniors using cannabis are among the 50 per cent of high school seniors who smoke. *Cannabis use among non-smokers is uncommon, so all efforts to reduce smoking will hit cannabis too.*

The age at which teenagers first try cannabis is getting younger. In 1987 the average age for first use was 17.8 years. By 1996 it was 13.5. But that is an average. It means that some are now trying cannabis when they are as young as nine or ten.

The figures are bad enough without exaggerating them, yet that is exactly what teenagers themselves do, both users and abstainers. Surveys show that they are all convinced that 75 per cent have tried cannabis and 25 per cent are regular users – a dangerous distortion we will return to when looking at prevention. The 25 per cent figure applies only to the oldest pupils, and abstainers are in good company, not an eccentric minority.

The typical attitude is that 'no one has died from taking pot'. Marijuana use is seen as low risk. However, as we will see in a later chapter, there is overwhelming evidence that for a good 24 hours after use a student's brain will not be functioning correctly. More seriously, as we will also see later, brain function can remain abnormal for six months or more after the last dose in those who have been regular users for a long period.

So here we have one in four of all senior high school pupils taking a drug which we know damages their mental ability the following day, and in more subtle ways in the longer term. And the brain areas affected are exactly those a student most needs to be able to do well in class. For example, cannabis use makes it more difficult for a pupil to focus in on what the teacher is saying, ignoring other distractions.

Solvents

Solvents are dangerous and commonly abused by young children. Around 900,000 people abused inhalants in America in 1993 with 70 per cent of users being young teenagers.[40] Solvent abuse tends to be localised around particular estates or schools. Around 4 to 8 per cent out of thirteen- to eighteen-year-olds have tried sniffing solvents, mostly just once or twice. Perhaps one in fifty will carry on for a few weeks or months, while one in a hundred will become a long-term user, often sniffing alone. Solvent use usually begins at the age of thirteen to fifteen. Deaths are common.

Stimulants and LSD

Five per cent of high school students use stimulants on a monthly basis and 10 per cent have done so in the last year. LSD was used by 8.8 per cent of twelfth graders in the past year.[41] Unlike amphetamines, LSD is capable of causing terrible long-term flashbacks. Not a good way to begin adolescence.

Cocaine

In 1996 one in fifty of all twelfth graders in America were using cocaine regularly, which was lower than the 6.7 per cent high of 1985. However, those who had ever used cocaine almost doubled in five years among eighth graders, reaching 4.5 per cent in 1996.[42] In other words, one in twenty have used cocaine by the time they leave school, and the age of experimentation is also getting younger. The mean age for first cocaine use is falling, from 23.3 years in 1990 to 19 in 1994.[43] Senior high school pupils using cocaine at least once in their lives shot up from 7.1 to 8.7 per cent in a year.

Heroin

A 1996 survey found that 1 per cent of twelfth graders had used heroin in the last year, and 0.5 per cent had done so in the last month. That means on average *one in every two hundred pupils in high school is main-lining heroin*. These figures also tell us that many teenagers have tried heroin a couple of times and didn't want to carry on, giving up before addiction became established.

Numbers using heroin at least once doubled in eighth and twelfth graders from 1991 to 1996, reaching 1.8 per cent and 2.4 per cent respectively.[44] One in fifty eighth to twelfth graders said that they had used heroin at least once.[45] So heroin is a significant problem in pre-adults, and a growing one, likely to increase further as prices fall following bumper harvests.

These cold statistics become a terrible reality for a teacher in a classroom who suspects that two or three are regularly using crack, cocaine or heroin at the age of fifteen or sixteen. What do you do? Throw them out? Try to talk to them? As we will see, there are no simple answers.

Where teenagers take drugs

You might think after what we have seen that going to school is a risky experience, but among sixth to twelfth graders the *least* common place to take drugs is school. Compared to other settings, school remains a protected place.

- 17 per cent said they smoked dope at a friend's house
- 14 per cent elsewhere in the community
- 10 per cent smoked in a car
- 8 per cent at home; and only
- 4 per cent at school

So most drug use occurs outside school hours, at night or weekends when in theory parents are in charge. However, school is where people talk about drugs: taking them, where to get them, how to get them, what they do, when to meet up again.

It raises a big question about parental awareness. If a thirteen-year-old boy goes round to a friend's house, one might assume that there is an element of parental supervision when he gets there. But is there? And what if your own children invite someone back? Is there an adult in the house? Of course, young people can do whatever they want wherever they want if they try hard enough, and cannot be supervised every moment of the day or evening, but there are times when one wonders if a drugs problem has not been made worse by long hours worked by both parents or guardians.

Taking more to get higher

Drug use is getting heavier, as well as more frequent. Teenagers are getting higher than before as well as using drugs more often. Almost three out of four seniors said they got 'very high, bombed or stoned' when smoking marijuana compared to only six out of ten eight years earlier.[46]

Twenty-five per cent unfit to work but fit for school

The net result of all this drug use is that by the end of 1997, one in four of all senior high school pupils would have found it difficult or impossible to pass a pre-employment drug test. Very few schools carry out drugs testing. Yet one might argue that education is just as important as productivity in the workplace, and that use of illegal drugs by pre-adults is such a serious matter that the school environment should be *stricter* than the 'adult' factory floor or office. The reality is that in most schools the risk of detection is effectively zero, whether for buying and selling on the school premises, or for consuming drugs before, during or after school.

Drug-related violence hits schools

However, this level of drug abuse among teenagers has brought new tensions. Fights, feuds and gang warfare have swept off the streets and in through the school gates, whether in the US or the UK. When significant numbers of young people are addicted to an illegal and very costly habit there is likely to be trouble.

Five per cent of pupils take guns to school

Drug-related killings in or around school are bound to increase. In 1996 around one in twenty US high school pupils said that they had carried a gun to school, while 12 per cent had joined a gang. Forty-two per cent said that they had threatened to harm someone, and a quarter had been in trouble with the police. There is a direct link to drug abuse by those at school: it is more common among those bringing in guns, joining gangs, or in trouble of other kinds.[47]

So then, the writing is on the wall. We cannot ignore the current situation in US high schools. It requires urgent, multi-level action, as will be outlined in later chapters. But is the US a special case? Could the same happen elsewhere, in Britain for example? The answer is that in British schools the situation is already alarming, a reflection of drug use across the country.

SIZE OF THE UK PROBLEM

The UK drugs problem is less serious than that in the US but it has been catching up. British surveys suggest that 45 per cent aged sixteen to twenty-nine have now used illegal drugs, 24 per cent have done so in the last twelve months, and 15 per cent in the last month.[48] There is one glimmer of good news: levels of drug taking were relatively stable between 1994–96. Nevertheless, this has to be seen in perspective: up to 1.5 million doses of Ecstasy are taken every week in Britain.

The Home Office believes that heroin addiction alone accounted for at least £1.3 billion of property crimes in 1997. One in five of all people arrested are heroin addicts. Heroin is getting cheaper, following large harvests of opium poppies by 200,000 farmers in Afghanistan.[49] The price of a 'wrap' of heroin fell sharply in 1998 to as little as a pint of beer, while heroin seizures leapt 135 per cent.[50]

Home Office and other studies have found that:[51]

- 70 per cent of men have tried an illegal drug by the time they are twenty-four
- 25 per cent across adults of all ages and both sexes have used an illegal drug on at least one occasion
- 10 per cent use illegal drugs in a year

- 5 per cent use illegal drugs every month
- 6 per cent of men are alcohol abusers (more than 50 units a week)
- 2 per cent of women are alcohol abusers (more than 35 units a week)
- 2 per cent are addicted to illegal drugs (mostly men)
- 13 per cent of 45- to 59-year-olds have used drugs at some time
- 40 per cent of under-35-year-olds have used drugs at some time

So then, a total of perhaps 8 per cent of all men are abusing either alcohol or illegal drugs or both – that's almost one in ten of the entire male workforce, and around 2.5 per cent of women. Mostly it's very well hidden, but the effects are there or will be in the future. One in ten of all men in your street. One in ten of your friends. One in ten of those in the office or factory. One in ten doctors in the hospital. One in ten taxi drivers. One in ten safety engineers. Do you know who they are? Does anyone know?

Numbers of addicts to heroin, morphine and cocaine

Drug addiction has soared since the early 1980s, yet by 1984 the British Medical Association conference was already suggesting that drug misuse was no longer an epidemic but a plague.[52] In the previous year there had been 142 deaths from misuse of controlled drugs,[53] 5,000 deaths from alcohol abuse, and at least 100,000 premature deaths from cigarette smoking.[54]

The number of addicts notified to the Home Office is always a fraction of the total, despite the legal requirement until 1997 on all doctors to report all those they know or suspect to be addicted to controlled drugs.

Official figures for those addicted to heroin, methadone or cocaine rose from 37,200 in 1995 to 43,500 by 1997. However, true numbers were probably five times that – well over 200,000 by

1997. The steepest rises have been in the under twenty-one age group.

- 75 per cent of new addicts are under thirty years old
- 25 per cent of registered addicts are women
- 16,000 addicts inject drugs (numbers falling)[55]

Drug-related deaths

Similarly, while official records show 1,600 drug-related deaths in 1994, the true total was probably at least twice that (excluding alcohol and tobacco). Doctors often fail to recognise the cause, or use a variety of terms on death certificates.

Deaths related to use of controlled drugs:

- 490   Directly due to drug use
- 440   Accidental poisoning
- 240   Other drug poisoning
- 330   Suicides using drugs
- 110   Deaths from AIDS

Drug offenders in Britain

This level of drug activity consumes a huge amount of police time. Around 100,000 people a year are arrested for drugs offences in Britain, and 90,000 for possession of cannabis, who are mostly just cautioned. Only one in five of all arrests are for drug trafficking. Heroin prosecutions are also rising fast. Between 1994 and 1995 there was a 42 per cent increase in heroin offenders to 4,200. Ninety per cent of all heroin offenders are male, and 35 per cent are under twenty-one. The average age is falling.

Highest drug use among lowest income group

Drug addiction is most often found in the poorest and the wealthiest in Britain. Each group needs a different approach to prevention.

- Those with household incomes of less than £5,000 a year are the most likely ever to have used heroin
- High levels of lifetime abuse are also found among those with household incomes of more than £30,000 a year
- Middle income households have the lowest levels of drug problems

Professional and skilled workers are more likely to take illegal drugs (and continue to take them), but unskilled workers taking drugs are more likely to take them *frequently* and to *inject*.

Area of addiction

Drug use also varies from area to area, so anti-drugs activity needs to be focused geographically. Seizure rates are highest in London, Wales, Merseyside, north-west England, Glasgow, Edinburgh and Dundee. Scottish notifications rose 140 per cent since 1991, faster than any other region, with 40 per cent coming from Greater Glasgow. Fifty-five per cent of all adults in Scotland have used illegal drugs in the past, despite intensive campaigns and treatment programmes there.

But drug marketing is also very intensive. In some parts of Scotland young people are being offered free drugs such as crack or cocaine, by addicted friends keen to recruit new users.[56] In parts of London crack users are openly stopping teenagers on the street with offers of drugs.[57]

Alcohol use and smoking also vary regionally. For example Scotland, Northern Ireland and the north-west of England score highest for tobacco use.

Drugs for Britain

Drugs for the British market come from a variety of countries via complex routes, each of which raises a host of political and practical control issues, as we will see.[58]

- Heroin – Near and Far East, Soviet Union, Colombia
- Cocaine – Colombia
- Ecstasy/Amphetamines/LSD – Holland, US
- Cannabis – Near and Far East, North Africa

Alcohol

One in twenty-five people in Britain are dependent on alcohol, twice as many as are dependent on drugs. Average consumption has almost doubled over the last 35 years, and most abusers are men.

The UK alcohol industry is worth £27 billion a year, of which £10 billion is regained by the government through tax. So, as with tobacco, the Treasury has a vested interest in keeping consumption high – short-term cash gain, long-term social costs. The average adult drinks 7.2 litres a year of pure alcohol, that's equivalent of around 140 pints of beer *and* fourteen bottles of wine *and* a few bottles of spirits.

The problem of alcohol dependency in teenagers has been made worse by products such as alcopops, designed to appeal to younger tastes. Seventeen per cent of eleven- to fifteen-year-olds drink regularly. Children are also affected by parental alcohol dependency, which is a common factor in family break up. Indeed, marriages where one or both partners have a drink problem are twice as likely to end in divorce.

Tobacco

It is highly fashionable to be an addict in Britain, especially among teenagers. Smoking in eleven- to fifteen-year-old girls is higher than for fifteen years, encouraged by glamorous models on catwalks holding cigarettes.[59] Every day 450 children in Britain take up smoking.[60]

Thirteen million smoke cigarettes in the UK – and numbers are rising again. Every year since the 1970s an average of 500,000 smokers have given up, but during 1996 and 1997 numbers rose by 340,000: high earners, those in their late thirties and early forties.

In summary then, Britain may not have a drugs problem as severe as that of the US but it is highly significant and is already having a major impact on at least 10 per cent of all households, or some five million people, as well as on many others in the workplace. What about British schools?

Drugs in British Schools

In school pupils, according to the Home Office, past drug use is now:

- One in twelve 12-year-olds
- One in three 14-year-olds
- Two in five 16-year-olds
- Half of 18- to 20-year-olds – a third of them using regularly

There are around 750,000 children in each school year. Based on the figures above a total of *1.75 million school pupils in Britain have used an illegal drug at least once*, of which at least 300,000 are doing so regularly. A survey of 27,000 pupils found that among fifteen- to sixteen-year-olds, 14 per cent of boys and 11 per cent of girls had taken drugs in the previous week. More than 60 per cent knew at least one drug taker. Drug takers are more likely to be pupils who are confident, outgoing, sociable and have part-time jobs. They are likely to be less studious than abstainers.[61]

How does this compare to the US? As we have seen, 11 per cent of twelve- to seventeen-year-olds in the US have used drugs in the previous month – but that's *less* than the British figure of fifteen- to sixteen-year-olds for the previous *week*. The figures are not directly comparable but if we assume that fifteen- to sixteen-year-old figures are not far off an average for a wider age range, then it suggests that drug taking in British schools is catching up fast with that in the US.

Therefore the same arguments apply as in the US for strident action to combat the drugs menace in secondary school education. We will return to this later. State and privately funded schools alike are being out-run by the drugs problem. Most have poorly developed strategies to cope, limited mainly to suspension or expulsion of a pupil caught in possession of illegal substances on school premises. Since this is extremely difficult without a tip-off, and since most pupils who know are far too scared to tell for fear of very violent retribution, the chances of a supplier being caught are exceptionally low.

The levels of intimidation in an average British comprehensive school are high. A headmaster was stabbed to death recently in London trying to break up a fight, and pupils regularly carry knives into school to threaten and protect themselves. Fights with knives are common outside school gates, on estates and outside homes, where punishment is carried out away from teacher interference. Death threats are common, often perhaps in jest, made not by individuals but by groups against individuals.

I was in a school recently addressing several classes on issues including drugs. I was assured by the most senior teachers that drugs were not a significant problem. But how could that possibly be so? Are their pupils drawn from a different city – a different country even – than every other school in the area? After the lessons were over I told them to think again. If a school says they have no problem, it is usually just a reflection of poor leadership and even poorer pupil-teacher communication. The result will be in many cases a growing and *uncontrolled* problem.

A huge barrier to tackling drugs in British schools is the fear of loss of reputation if, say, the press run big features following the break up of a drugs ring inside a school. Hence many schools have an unofficial policy of cover up and denial. The aim is to deal with these matters discreetly. But this makes aggressive action far harder to take because it is harder to justify.

Such schools are being held to ransom. There is an unspoken acknowledgment that rooting drugs out of the school could result in the school being punished by those who are caught. Any one of them could greatly damage the reputation of the school, revealing the truth about the size of the drugs problem: 'I'm not the only one – they just picked on me.'

There is only one way forward: embrace the problem together with other schools in the area so that none are humiliated by being singled out, and as far as possible agree collective drugs policies which are applied rigorously and consistently, with the backing of governors, teachers and above all parents. Pupils should also be consulted widely on these matters. The difficulty is actually introducing a change. Once it has been done, all new prospective pupils and their parents can be asked to sign up to the drugs policy as a condition of admission. We will return to these issues in later chapters.

Most pupils don't take drugs any more

One fact should provide encouragement. As we have seen in US schools, while one-off experimentation is common, it is still a minority experience. Even among the oldest pupils, abstinence is the dominant lifestyle. Two thirds of those who have tried illegal drugs no longer use them. Women tend to give up faster and younger. Numbers of male and female users are equal at school, while adult users are mainly men.

White pupils take more drugs than black pupils

There is less difference between White and Afro-Caribbeans than people think. Afro-Caribbeans between thirty and fifty-nine years old are more likely to have used illegal drugs than whites (25 per cent compared to 22 per cent), but this is reversed in sixteen- to twenty-nine-year-olds (34 per cent compared to 43 per cent). Younger Afro-Caribbeans are rejecting lifestyles of their parents' generation.

However, among sixteen- to twenty-nine-year-olds 4 per cent of Pakistanis and Bangladeshis are taking heroin – higher rates than for any other group.

In summary then, Britain has a very serious and growing drugs problem, particularly in the younger age groups. We have looked at the impact of schools, and compared the lack of controls there to tightening restrictions at work, particularly in America. We need to look further at this important change.

WORKPLACE – THE HIDDEN DRUGS CRISIS

Market forces rather than morality will have the greatest impact on drug taking in America over the next twenty years. Drug addiction among workers will flare up into a major third millennial human rights issue, with company owners insisting that addicts damage profits, and wanting to test, identify, counsel, treat or sack 'bad risks' – not just addicts, but regular users too.

Among the American workforce 24 per cent of men and 13 per cent of women aged sixteen to twenty-five use illegal drugs, falling to 16 per cent and 9 per cent for those aged twenty-six to thirty-four. All will be targets in future, as will those whose blood tests suggest heavy alcohol use.

Drug-related accidents and lost productivity costs around $100 billion a year.[62] Employers in America are already turning to draconian anti-drug policies, with drug-testing at the heart of them. Other countries with significant drug problems will be sure to follow, or else they will lose business.

Expect a loud backlash, with angry workers indignant at what they see as gross abuse of human rights and totally unwarranted invasion of personal privacy. But employers will win, every time – on simple economic grounds. Expect a revolution in workplace attitudes – not in a day or a year but over the next decade. Anti-drugs employment legislation will be in wide use in industrialised nations by 2015, as companies fight to compete with others with stricter drug-free employment laws, drug-free work forces and higher productivity.

The new anti-drugs push will not be law-based but sanction-based, with promotions and jobs at risk. The same has happened already to an extent with tobacco. It has now become almost impossible for a heavy smoker to get a job with a US Federal Agency. Workplace restrictions on smoking are so severe that a serious nicotine addict cannot survive without suffering withdrawal symptoms, which interfere with productivity.

This new 'market morality' against drugs is based on a series of US studies which found that substance abusers (including alcohol) are on average:[63]

- 33 per cent less productive
- 3 times more likely to be late
- 3.6 times more likely to be involved in a job-related accident
- 5 times more likely to file for Worker's Compensation
- 3 times more medical bills than non-users
- 10 times more likely to miss work
- In addition 25 per cent steal from their employers

Cocaine addiction is particularly disruptive in the workplace.[64]

- 75 per cent of cocaine addicts use drugs at work
- 64 per cent admit it hurts work performance
- 44 per cent sell drugs to other staff
- 18 per cent steal from co-workers to fund a habit

★ ★ ★

These figures are averages – but what about the impact on an individual company? The US Postal Service found among workers who used illegal drugs:[65]

- Absenteeism was 66 per cent higher
- Use of health services was 84 per cent higher in dollar terms
- Disciplinary actions were 90 per cent higher
- Staff turnover was higher

General Motors found that drug-using staff averaged 40 days sick leave a year compared to 4.5 days for non-users.[66] Utah Power and Light found that new staff testing positive for drugs at interview were five times as likely to have accidents as those who tested negative.[67] The State of Wisconsin calculated that their addicted staff members were running up extra costs and productivity losses equal to 25 per cent of each person's salary. Often the effects of addiction are not so obvious to those running the company – or at least the real reason for problems with performance:[68]

- Diverted supervisory and management time
- Friction and tension in teams
- Damage to equipment
- Poor decisions
- Damage to company image
- Staff turnover

Drugs programmes at work save money

Drugs programmes at work help staff retain their jobs, improve productivity and morale – and save money. The State of Ohio found that comprehensive drugs programmes in the workplace resulted in:

- 91 per cent reduction in absenteeism
- 88 per cent decrease in problems with supervisors
- 97 per cent decrease in on-the-job injuries

These are spectacular achievements at relatively low cost. However, the fact remains that employers will be keen in future to do all they can to make sure that they recruit new team members who are 'drug free'. What company wants to employ a drug user or an alcoholic if there's someone else who is just as qualified for a new position? It's not just efficiency and safety of others, but also general health. That means lower premiums for companies providing health cover or pensions and other benefits. Insurance underwriters are already asking about anti-drugs programmes and are imposing penalties on companies without them. The stricter the regime, the lower the premiums. In future companies won't be able to afford *not* to implement full anti-addiction programmes.

UK Workplace

Alcohol-related problems alone cost British industry an estimated £2 billion a year from absenteeism and poor work performance (not including 25 per cent of workplace accidents linked to or caused by alcohol). Alcohol-related sickness absence alone accounted for £1 billion. Recent studies have found:[69]

- 75 per cent of employers say alcohol misuse is a problem at work
- Up to 25 per cent of accidents at work are caused by intoxicated workers
- 8-14 million days a year are lost because of alcohol-related problems.
- 7 per cent of men and 3 per cent of women admit that their work has been affected by drinking over the last year
- 11 per cent of men and 6 per cent of women drink alcohol during working hours each week

- 4 per cent of men and 2 per cent of women have taken time off work with a hangover in the last year
- 7 per cent of men and 3 per cent of women said that their work has suffered because of drinking in the last year

The drug-work problem is particularly serious in Scotland, where 65 per cent of all eighteen- to twenty-five-year-olds have used controlled drugs, and 25 per cent of those taking drugs are holding down jobs.[70]

Doctors at risk

Drug addiction affects millions of people every year whose lives depend on the skills and judgment of others – whether being driven in taxis, on buses, crossing the road, or visiting the doctor. Indeed the medical profession is just one of hundreds of examples where addiction affects the welfare of the public. I want to look at addicted doctors in some detail, as an example of issues which apply to many other groups.

Alcohol abuse among doctors is common and places a patient's health at risk. This has long been recognised. In 1986 the Royal College of General Practitioners declared that doctors had three times the rate of alcoholic liver cirrhosis as the general population.[71] A 1985 study found that 12 per cent of male and 45 per cent of female GPs were drinking dangerous amounts of alcohol.[72] In the mid-1980s it was estimated that there were between two and three thousand alcoholic doctors in England and Wales alone.[73]

Although doctors abuse other drugs less often than alcohol, a significant proportion of those abusing alcohol go on to develop a drug habit. In the US, one survey found that half of all alcoholic doctors became addicted to illegal drugs.[74] Another study found that one in fifty anaesthetists was drug addicted.[75]

The latest report by the British Medical Association says that one doctor in fifteen is addicted to either alcohol or drugs. That amounts to more than 7,000 doctors.[76] However, the BMA News

Review recently put the figure at 13,000, more than one doctor in ten.[77] These reports rely on self-assessment questionnaires, so the real total is likely to be even higher.

So how do you feel about the thought that if there are two doctors assisting in an operation plus an anaesthetist, the risk of you being cared for while unconscious by an addict–doctor is on average 30 per cent, by a doctor who may be intoxicated now, or suffering withdrawal or from a hangover? Yet there is no testing mechanism, and doctors are past masters at being able to hide their own symptoms.

Doctors are particularly at risk of drifting from alcohol abuse to self-prescription of controlled drugs. They are often highly stressed, the taboo against injecting and opiates has been eroded, and they have easy access to supplies.

The big question is what to do? The other day a medical friend of mine told me a colleague had turned up to a lunch-time meeting stinking of alcohol. But what should she do? If he was too drunk to drive a car, surely he was too drunk to make life and death decisions about treating sick people? She could secretly inform the British Medical Association, but what would they do? If they started making checks the suspicion would probably fall on her, in a small medical team, and working relationships could become impossible.

My own view is that I do not want a drunken surgeon to operate on me, nor do I want a heroin or cocaine addict to make decisions about what dose of medicines to give my young child. It is absurd that with almost one in ten doctors addicted to alcohol, cocaine, heroin or other drugs, there are no agreed methods for detecting and dealing with addiction.

The only satisfactory solution is for every doctor to be subject to random drug and alcohol testing, as a condition of employment. Health authorities must have the right to randomly breath test any doctor at any time while on duty, with or without suspicion. There should be severe discipline for someone at work who is 'over the limit' for alcohol – as for driving a car. There should also be tough sanctions for a doctor testing positive for illegal drugs, if in the view of the disciplinary committee judgment is likely to have been impaired with matters of life and death in patients' lives.

As in any such situation, discipline and compassionate care for the individual should go hand in hand. But the current situation is intolerable and must be affecting patient care. There is no need to forbid a doctor to practise because of overstepping the mark.

The best course would be to offer a severe warning, perhaps with a fine of some kind, administered by the General Medical Committee, with agreement that random testing will be more frequent. The costs of re-tests should be paid by the doctor. There should also be compulsory counselling, offering treatment and support. If the doctor is intoxicated again while at work, he or she should be suspended immediately until the GMC is satisfied that the problem is dealt with.

Unfortunately at present drug and alcohol testing is so lax that it is almost impossible to prove where medical mistakes are linked to abuse. Cases come to trial years later, and no tests are conducted at the time. This is wrong. Whenever a serious medical error is spotted immediately, the doctor should be required to give a blood sample.

Access to treatment needs to be made easier. Treatment should take place at a specialist unit alongside other addicted health care professionals, and post-treatment supervision needs to be closely managed.

But if we say that doctors should be randomly tested and subject to discipline as well as offered help, then why not others? Bus drivers, railway workers, dentists, engineers, fairground operators, life guards, dentists, nurses, security guards, bankers, financial advisers, car mechanics, airline pilots, cabin crew, ground maintenance staff, lawyers, accountants, electricians, gas fitters, machinery operators, factory workers – all these and more affect the health, safety and welfare of others if performance falls.

One concludes that employers in countries such as America and Britain, with big addiction problems, have a public duty to begin testing employees on a random basis, as part of a comprehensive addiction programme. We will look at some of the huge ethical dilemmas involved in a later chapter.

oOo

In summary, drug and alcohol abuse is widespread and has a colossal impact in school, at college and at work. All three places will need to consider urgent introduction of new policies to identify, help and support those with an addiction, and to discourage new users and non-addictive use.

In a world where most things are measured in money, we need to look further at the true cost to society of addiction. Then arguments aimed at governments about spending big money on drugs programmes begin to make economic sense.

The True Cost of Addiction

IMPOSSIBLE TO PRICE HUMAN SUFFERING

For millions of families whose every waking moment is dominated by the addiction of a close relative, you can never put a price on human suffering. How can you calculate the value of wasted cocaine years, of a burned-out alcoholic brain, or of a life lost through an accidental heroin overdose? How do you assess the living nightmare of a young girl, forced to feed a crack habit by selling her body to crack dealers for unlimited sex? Such things are beyond price. And yet all these things have enormous measurable costs to the whole of society, to the government for example, through added health bills, years of economic life lost, law and order and other things.

Drug use is far too serious to ignore as a public health issue yet budgets for prevention and treatment are nothing like enough in most countries. But governments on tight budgets need to be persuaded by every means possible that every dollar spent saves several other dollars. The same applies to companies, institutions, non-profit bodies, churches – in fact every organisation that employs people. Prove addiction costs more money than prevention and care, and every employer becomes an agent of change, as part of a global movement to fight illegal drugs and alcohol abuse.

Therefore it is absolutely essential to count these costs with care, in detail, not sweeping over the problem with vague generalisations. We need to dig deep. We need to probe every area of daily life in towns, cities and rural areas. The result is a list of figures and facts which on their own mean far less than when they are all assembled in one place. Together they paint a very disturbing picture of life in the closing years of the second millennium, in a society gripped by a cluster of addictions and their consequences. So then, how does it all stack up?

CONTRIBUTION OF DRUG TRADE TO GLOBAL ECONOMY

First we need to look at the macro level, the effect on whole economies, before tracking down to local and personal factors. Drug trafficking is now $400 billion a year, or 8 per cent of all international trade, according to the United Nations.[1] *That is more than the entire global trade in iron, steel and cars, or equal to all world trade in textiles.* However, there is one very big difference: this $400 billion cargo weighs just a few thousand tons compared to hundreds of millions of tons of lower value goods. This presents an impossible challenge for customs officials, as we will see. However, locating drugs money is even harder.

At any time around $5 billion is sloshing around the international monetary system as dirty money, some of it filtering into legitimate business where 'innocent' executives and shareholders also land up making their own profits.

Drugs trading is a world-class, highly profitable mega industry, a huge mass market retail operation. The mark-up from grower to retail seller can be as high as a hundredfold. For example, a kilogram of heroin in Pakistan costing £850 from source would fetch £72,000 in London.[2] No wonder the dealer on the street makes a decent profit too, typically:[3]

- 240 per cent for amphetamines
- 300 per cent for crack
- 100 per cent for heroin

So where does all the drugs wealth go?

Money from drug dealing is often ploughed back into more drugs – for personal use. The dealer-user sells some and his profit margin is his own share. Many smaller user-dealers are selling at cost, or just enough above that to pay for their own habit and no more.

Further up the chain the deals are big, far larger than any user could use on personal addiction. Here there are warehouses, syndicates, co-operatives, large networks. Most profits from street use are therefore funnelled upwards with cuts at every level along the way, including slices for those who act as security for big deals and who guard or move drugs around. At every level the drugs trade corrupts and subverts.

The drugs trade is a multi-layer operation, like a pyramid:[4]

- Large importer A
- Wholesaler B (may be a part of A's group)
- Small distributor C
- Large retailer D
- Retailer E
- User F

User F may be selling small amounts on a non-profit basis to friends. Retailers D and E may be users themselves, so there may not be much distinction between a user and a dealer at the lower levels.

Taking a cut with impurities

The quickest way to make a bigger profit is to buy and then dilute the stock, before selling it by volume at the same or higher price. The additives are often far more dangerous than the drug itself – especially if injected. Non-sterile talcum powder is bad stuff to have in the blood stream. The UK average purity in 1995 was as follows:[5]

- Cocaine 53 per cent – cut with lactose, glucose, mannitol, procaine
- Crack 80 per cent +
- Heroin 43 per cent – cut with lactose, glucose, mannitol, chalk dust, caffeine, quinine, procaine, boric acid, talcum powder, vitamin C
- Amphetamine 10 per cent – cut with caffeine, ephedrine, paracetamol, glucose, vitamin C, chalk powder, talcum powder

But then where does all the drug wealth go? The answer is that this cash-based economy spirits into thin air, as hard currency is converted again into goods: property, cars, small businesses, computers – or into deposits in offshore anonymous bank accounts.

The United Nations Drugs Control Program estimates that *more than half of the world's offshore money transits are drug-related.* Around $1.5 trillion of external assets are invested offshore (1993 figures) the equivalent of around 30 per cent of the entire wealth of all the funds invested in industrialised nations in normal bank accounts. Offshore investment funds have more than $1 trillion of assets under management.

Internationalisation of money laundering has been easier with recent integration of financial markets. Drug groups have also moved operations to countries where control is weakest, and legislation absent or ineffective.

The Internet is making things even harder. New technology already allows very large sums to be moved around secretly using encryption methods so secure that intelligence agencies can't crack them for months. Indeed entire drug operations from production to warehousing to transport and retail distribution can now be managed on-line, from any PC or mobile data-phone anywhere in the world, using public phone lines, with almost zero risk of interception.

It has never before been possible to be in constant touch with thousands of people involved in criminal activity, co-ordinating their every move with complete intelligence on the exact location of every one of them to within three metres anywhere on the surface of the earth. And all of this can run from a boat in the Mediterranean, or a train moving at eighty miles an hour in a tunnel under the Swiss Alps, at low cost and with ultra-high security.

Power to buy whole nations

Money laundering at current rates already has the power to undermine the integrity of the international banking system and destabilise entire nations. It's hard to understand the giant scale of this problem. To put it in perspective, let us take just 60 per cent of that $2.5 trillion of offshore drugs money. What does it look like?

- More than the entire combined GDP of Germany and Canada
- 8 times the combined GDP of Malaysia, Singapore, Thailand, Philippines
- 40 times the GDP of Colombia
- 280 times the GDP of Burma (Myanmar)
- 300 times the GDP of Costa Rica

In other words, *if all that offshore drugs wealth was assembled in one place, it would be worth more than three hundred times the entire factory production, farming output and services industries of a country like Costa Rica.*

Now we can understand why some suggested that the recent currency collapses of Thailand and other nations could have been influenced by the Drugs Factor. It is naïve just to point the finger at known speculators and general economic conditions, when the possibility is that drug-related organisations controlling vast offshore funds also played a significant role. After all, they want a return on investment like anyone else, and are also playing the market.

However, an international drug syndicate may see things rather differently to the rest of the market. Changes in border restrictions, the arrest of most of a big network, closure of several large opium refineries, shift in global drug-taking habits – all these things could mean pulling currency out of one nation and placing it in another. Thus a drugs wild-card can be operating in addition to all the commonly understood market forces.

The market operates by trying to outguess what others are going to do next – buy or sell? Expect far greater attention to the Drugs Factor in future, to how drug-dealing owners of these vast offshore funds think and react.

But it's not just the impact of huge investment funds. Drugs syndicates can land up owning entire chains of hotels, industrial estates, galleries of art, power companies and commercial airliners – this wealth has to be placed somewhere.

But these are the *earliest days* of global drugs trade. As we have seen, this a relatively recent problem. With every decade that passes, hundreds more billions of dollars are paid to buy drugs, most of it taken as profit between what the farmer is paid, and what the punter on the street is charged. Thus every year the total power base of the drugs industry grows larger, the criminal elements in society become stronger.

Proportion of GDP

What about the drugs economy inside a nation as a proportion of GDP? The UK heroin and cocaine trade alone is worth more than 0.2 per cent of GDP,[6] so the whole UK drugs economy must be at least 0.3 per cent. The US is higher and Australia slightly less. Total figures for retail sales therefore could be (minimum):

US GDP	$6,737 billion	0.5 per cent = $34 billion
UK GDP	$1,000 billion	0.3 per cent = $3 billion
Australia GDP	$300 billion	0.2 per cent = $0.6 billion

Some would place the US figure higher at $46–$50 billion or 0.7 per cent GDP.

US COST TO SOCIETY OF DRUGS AND
ALCOHOL ABUSE

Total social and health costs of dealing with the *consequences* of illegal use of drugs in the US has been estimated to be a further $66.9 billion a year. The total social and health costs to US *society* of dealing with alcohol and illegal drug abuse has been estimated as $167 billion.[7] The US spends around $10 billion a year on supply reduction, and $5.5 billion on demand reduction. What this means is that *every man, woman and child pays almost $1,000 annually to cover the extra health care, law enforcement, car accidents, crime and lost productivity caused by drugs.*[8]

- Illegal drugs $66.9 billion
- Alcohol $100 billion – including 500 million lost days at work a year
- Tobacco $72 billion

If you add the *health and social* costs of tobacco, the total becomes around $240 billion.

So then, the total costs of illegal drug purchases, and society costs, come to around $100 billion, or 1.5 per cent of GDP. If you add the society costs of dealing with tobacco and alcohol abuse (not including purchase costs), then the total becomes more than $270 billion, or 4 per cent of GDP – more than all America spends on schools or housing.

In addition America spends $40 billion on buying cigarettes. We also need to add a proportion of all alcohol sales, by those who are alcohol dependent, perhaps a further $30 billion. *The total cost of illegal drug use, smoking and alcohol addiction then comes to at least $340 billion or 5 per cent of US GDP.*

Deaths from drink-driving

Here are a few alcohol costs. *Alcohol-related crime cost society $11.3 billion in 1990* – including direct crime costs, lost wages of victims, costs of prison.[9,10] The number one substance abuse crime is drink-driving – 1.4 million arrests in 1995 at a cost of $5.2 billion for arrests and prosecutions. Eight young people every day die in alcohol-related car accidents.[11] In 1996, 7,800 drunk drivers aged sixteen to twenty were fatally injured.[12] The accidents they have are worse than the average, with greater risks of injury.[13]

Drug-related deaths

Drug-related costs are also vast. Forty per cent of deaths from illegal drugs happen in the thirty to thirty-nine year age group[14] – men more than women and blacks more than whites.[15] AIDS is the fastest growing cause of drug-related deaths. Thirty-three per cent of all new AIDS cases in the US are among drug-injecting users and their sexual partners.[16]

Drug-related medical emergencies

More than half a million visits to hospital emergency rooms a year are drug-related.[17] Visits caused by heroin use rose from 34,000 in 1990 to 76,000 in 1995.[18] Heroin-related admissions rose 124 per cent from 1990 to 1995, cocaine admissions remained high and amphetamine admissions soared from 5,000 to 18,000 between 1991 and 1994.

Birth defects and infant mortality

One in twenty pregnant women uses illegal drugs during pregnancy – around 221,000 a year.[19] Marijuana is used by 3 per cent or 120,000, cocaine by 1 per cent or 45,000.[20]

Babies born to drug abusers can be drug dependent themselves at birth or have other problems. Pre-natal drug exposure can affect development in the womb, and many babies continue to face risks from further drug taking by their mothers. Mothers who are addicted may not be able to care for their children as well as they would have normally, and multiple separations are common.

Drug abuse by mothers brings a higher risk of miscarriage, stillbirth or death shortly after birth up to the first year of life. One large study found infant mortality rates up by around 50 per cent in drug abusing mothers (14.9 per million) looking at a population on Medicaid (low income). Cot deaths were 2.5 times as common.[21]

Drug-related crime

One in 144 of the entire American adult population is in prison today for a crime in which drugs and/or alcohol were involved – 1.4 million people out of a total of 1.7 million. Taxpayers are spending $30 billion a year keeping them in gaol.[22] Companies are spending $90 billion a year on private security, mostly to keep those out of gaol away from their property.

Drug-related crime cost the American people $46 billion in 1990 – including direct crime costs, lost wages of victims, costs of prison, losses to the economy of those engaged in crime rather than legal employment.[23]

Ten per cent of federal prisoners and 17 per cent of state prison inmates say they committed crimes to pay for drugs.[24] One in ten murderers in New York State say that their cannabis use in the hours before the killing was a significant factor in what happened.[25]

Eighty per cent of those in US prisons are high on drugs or alcohol when arrested, steal to buy drugs or have a history of drug and alcohol abuse. One in ten prisoners uses drugs in gaol, usually marijuana.[26] Since 1996, prisoners have been required to test drug-free to win parole.

Despite the disturbing level of addiction and abuse among those in prison, *investment in treatment programmes is completely inadequate.* The number of inmates needing drug treatment has increased by around 50,000 every year to 840,000 by 1996, while the numbers in drug treatment programmes has been almost unchanged.[27] Just 13 per cent were receiving help of the 70–85 per cent of inmates needing it. What is going on? We know that almost all of these offenders will return almost immediately to previous patterns of addiction and drug-related crime, even after months or years of enforced abstinence in prison.

This is a very expensive national network of long-stay facilities, every one of which should become a huge rehab project. After all, only 20 per cent of prisoners would not qualify to be offered the treatment package.

Drug trafficking also causes a huge amount of crime:

- Competition for territory
- Quarrels among dealers
- Location of drug markets in disadvantaged and poorly policed areas
- Gun culture with many weapons carried by users and dealers
- 5 per cent of all murders in 1995 were drug-related (1,010)[28]

As we have seen, money laundering undermines society – drug dealing generates billions of dollars a year. Sixty per cent of cases investigated by the Inland Revenue Service in 1996/97 were drug-related.[29]

Cost of preventing entry in US

A key control strategy is to restrict supply with seizures at borders and points of entry such as airports, but this is costly. *Customs posts are completely overwhelmed by the global revolution in low cost travel.* Every year 60 million people enter the US on more than 675,000 commercial and private flights, another 6 million by sea, and 370,000 by land; 116 million vehicles travel across Mexican and Canadian borders; 90,000 merchant and passenger ships dock each year, carrying 9 million shipping containers, 400 million tons of cargo. And a further 157,000 smaller vessels visit ports.

Mexico's border alone is an impossible problem with 84 million car crossings, plus 2.8 million trucks, 232 million drivers and passengers. All pass through 38 ports of entry scattered along a 2,000 mile frontier. Drug-runners just cut across wherever they will, terrifying ranchers and those living in rural areas. The risks of arrest at an official border crossing are minimal.

The US government threw almost 2,000 extra people at the problem in 1997, together with new detection technologies, sensors, infrared sighting devices, but all with limited success – how can you hope to succeed against such traffic flows?

The same is true of any busy international airport. The volumes of baggage and the speed requirements for loading and unloading are impossible to overcome. And with a kilogram of heroin worth $250,000, *a single suitcase can contain over $5 million, while a person can hide $100,000 of heroin on or inside his or her body with little difficulty.*

- Chicago O'Hare 65 million passengers
- London Heathrow 47.6 million
- Frankfurt 31.8 million
- Amsterdam 20.6 million
- Tokyo 18.9 million

Then there are the sea ports. North Atlantic sea trade has grown to 1.3 million containers a year.

Cargo traffic in millions of tons:
- Rotterdam 293
- Singapore 290
- Hong Kong 147
- London 52
- New York 47

Even if there is a major crack-down on one route, traffickers rapidly move to a softer option. There is always going to be a way. The fact is that many countries are awash with drugs, which is why purity is rising as prices are falling. There is far more to go round than needed. The markets are becoming flooded, while the level of seizures is too small to affect street prices for long – the only real test of effectiveness.

COSTS OF DRUG ABUSE IN BRITAIN

So what about the costs of drug abuse in Britain? We have already seen that the total UK drugs economy is worth around 0.3 per cent of GDP or £3 billion a year. In addition, at least £3 billion is spent dealing with the social and health costs, and there are more than £6 billion of other costs to society. That makes a total of more than £10 billion, or around 1.5 per cent of British GDP – a significant drain on the nation. If you add on drug costs to society plus smoking, *the total cost of drug addiction in Britain is more than £30 billion a year, or 4 per cent of GDP.* Let us look at some of those costs.

Smoking

Smoking is estimated to kill around 120,000 a year in Britain, shortening life on average by at least ten years. That's 1.2 million years of life lost. Normal government actuarial calculations would be that for every year of life lost, the economy shrinks by the wage of the person who is not now earning. The average annual salary is around £17,500. Therefore if just twenty smokers have to stop work five years before retirement because of smoking-related ill health or early death, the loss is around £1.7 million. The numbers soon start to climb.

Most smoking ill health and most of the 120,000 smoking deaths a year are among those retired. But if we take a figure of 20,000 people, who are unable to work for an average of five years each (mainly because of death before retirement), then the economic cost would be almost £2 billion a year.

The cost of caring for those with tobacco-related illness is around £1.6 billion – a significant proportion of the £35 billion a year spent on health.[30] Against that many smokers argue that tax revenues on cigarettes more than compensate for the extra workload. Similar arguments have been made in the US. They also argue that people who die from smoking aged 70 are less a drain on the state than those who live till they are 90.

We can dispute the exact figures but the fact is clear: smoking robs people of health and life, and both of these are devastatingly high costs to the individuals, to their families and friends, as well as to society.

Alcohol

Alcohol abuse dominates law and order enforcement in many areas, and wrecks millions of British lives. Alcohol abuse alone is far more disruptive than all the rest of substance abuse combined.

Alcohol kills 31,000 a year – 28,000 deaths a year are alcohol-related (plus a further 3,000 are deaths where alcohol is listed as a cause on a death certificate), and 28,000 include suicides, accidents, cancers and strokes. Alcohol-related accidents at home – for example falling downstairs – and head injuries are the most frequent result.

While deaths from alcoholic liver damage are usually in older people, deaths which are alcohol-related are spread across the age groups more evenly. If we say that the average alcohol-linked death results in a loss of five working years, then the cost to society in actuarial terms each year, based on lost earnings, could be more than £2.5 billion.

Alcohol-related health costs in Britain have been estimated by Alcohol Concern to be around £150 million a year,[31] or 4.3 per cent of total health spending.

- 25 per cent of male hospital admissions are alcohol-related
- Deaths from liver disease are ten times the normal rate among heavy drinkers
- Drinking excessively is a common cause of high blood pressure, strokes and obesity
- 3 per cent of all cancers may be linked to alcohol
- Alcohol is a factor in around 15 per cent of all road deaths, 26 per cent of drownings and 39 per cent of deaths in fires
- 4,500 people are admitted because of mental health problems every year due to alcohol
- 65 per cent of suicide attempts are linked with excessive drinking

There are many links between alcohol and crime: alcohol-defined crimes such as drink-driving, public drunkenness and others; disinhibition; links to violence and so-called 'Dutch courage'; and crime to pay for drink.

Drink-driving

Drink-driving accidents have fallen 40 per cent in ten years to around 10,000 a year in the UK, despite a 30 per cent increase in motoring. However, these crashes still kill eleven people a week. The annual cost of drink-related traffic crime has been estimated to be £50 million.[32]

Drink kills pedestrians and cyclists too. Fifteen per cent of all those injured in road traffic accidents have been drinking in the previous four hours.[33]

Other alcohol-related crimes

Alcohol causes crime – on a breath-taking scale.[34,35] It is easy to be blinded by lists of statistics, but when reading the ghastly catalogue below, just reflect what a difference it would make to society if there were no alcohol abuse – or even a 50 per cent reduction. Alcohol use is associated with:

★ ★ ★

- 65 per cent of all murders (33 per cent of murder victims have been drinking)
- 75 per cent of all stabbings
- 70 per cent of all beatings
- 50 per cent of all domestic violence
- 33 per cent of burglaries
- 50 per cent of street crime
- 85 per cent of crime in pubs and clubs
- 44 per cent of all violent assaults
- 30 per cent of sex offences
- 30–40 per cent of child abuse cases

We cannot turn away from these figures. They provoke profound questions about the future. In the light of these facts it is even more shocking that the real cost of alcohol continues to fall, while access to alcohol has never been easier. Drunkenness has become an accepted way of life, although publicly discouraged. We cannot go on like this. The cost is too high. But there is more.

Facial injuries

Just one example of large-scale alcohol-related injury is facial cuts. As a casualty officer I have seen entire emergency departments grind to a halt as ten or more drunken lads stagger in with bleeding faces, each of which will need perhaps half an hour to an hour of a doctor's or nurse's time to stitch back together again. Every Saturday night the same thing happened, around 2.30 in the morning as the local night club crowds began to leave.

Half a million people in Britain suffer facial injuries each year, severe enough to need medical help, 125,000 of them in assaults.[36] Half of all facial injuries in the fifteen- to twenty-five-year-age group happen after victim or aggressor have been drinking, and usually take place in bars, clubs or in the streets. Alcohol increases aggression in some and vulnerability in others, a dangerous combination.

Outside the home, four times as many men as women are facially injured, but this is reversed at home, where almost half of all facial injuries occur in women and half of these are linked to drinking.

A nation of drunkards

There would be a dramatic fall in all the offences listed above if the nation were very moderate in drinking, instead of the reality where, as we have seen, 6 per cent of men are drinking more than 50 units a week.

- Around 60,000 are cautioned every year for drunkenness, commonest age nineteen–twenty
- One in five of all people arrested and brought to Charing Cross police station in 1994 were charged with drunkenness
- Half of all incidents of disorderly behaviour in urban areas happen just after pubs close, mainly on Friday and Saturday nights, usually involving young men
- Fear of alcohol-related crime discourages large numbers of older people from walking around city centres in the late evening, especially at weekends
- 30 per cent of those on probation have severe alcohol problems, and 70 per cent of those were inebriated when they committed their last offence
- Almost half of those on remand have a significant problem with alcohol, together with one in five convicted prisoners – one in ten are alcohol dependent

Illegal drugs and crime

In comparison with alcohol and tobacco, the total impact on Britain of illegal drug use may appear at first to be relatively small. However the links to property crime are huge.

A Department of Health survey of 1,100 addicts found that they had committed more than 70,000 separate crimes in three months before entering treatment.[37] *Twenty per cent of all criminals use heroin, and heroin users are stealing £1.3 billion a year in property to pay for their habit.*[38]

The 20 per cent using heroin are responsible for 80 per cent of all property crime, more than 800,000 burglaries, more than 1.7 million other reported thefts, not including stolen vehicles.[39] In Lancashire, for example, that amounts to a loss of £147 in every household every year. It is possible that the crime wave may decline in the short term with lower heroin prices, but lower prices will increase consumption and the number of users. Heroin for the price of beer can only make the problem of addiction worse.

Cost of the legal system

A significant part of the legal system is needed just to deal with drug-related crime. That is a proportion of total costs of £14 billion a year, including £7 billion on policing, remand and borstals, £1 billion on legal aid and £0.3 billion on probation costs, £1.5 billion on prisons – around 6 per cent of all government spending.[40]

One in a thousand of all adults in England and Wales is in prison at any time, rising rapidly (10 per cent from 1995 to 1996), and the greatest increases are among those with drugs offences – from 8 to 13 per cent from 1995 to 1996 alone.

Fifteen per cent of men in prison have been gaoled for drugs offences, 14 per cent for burglary and 14 per cent for robbery. However, as we have seen, 80 per cent of burglaries and robberies are to pay for drugs. *So around four out of ten men in prison are there because of illegal drugs* – trading, buying, selling or stealing. This fits with another finding that 40–70 per cent of convicted prisoners report using drugs shortly before being arrested. One in three women prisoners is inside for drugs offences, with more there for drug-related theft or burglary or prostitution.

Twelve per cent of male and 24 per cent of female prisoners are addicted to drugs or alcohol when taken into custody. Ten per cent of prisoners say they were injecting before entering. Between February 1995 and January 1996, a pilot scheme for compulsory testing of prisoners (urine samples) found that 1,435 out of 3,785 were positive for drugs (38 per cent) of which 81 per cent were for cannabis, 9 per cent for heroin.[41] That suggests that around 3 per cent inject heroin in prison, often in situations where they are likely to share needles. But providing needles in prisons is almost impossible without jeopardising safety and security. Bloody needles and syringes become highly feared offensive weapons when others suspect the blood is HIV infected.

Clearly this level of drug consumption requires money, favours, and extensive outside and inside help. *High levels of drug taking destabilise prison life and subvert every level of day-to-day activity.* On the other hand, aggressive clampdowns can also trigger unrest. Many prisons are controlled by a small number of well organised and aggressive drug barons who rule for favours.

Private security firms

One direct result of soaring property crime from drug addiction has been a boom in private security firms. As we have seen, in the US the bill for private security is now $90 billion compared to $40 billion for the police, while there are two security guards in Britain for every police officer. Eighty per cent of this effort in Britain is to prevent drug-related crime.

Illegal drugs and health

Emergency admissions and treatment

Emergency admissions to hospital wards are common in British
drug users. Every year thousands are admitted:[42]

Drug psychosis	2,951
Drug dependence	5,092
Non-dependent use of drugs	10,269

Special health issues

The bill for care and prevention of HIV/AIDS is in excess of
£210 million. Those with AIDS through the use of drugs constitute
around 6 per cent of the total. Other sex diseases are also more
likely to spread among drug users who may be too intoxicated to
care about risks.

Hepatitis C has spread rapidly through needle sharing – indeed
it is the commonest route of transmission. Sixty per cent of drug
injectors attending UK drug services are now carrying hepatitis C.
Up to 400,000 people in the UK may have been infected through
sharing injecting equipment.[43] Hepatitis C is a major problem
world-wide. In most developed countries with incidence it is
around 1–2 per cent, and is predominantly blood-borne.

Eighty-five per cent of those infected develop chronic infection,
usually chronic hepatitis, and of these one in five develop cirrhosis
eventually. In the US hepatitis C already kills 8-10,000 people a year.[44]

Health costs of stressed partners and other family

Each drug user who dies at a young age is a loss economically to
society. Actuarial tables for loss of earnings for someone dying aged
thirty-five are around £400,000.

Social support for drug users

Drug abuse costs the State heavily in social welfare support. There is very little data on the social situations of those using illegal drugs, however the Yorkshire Substance Abuse Database reported the following in 1996:

- 83 per cent unemployed
- 84 per cent of those who do have jobs are manual workers (skilled/unskilled)
- 46 per cent live with parents
- 30 per cent live with partner
- 25 per cent live alone

So most male drug users consume enormous amounts of social support and welfare payments, with most being out of work. Women drug users often have dependent children as well:

- 70 per cent have dependent children at home
- 20 per cent have children elsewhere
- 10 per cent have children in care

Then there is the cost of housing. Very few own their own homes and many have no homes at all. One reason for this is debt: addiction means bills are unpaid, people are thrown out of council properties and find it hard to get new landlords to take them on. This is all part of the downwards spiral.

- 6 per cent homeless
- 14 per cent owner/occupier
- 22 per cent rented
- 24 per cent other
- 34 per cent council tenant

Social workers and health visitors

Then there are other social costs, for example rehabilitation and child protection. Under community care regulations, social services are responsible for funding residential rehab placements for addicts. They are also responsible for child protection. Although the 1989 Children Act stresses the need to try to keep families together, many women are scared of coming forward for help in case they lose their children or a baby yet to be born. We also need to add a proportion of the cost of citizens advice centres, child therapy, family support agencies and the rest.

Damage to education programme

As we have seen, drug addiction at school causes loss of concentration, delinquency and encourages truancy – all of which cost money in terms of wasted education. Suspensions, expulsions and other disciplinary measures distract teachers from what they are really called to do, which is to teach. Drug-using pupils can also be a continuously disruptive influence in class.

oOo

So then, the costs of addiction to society are a major burden, whether the costs of crime, health care, social support, prevention and treatment. We can have only one response, which is to do more to tackle the problem, and so reduce these costs. However, there is a very strange paradox: drug addiction can also have *positive* effects on the economy.

BENEFITS OF DRUG ADDICTION TO ECONOMY

It may seem a little strange to count the benefits to the economy from drug addiction, but unless we address these as a central issue, the problem of addiction will continue to grow. The truth is that addiction in some ways can be very good news to many governments, including that of Britain, creating jobs and helping exports. For example, a million jobs in Britain alone depend on the alcohol industry.[45]

How many jobs would be lost if alcohol consumption fell? This is the main reason why alcohol has become cheaper in real terms over the last twenty years. The problem has been made worse by European partners such as the French who have insisted on standard taxes on alcohol throughout the EC – low ones to protect their own wine-making economy.

Every measure designed to restrict sales of abused substances directly affects the economy. Interests may be wealthy, powerful and organised, as in the case of the tobacco industry. After all, we are talking about a significant element of GDP.

Then there are emerging economies like Afghanistan or Myanmar where drugs trade is absolutely vital to foreign currency earnings. Mexico, Colombia and many others have a huge disincentive to attacking the production and export of one of their main cash crops.

In many countries democratic government is being undermined by the drugs trade. A recent EU commission found evidence of this in several Caribbean countries in 1996.[46]

Mexico is so hooked on drugs money that the profits from illegal trade would make the difference between boom and bust. Mexican gangs have overtaken Colombians as the most powerful drug cartels in America, supplying around 770 tons a year of cocaine, 6.6 tons of heroin and 7,700 tons of cannabis – 70 per cent of all drugs entering the US.[47] Drug cartels are hiring former US military officers at up to $500,000 a year for expertise on such things as burst transmissions, bug interception and detection, and intelligence on highly classified drugs operations.[48]

It's not just the producing nations who benefit. Every country through which drugs pass, and whose citizens take profits en route, benefits economically from the trade. Of course, at the same time, they acquire a drugs problem of their own.

The end of the Cold War has opened up new routes and markets, as part of the unstoppable forces of globalisation. For example, the abolition of apartheid in South Africa has helped grow the local market for heroin, cocaine, cannabis and mandrax.

Opium

Most opium destined for Europe comes from the 'Golden Crescent' of south-west Asia: southern Afghanistan, northern Pakistan and eastern Iran. In 1994 Afghanistan overtook Burma as the world's largest producer, with a crop of 3,400 tons.

Opium is by far the most valuable cash crop that Afghan farmers can grow. Lack of central government control and political strife have allowed unhindered growth of opium cultivation and heroin refining.

Most of the Afghan and Pakistani opium is refined in Pakistan into approximately 350 tons a year of heroin. While some is consumed in Pakistan, 20 per cent goes to the US and most of the rest to Europe. Around 4 tons of heroin is made in Lebanon a year, from imported base.

North American, Australian and Japanese opium markets are fed from the south-east Asian 'Golden Triangle' – highlands stretching from north and east Burma to the north of Laos and Thailand. Total production of opium here is around 2,500 tons a year.

Burma alone accounts for 90 per cent of the region's opium production, Laos 9 per cent and Thailand 1 per cent. This opium is equivalent to 250 tons of pure heroin. Much of the refining takes place on the Thai-Burmese border.

Secondary producers for the American market are Mexico, Guatemala and Colombia, where cocaine syndicates are diversifying into heroin. Crop eradication programmes in these countries have destroyed large areas of cultivation by spraying weedkiller on to fields from planes.

Every driver, every supplier of a lorry, every packer, every distributor and every courier benefits along the trafficking chain; every airline that carries a courier, every shipping company handling a container of cannabis; banks, finance houses, industries owned by money laundering operations – all become involved in profit sharing whether they realise it or not.

Heroin

Most south-west Asian heroin bound for Europe travels overland from the Afghanistan-Pakistan border in heavily armed convoys of trucks to Iran, where it is transferred into container lorries to go across Turkey and central Europe.

The traditional route via Bosnia has been disrupted by fighting, replaced by Bulgaria, Romania and Hungary, and increasingly through Albania to Italian ports. A second route is via the former Soviet Asian republics. Other routes include India then air or sea to Europe, or sea via the Gulf, or Africa via air to Europe (couriers are usually West African).

Most south-east Asian heroin travels overland to Thai ports and then in shipping containers to North America and Australia. Other routes link Hong Kong, southern China, Vietnam and Cambodia.

Cocaine routes

Cocaine is mainly produced in the Andean region of South America. Fifty-six per cent of coca leaf production is in Peru, 20 per cent in Bolivia and 11 per cent in Colombia. Total global production is around 750–900 tons a year, mostly destined for North America and Europe.

Cocaine bound for Europe is exported mainly through Venezuela, Ecuador and Brazil, and unloaded at Rotterdam in the Netherlands, Mediterranean ports such as Genoa and Barcelona, and in the Baltic states. Small ships are also used.

The North American traffic is mainly via light aircraft up the Pacific coast, with other short flights to dropping points in the Caribbean, where cargo is picked up by small boats. However, traffickers are increasingly brazen, as seen with multi-ton shipments of cocaine on commercial-sized planes from Colombia to large airfields in Mexico.

Cannabis routes

Most European cannabis comes from Morocco, where production dominates the Northern Rif Region economy. The annual crop is around 350,000 tons of raw plant (kif), equivalent to 35,000 tons of herbal cannabis. Most kif is turned into resin and hashish oil, or consumed locally.

Other routes are from the Lebanon, less since crop eradication was introduced, and Pakistan. US cannabis is grown in-country and in neighbouring nations such as Mexico. Moroccan cannabis reaches Europe mainly via the straits of Gibraltar to Spain. A second route is via Morocco to Spain or northern Europe.

Synthetic drugs

Synthetic drugs can be made anywhere, so unlike crops such as cannabis they do not need long-distance routing. This allows greater profit margins. Synthetic drugs such as LSD, Ecstasy, amphetamines and others are mainly made where they are consumed. Exceptions are Poland, which is a big exporter of Ecstasy and other synthetics to western Europe, and India, which supplies southern Africa with mandrax.

Changes in production and routes

Central Asian states have seen growth in heroin and opium production and trafficking since the collapse of the Soviet Union. The climate is ideal for both opium and cannabis. Opium poppies are wild flowers in Kazakhstan and Uzbekistan, while a potent variety of cannabis grows as a weed in Kazakhstan and Kyrgyzstan. Most wild plants are never harvested, but cultivation is becoming more commercialised.

Extra controls in Thailand and the opening of trade in Vietnam have resulted in a shift of routes. China is also seeing an increasing problem, especially in Yunnan, Guangxi and Guangdong, which lie on the route between the Golden Triangle and Hong Kong. A severe Chinese crackdown has failed to stem the flow.

In Colombia and Bolivia the governments have publicly announced their own ambitious eradication plans for coca production. Colombia aims to rid the country of all cocaine production within a few years. However, as we have seen, the economic pressures from lost production make the promises hard to fulfil.

Cocaine exports are of major importance to Colombian foreign exchange earnings, and contribute directly to the standard of living of the Colombian people – or at least to some of them. In addition, the country has 600,000 cocaine addicts of its own. The problem of addiction in producing countries is a major hurdle to overcome, since local people are committed to making and selling in order to supply not only income but their own dependency.

This is also a factor in Pakistan which had 5,000 heroin addicts in 1980 but over a million by 1990 and three million by 1994. This is in part a direct result of the overflow from opium factories based on Pakistan soil near borders. Transit countries are also hard hit by addiction as payment tends to be in drugs rather than currency, and those addicted are willing to take huge personal risks for a generous supply.

oOo

In summary then, addiction is costing wealthy nations a fortune. The detailed analysis we have seen proves beyond all doubt that far stronger measures are needed. We cannot afford to continue with more of the same, with just a fine tuning of existing drugs programmes. We need a quantum leap, a major shift in thinking by governments and institutions as well as by millions of ordinary men and women. We cannot go on running blindly from the reality, believing somehow that because the problem is not new it requires no new approach. While it is true that the problem of addiction is ancient, it has never been more pervasive and deeply rooted than today. We also need to recognise that for every ten losers in the world of addiction there is another who gains. Every anti-drugs policy needs to take into account the pro-drugs factor that drives the industry forward, especially in the poorer producing nations.

But before we look at individual drugs and how they act, and then at prevention and cure of addiction, we need to ask some fundamental questions about pleasure seeking, fulfilment and the kind of world we want to live in. Are we all addicted to pleasure?

3

Addicted to Pleasure

The most basic human instinct is for survival and the most basic drive is pleasure – or the satisfaction of human appetites whether for food, drink or sex.

In every one of us there is an innate restlessness in the pursuit of something better, more perfect, more complete. Some people feel it as a desire for material things – bigger house, car, more possessions. For others the desire is for 'softer' experiences such as love, affection, understanding or for spiritual revelation.

This restlessness is fed by the hope of what may be just beyond our grasp, just around the corner. When hope dies, depression is never far away, the spirit is crushed, energy melts and life seems to have no purpose beyond existing for the day.

Animals without hope can be seen in cramped zoos where they pace and turn, having lost all direction. They have no need to hunt for food, nor to escape threats from predators. Humans in prison cells can also die a death of the spirit. I will never forget my first visit as a doctor in training to Wormwood Scrubs prison in West London where there was a mixture of life prisoners and those on remand or doing short sentences. It was easy to tell who the 'Lifers' were. They were institutionalised, boxed, caged in their minds, with glazed eyes and numbed reactions.

WHEN PEOPLE LOSE HOPE, ADDICTION IS A RISK

When people lose hope, drug addiction becomes a great risk. When people cannot find rewarding work and feel their existence is meaningless, a chemical or liquid cosh to anaesthetise against reality becomes very attractive. That is why it is no surprise to find the highest levels of drug addiction of various kinds among some of the poorest and most marginalised in our society. Time and again surveys show convincingly that good education and career prospects, together with happy personal circumstances, are protective against drug addiction.

The trend is different for alcohol abuse: for men, an increased risk is not associated with any particular social status, except for senior managers on high incomes; for women, the risk of alcohol abuse is greater for those who are in a professional household, working full-time or of an increasing age.[1]

Drug addiction is often a sign of something far deeper, and when a community shows high levels of addiction, it indicates a sickness at the very heart of daily household life. It is far too easy to focus on simplistic anti-drug campaigns while ignoring the underlying factors that make widespread drug use almost inevitable, particularly among the young.

CUTTING SUPPLIES WILL NOT DEAL WITH DEMAND

It is not enough to say that the drugs problem is caused by low cost supplies swamping our streets. Dealing with the supply will reduce but not control the problem. With our shrinking hyper-mobile world has come the destruction of stable relationships, an erosion of patterns of life and a neglect of helpful traditions.

These factors lead not only to addiction but also to a hundred other social ills which threaten to bankrupt or destroy society as we know it today. We can expect governments to spend and tax on a grand scale in a huge effort to deal with these underlying issues.

The human brain is wired for positive living, with well-developed pleasure centres. Using the latest imaging technology you can watch someone's brain activity change as he or she feels happy or sad. So what happens when we use plant extracts and other substances to activate these pleasure centres? Is psychological dependency inevitable?

History of drug use

Drug use is an ancient activity. From pre-history human beings have known that certain plants were good for eating while others were deadly. Between the two were plants with mixed effects, including those that altered the mind. Animals also grazed on a variety of plants and learned the differences, as they still do. Recently there was a report in India of cows that got stoned eating sativa (wild cannabis).

Alcohol consumption is as old as civilisation. Stored fruit juices have a habit of fermenting naturally, while winemaking is mentioned in Egyptian papyrus records dated 3500 BC. The distilling of spirits is only a thousand years old.

Six-thousand-year-old Summerian texts mention opium poppies as joy plants, and opium arrived in China in the seventh or eighth century, probably from Arab traders. It was used as a medicine until the seventeenth century, when people began to smoke it. Later the Portuguese and British supplied China with opium, a trade resisted by the Chinese, leading to the Opium Wars. In the post-war settlement China gave Hong Kong to the British for a hundred years.

Five thousand years ago the Andean Indians in Peru and Bolivia were chewing coca leaves, the raw ingredient for cocaine production. Spanish settlers disapproved, but brought coca back to Europe. Cocaine was first synthesised in 1855, but not recognised fully in medicine until 1880. At one time Sigmund Freud encouraged its use as a tonic, and until recently it was a standard ingredient in a British painkilling cocktail, the so-called Brompton Mixture used to treat those with advanced cancer.

Records of cannabis use go back to a compendium of medicines made for the Chinese Emperor Shen Nung in around 2727 BC. It grows in many parts of the world and has been used by many ancient peoples in Africa and Asia. Egyptian mummies and burial tombs show traces of it. Cannabis has been widely used to make rope and cloth (hemp) and in medicine. Queen Victoria is said to have used it in a tincture form (in alcohol) to relieve period pains. It was used legally until 1928.

Cannabis became popular again in Britain with the arrival of West Indian immigrants, and in the fashionable Soho clubs from the 1950s onwards. Cannabis use in the Caribbean dates back to the abolition of slavery and the influx of workers from India. It acquired a socio-religious status, mainly because of the association with the Rastafarian movement, a sect which identifies with the late Ethiopian Emperor Haile Selassie, one of whose titles was Ras Teferi. Cannabis (known there as ganja) is not associated in the popular Caribbean culture with the evils of other drugs such as cocaine. However, many clinics in Jamaica are now dealing with problems relating to ganja use.[2]

Caffeine also has a long history dating back to the Aztec leader Montezuma, who greatly enjoyed a hot drink from cacao (chocolate is derived from this). Coffee is mentioned in the Koran and comes from Africa and the Middle East. Tea has been used in China for many hundreds of years.

Tobacco use is comparatively recent, with first records dating back to around 500 BC (Mayan civilisation), although it was probably used for a long time before this. Sir Walter Raleigh introduced it to England in 1586, as a medicine. Cigarettes only arrived after troops brought them back from the French and Turkish armies during the Crimean War. The world's first automatic rolling machine was made in 1881, which opened the door for mass production at low cost, and to national tobacco addiction.

By the mid-eighteenth century British gin production was in full swing, supplying an epidemic of heavy spirit drinkers with many deaths. Distillers competed to make the strongest drink possible at the lowest cost. In 1751 Parliament took action and imposed high duties on spirit sales. Nevertheless, throughout the nineteenth century alcohol abuse continued to be a common means of escape for millions of industrialised men and women living in miserable conditions. Alcohol became a well recognised social evil. This led to the temperance movement and to restrictions on licensing hours.

History of the American Prohibition Movement[3]

Many societies tried banning alcohol: from the ancient Aztecs to ancient China, feudal Japan, the Polynesian islands, Iceland, Finland, Norway, Sweden, Russia, Canada and India – but only a few tried national prohibition.[4] The American experience is widely quoted by those in favour of freedom.

1820s	Religious revivals create movements to end slavery and drinking
1825	Temperance movement sets goal of total national abstinence
1838	Massachusetts law passed banning spirits sales of less than 15 gallons
1840	Massachusetts law repealed
1869	Prohibition Party formed in US
1892	Prohibition Party wins 271,000 votes on a single issue
1906	Renewed attack on liquor sales
1906	Anti-saloon league forms
1914–18	Temporary Wartime Prohibition Act to save grain use for food
1919	National prohibition sweeps America
1920–32	Prohibition enforced only where population sympathetic – consumption of spirits rises as a proportion of alcoholic drinks
1933	Prohibition ends after increasing criminal production, bootlegging (illegal sale)

Prohibition in the US was a short-term effort against a long-term problem and was a failure. This failure is often cited as a reason why laws against drugs should be abolished. However, the two issues are completely different.

It is true that many people died from illegally produced liquor. The law was very difficult to enforce on a population that didn't accept prohibition as necessary or desirable. Prohibition cut across a tradition of alcohol drinking going back to the first days of American history. The ingredients for brewing were universally available, and the brewing of wine, beer or spirits was a part of folk tradition.

However, alcohol use in the 1920s was a completely different issue to using illegal drugs today. For a start the history of widespread drug use is very recent. Many of these drugs are imported or manufactured rather than made as a result of back-garden local efforts. As we have seen, most people do *not* use illegal drugs, and most have never tried them, even once. In contrast, most people had tasted alcohol in the 1920s and the majority drank regularly. Trying to make one of the oldest pleasures completely illegal, when enjoyed by the majority, was ambitious and doomed to failure from the start.

The temperance cycle took a hundred years from start to finish. It is still alive. In March 1997 women in New Delhi took to the streets to campaign for severe restrictions on alcohol – which they won, with bans on drinking in many public places. Finland also adopted prohibition from 1913 to 1931.

Many Islamic nations today are strictly teetotal. The ban is absolute and controls are severe. Prohibition works in these countries because their history and cultural attitudes to alcohol have always been different, with abstention from alcohol a fundamental teaching of the Islamic faith. In contrast, countries like the US have been dominated by a Judaeo-Christian ethic, which teaches that alcohol in moderation is a welcome part of normal day-to-day life. Jesus drank alcohol, and used it in the Last Supper, while the Apostle Paul urged the ailing Timothy to drink a little wine to help his digestion.[5]

We will return to lessons from prohibition when considering laws in a later chapter.

Nineteenth-century opium

It seems extraordinary today that people were so blind to the dangers of opium when it first began to be used in Europe in higher society circles. The history of drug use is that time and again a substance is discovered to be pleasurable and thought to be relatively harmless, for ten, twenty, fifty or more years, until the painful truth dawns. It's the same in medicine, with terrible mistakes made over prescribing highly addictive drugs like Valium to a whole generation. At the time the dangers were not recognised.

This should make us very cautious indeed before giving drugs like cannabis, Ecstasy or Viagra a fairly clean bill of health. Their obvious short-term health risks are low compared to many other drugs as we will see, but these are still early days.

Opium was a fashionable and respectable drug widely used in Victorian times, so much so that Sir Arthur Canon Doyle could create a household name detective hero, Sherlock Holmes, and portray him as an opium addict without fear of hostile reaction. The commonest form was as laudanum, opium dissolved in alcohol although it was also swallowed in pills. Both the poets Byron and Keats were opium users. Heroin was created in 1874, and became illegal in the UK in 1920.

At the very time that alcohol fell under prohibition in the US, and many other drugs were declared illegal, a host of new synthetic drugs began to emerge. This was the start of a new drug culture which continues to accelerate today.

Twentieth-century drug creation

- 1914   MDMA (Ecstasy) made as appetite suppressant; legal in US until 1985
- 1920s   LSD made by Dr Albert Hoffman
- 1940s   Anabolic steroids used
- 1940s   Amphetamines widely used to keep troops awake
- 1950s   Legally made amphetamines used by those wanting to lose weight, students, truck drivers and athletes. LSD used in psychiatry with disastrous effects
- 1960s   Tranquillisers such as Librium and Valium

The dawn of the 'drugs era' – 1960s–1980s[6]

Drug misuse only became recognised as a significant problem for the whole of society in the 1960s, with growing consumption of heroin in London and beyond, along with amphetamines, cannabis and LSD, which together typified the 'psychedelic' fashions of the late 1960s.

By the 1970s heroin use was continuing to grow, together with barbiturates and methaqualone, illegally manufactured amphetamines. Solvents had found their way into widespread abuse, and cannabis continued to grow in popularity, while LSD was used mostly by those identifying with the alternative culture of the previous decade.

The 1980s saw the arrival of large quantities of smokable heroin, which made it far more popular as a drug, especially among a younger generation from lower income backgrounds who were reluctant to use a needle. However, many switched to injectable heroin because it was cheaper.

By 1986 AIDS was a major worry, and this forced a move from prevention to harm reduction with needle exchanges and other measures (see later). It also became clear that the areas of the UK worst affected by drug addiction were those of greatest economic and social needs, such as inner-city housing estates in London,

Manchester and Liverpool and outer areas of Glasgow and Edinburgh.

The 1990s dance culture

A more recent change has been the emergence of an all-night dance culture, associated with 'Ecstasy' which first appeared in Britain in 1985 before explosive growth in popularity in the 1990s. Another trend has been growing use of a wider range of drugs, some not covered by older regulations, such as ketamine, amyl nitrite and more recently Viagra. Solvent deaths have fallen, and fears of a crack epidemic have not been fulfilled. However, crack and heroin remain major problems, as we have seen.

PLEASURE MEANS HEALTH AND SURVIVAL

The pursuit of pleasure helps guarantee human health and survival – even the pleasure of picking a skin lesion or of excreting. If these activities were not wired to the pleasure centres of our brains, the only motivation we would have for various mundane activities would be the avoidance of pain. Food, reproduction, social activity – all aspects of normal human life create pleasures. When the natural activity/reward system breaks down then life itself becomes at risk, and normal processes grind to a halt.

Wiring monkeys for happiness?

The pleasure centre in the brain has been intensively studied, particularly by those looking to understand addiction. In one famous experiment, electrodes were inserted into the pleasure centre of a monkey's brain so that small electrical pulses were delivered on pressing a lever. Several monkeys became instant pleasure addicts, choosing to spend their entire waking lives pressing the levers. Obtaining intense pleasure displaced every other activity including feeding. The pleasure centre was so overwhelmed by hyperstimulation that all normal stimuli failed to be rewarding e.g. full stomach when hungry. All motivation to eat disappeared. The monkeys died.

Happiness can be bad for you

Drugs are artificial pleasure inducers. The greatest seductive power of a drug lies not in its ability to create physical dependence and withdrawal symptoms, but in hyperstimulating the pleasure centre.

There are many psychoactive substances. Some are so pleasurable that users much prefer to be intoxicated than sober. This is nothing to do with physical tolerance, dependence or addiction. The first time someone uses a drug he or she will have little idea about how the experience will be. Contrary to the myths, addiction after a single dose of even the most powerful drugs is unusual, and initial use is not always enjoyable. The experience of drug use is greatly influenced by the setting and the previous mood of the user, as well as by previous exposure, for reasons we will see later.

An epidemic of unhappiness in a materialistic world

We live in a strange paradox, at a time of extraordinary wealth and health in industrialised nations, yet of unprecedented misery and dissatisfaction, judging by divorce rates, agony columns, soaring stress-related disorders, depression and suicides. Psychotherapy and counselling are boom industries, a sign of the times, helping a generation cope with painful reality.

Chronic disease and debility

While life expectancy has increased, so have the years of loneliness, isolation, chronic illness, muscle wasting, partial mobility, deafness, fading vision, physical dependency and feeble mental powers. There is a growing market therefore for 'happy pills'. Anti-depressants are often only partially effective, taking sometimes six weeks or more to have their full impact. As a doctor I know that a fast-acting mood elevator to give to those who are feeling miserable could be very useful – in theory.

Features of an ideal 'happy pill'

- Creates happy feelings in neutral or unhappy situation
- No damage to any organ or system
- Health-enhancing properties
- No habituation or tolerance
- No physical dependency or withdrawal
- Low cost
- Long acting and reversible (Naloxone-like antidote to produce instant sobriety)

Humans who cannot feel pain

So what would happen if people could take a drug that relieved all emotional and physical pain and distress? The answer is that the person would not survive long.

There is a very severe inherited condition, the Riley-Day Syndrome, where a child is born with damaged sensation so that he or she can hardly feel any pain. Pain is a normal warning sign of slight injury and is first felt as mild discomfort. You are experiencing it as you read this book. Every few minutes your senses tell you to shift position slightly to even up the blood circulation in the skin. If you did not you would very quickly land up with pressure sores. We automatically turn over when asleep, and make hundreds of other postural adjustments, shifting weight from one leg to another when standing, and resting weary muscles after an energetic day.

When someone lacks this continuous feedback to the brain from skin, muscles and bones, the result is that they burn, cut, and bruise themselves. So pain keeps us healthy, constantly disciplining our daily lives. Relieve all pain, and risk your whole future. And the same is true of emotional pain. Happiness and sorrow in our relationships are vital to healthy community life.

You cannot have love without grief. It has been said that the greatest gift you can possibly give to someone who is dying is the knowledge that you will miss him or her when they are gone. Grief is a direct expression of our love, of missing the person. On a day-to-day basis, grief caused by separation is what drives the engine to invest time and energy in a relationship. Marriages where spouses never miss the other's absence are at high risk of divorce.

What happens to humans able to live in constant ecstasy?

So what happens to people who are able to live (hypothetically perhaps) in constant ecstasy? They will never be distressed by the lack of anything. They will forget to eat, won't pay bills, won't worry about whether friendships or relationships are falling apart – in fact they won't be able to focus on any problem in life, until the nightmare moment arrives when the dose wears off.

Someone in the ultimate happy state will be so contented when intoxicated that she not be able to remember or even imagine what it will be like to wake up tomorrow and need another dose. Nor will she have any strategy to get another one, because she will not be able to feel the slightest concern or motivation to think about the future. So then, stress and worry keep us healthy, just as in the animal kingdom, stress and worry (the need to find food, shelter and stay away from danger) keep them fit and healthy.

What happens to humans who have had a fleeting experience of unimaginable pleasure?

Now we begin to understand the basis of psychological dependency or addiction, where there is no physical dependency or withdrawal. If a human being has a fleeting experience of unimaginable pleasure, then the person is almost certain to want more, seeking to repeat the experience until some unpleasant problem emerges or the pleasure effect fades.

An example of this cycle of pleasure seeking is orgasm, which in men at least is governed by the law of diminishing returns, as multiple orgasms over a limited period become progressively less intense. Just as well, or those engaging in sex would be at risk of dying of sheer exhaustion. The new drug, Viagra, introduced in 1998 as a treatment for impotence, became a runaway success with a million men taking it in the US in the first three months – mostly with no medical condition. Men and women reported spectacular results and overnight a new recreational drug was born. But sixteen men died in less than sixteen weeks. Expect growing worries about addiction and many more 'performance enhancers'.

However, sexual addiction is a well-recognised condition, and a large number of organisations exist to help deal with it in the US.[7] Key features of the sex addict can be:

- Feelings of insecurity . . . so
- Feeling that nobody can accept the person as he or she really is
- Feeling that personal needs cannot be met by dependence on others
- Feeling that sex is the most important sign of love or that sex is the most important personal need

Every other source of pleasure is measured against the utopia

Where someone has experienced a pleasure more intense than any felt before, the person will continue to measure all future experiences against this yardstick. This is likely to drive the person back to the same place again, even if the after effects were unpleasant.

One reason for this is the selectivity of human memory, different from the near-total amnesia afflicting some after a severe drinking bout. Part of our coping mechanism is that painful memories often fade faster than pleasant ones, with the exception of severe psychological trauma. Hence the saying that 'memory is kind'. This distortion can encourage further self-damaging behaviour.

Is true ecstasy the absence of pain?

Pain and happiness are linked. Some find that pain is pleasurable, both giving or receiving it. However, most people recognise that exquisite pleasure can come from the relief of pain as well as from the presence of happiness.

One example is hunger or thirst. When you are ravenous, even the simplest meal is highly pleasurable. When you are climbing a steep mountain, a short rest seems like heaven. So the normal pain of life sharpens our enjoyment of the pleasures of life. No pain means only partial pleasure.

This pleasure-pain-pleasure cycle becomes extreme in the case of an addict, with bouts of acute withdrawal and intoxication. When the craving is severe, the intensity of the contrast heightens the reward from taking the next dose. So drug-taking often creates a new kind of hunger, sometimes an appetite with vicious power. To make matters worse, the person's perception is damaged by the drug, making them even less able to cope with unpleasant symptoms.

All pleasure inducers can be addictive

In theory all pleasure inducers can be addictive, whether sex, sport (adrenaline and cortisol levels higher), gambling (adrenaline rush), leisure or inactivity (encephalin release).

But is private pleasure just a private matter? Is what we do on our own a moral issue? Should society be concerned about drugs people use in privacy at home? Is it so wrong to be happy? No damage to others. No damage to self? These questions will return time and time again in the next millennium as more drugs become available with ever more sophisticated and rewarding properties, and as society continues to wrestle with the results of addiction.

THE ROOTS OF ADDICTION

So how did we land up in a situation where perhaps the majority of the country are enslaved to one kind of addiction or another? People use drugs for a variety of reasons, not just because they give pleasure.[8]

- Just curious
- Sense of adventure
- Enjoyment
- Belief that the drug helps physical or mental performance
- Belief that the drug is harmless
- Belief that the drug will help depression
- To cope with trauma, e.g. child sex abuse or school failure, or relationship problems
- Sensation seeking
- Drug use by other family members
- Peer pressure – influenced by peer selection. For example, most youths who smoke tobacco are making conscious decisions to be with a peer group dominated by smokers[9]
- Rebellion against authority/parents
- Positive images in the media
- Access, availability and relatively low cost – cannabis, a few joints for £5, LSD trip £2.50, pint of lager £1.80
- Alternative economy in deprived areas – small-scale supply business

Risk factors for drug abuse

Tobacco smoking

As we have seen, tobacco use is a major risk factor for using cannabis, and therefore other drugs as well.

Time

Spending leisure time with drug users is the commonest route to personal use.

Stressful life

Drug taking is often a means of escape from difficulties and pressures.

Drug availability

The greater the availability, the more likely the use – whether by the child taking a cigarette from a parent's pocket or handbag, helping himself to whisky from the drinks cabinet, or smoking a joint being passed round at a party.

The race factor

Patterns of abuse vary among cultures and ethnic groups. For example, cannabis use is more common among some groups of Rastafarians, who themselves are usually Afro-Caribbean in ancestry.

It's in my genes?

There is strong evidence for a genetic influence on the risk of addiction. It seems that some brains are particularly prone to addictive patterns.

Sons of alcoholic fathers who are brought up by sober foster parents are still eight times more likely to become alcoholics than their fostered siblings born of a non-alcoholic father.[10] As many as seven out of ten alcoholics may carry the Dopamine D2 receptor A1 gene, compared to only one in five of the general population. The gene is also more common among cocaine addicts.[11] It may be linked with other kinds of sensation-seeking or compulsive behaviour.

The so-called 'alcoholism gene' has been used to win a defence case in American courts. John Baker was a successful Californian lawyer caught embezzling his client's money. He was brought before the Bar Association and excused himself by saying that his father had American Indian blood. American Indians have a well known inability to break down alcohol, and are therefore more susceptible to becoming intoxicated. He was suspended, not banned.

An addictive personality

Addictive personalities have also been described, where the person has a tendency to all kinds of addictive and compulsive problems.

If addiction is influenced by genes or personality, can these effects be 'cured'? An important step is for the person to recognise that they may have this tendency, and then to be on the alert for situations which could create problems. So for example, someone who has overcome an addiction to alcohol could then land up addicted to gambling.

Another question is whether susceptibility to addiction can be identified before addiction develops, as part of a prevention programme. Such techniques are not well developed at present, but we can expect pre-addiction counselling to be offered in the future, based on personality profiles, especially of teenagers.

Sensation-seekers

Sensation-seekers can be clearly identified as a group of people for whom new experiences are particularly important. Sensation-seeking has become part of the culture as an end in itself, along with self-development and self-realisation. Bungee jumps, sky-diving, white water rafting, hang gliding – all these new fads are billed as 'the ultimate adrenaline rush'. Extreme excitement (which usually contains an element of danger) can itself become addictive. Drug taking then becomes just another sensation area to explore, also with an element of danger, even if only the excitement of discovery by the police. Once again, sensation arousal may be linked to our genetic make-up.

Once an addict, always an addict . . . is a lie

As we have seen, the statement 'Once an addict, always an addict' is a lie and a curse. Most of those addicted to various substances do change. Even if they are unable to break the habit completely, they may reduce the level of abuse. Indeed, if you follow up a large number of young adults addicted to various substances, significant numbers will no longer be using them ten or twenty years later.

One of the most remarkable transformations among heroin injectors has been seen in sharing needles and syringes. Half of all drug injectors in Edinburgh became infected with HIV this way between 1983 and 1985, some 1,400 people. In 1986 a high-profile AIDS campaign was launched across Scottish cities, targeted at all drug users. They were warned of the dangers of sharing, taught how to sterilise equipment, and told where they could exchange old needles for new. In practice only 70 came back for every 100 given out, but the scheme achieved a primary aim, which was to ensure that those determined to inject drugs could do so safely.

Despite much cynical comment about drug addicts not being motivated to take care of themselves or others, the programme was a spectacular success. As a direct result HIV levels have been falling among drug injectors for some years and are now at their lowest level for a decade in cities like Glasgow. Many of those infected have become ill and died, while those uninfected have remained so.

WHAT'S GOING TO HAPPEN?

The biggest question of all is what is going to happen to drug behaviour in future? How will smoking and alcohol be viewed in the 2020s? What is going to happen about crack and heroin, and how will new designer drugs alter the picture?

The answer is that drug use is related to everything else going on in society. Expect therefore that patterns of addiction will follow other major trends. However, drug addiction is becoming a key factor in its own right, influencing behaviour, attitudes, working practices, patterns of health care and economic growth.

Context of the new millennium

The millennium itself is a highly significant event. Every decade has its character and every century its own image. The human mind tends to separate the past into these artificial time frames. But the millennium marks the end of a year, decade, century and millennium in the same instant.

For example, when it comes to music or fashion, the sixties, seventies, eighties, and nineties have had their own strong identities. We say that a song or dress is 'typical eighties' for example. However, it is hard to imagine in the year 2006 people describe a new building as 'typical twenty hundreds'. They might describe a new building as early twenty-first century, but are more likely to label it early third millennial – catching the hopes, fears, aspirations and dreams of the new millennium.

Expect therefore major shifts in attitudes, social conventions and expectations in the years following. In the late 1990s a way to insult a boss was to tell him he was still stuck in the 1980s or 1970s – or perhaps in the nineteenth century. But by the year 2010 the insult will have changed. 'You're still stuck in a late-twentieth-century time warp . . . you need to get into the third millennium.' The millennial dividing line will mark a watershed in human history and will directly affect the way people see drug taking, tobacco, alcohol and other issues.

The bigger picture

I have described elsewhere in *Futurewise* the six faces of the F.U.T.U.R.E.[12]

Fast

The world is speeding up. Computer technology, the digital society, Internet, networking, acceleration of scientific discovery, political change, economic crises – it's all changing faster than ever. As a result, growing numbers of people will want to opt out, to use drugs to help them relax after hyper-intense bursts of activity, and to help keep them going when exhausted.

Urban

Our world is increasingly urbanised, with anonymous neighbours, family break down, elderly separated from children and partners separated from partners, more living on their own. Inner-city estates have become ghettos of deprivation and despair, with high unemployment among the young and alienation from all forms of authority. All these factors will make the spread of drug abuse more likely.

Tribal

As the world disintegrates on the one hand and becomes more globalised on the other, people and relationships are getting left behind. Yet there is a powerful need to belong, to identify, to be a part of a family, a group, a gang, a community, a tribe. Tribalism is perhaps the most powerful force in the world today, whether seen in Northern Ireland or Bosnia or among football supporters. Drug use is often an expression of tribalism: the ceremony of passing a needle and syringe among a group of intimate friends, the sharing of a joint, joining the ecstasy/dance culture. Drug use can be a way of identifying with a particular group, of finding an identity. It can also dull the sense of isolation and emptiness when you can't find one.

Universal

The world is getting smaller thanks to the transport revolution and changes in technology. Trade barriers are crumbling, together with restrictions on the movement of goods and people. As we have seen, money flow from one country to another has never been easier to do or so difficult to track, using encryption and Internet technologies. All these factors make transport of illegal drugs more difficult to prevent and payment more difficult to detect. Universal cultural norms mean that drug patterns in one country quickly spread to another. What happens in the drug-swept US today, and US reactions to it, are both indicators of future trends in other nations. A prime example of this is the head of steam building up in America over the importance of testing for drugs at work, and the insistence that tobacco companies should pay for making people ill.

Radical

With the death of left/right politics has come the beginning of new political movements, not based on old ideology but on single issue groups which are growing in power. Take the row over Nazi gold, which was driven by pressure groups in the US and resulted in Swiss law and banking practices being changed. Or take the Brent Spar oil rig which Greenpeace fought to prevent being sunk by Shell in the North Sea. Once again, a relatively small number of people overturned German and British government policies, helped by a mass boycott of Shell products.

The lesson is that governments are increasingly vulnerable to well organised protest groups. And the pro-legalisation of cannabis is a single issue as powerful as any other, since a change in the law would change the criminal status of around one adult in ten in many nations. Expect therefore that single issue groups on every side of the debate will grow and that governments will change legislation not according to manifesto or deep conviction but as a response to popular demand. Perhaps we will see some legal questions decided by a referendum, the ultimate tool of government when single issues need to be agreed on.

Ethical

A consequence of this fast, urban, tribal, universal and radical world is the impact on people, relationships and spirituality. Profound questions are being asked. What is the point of all this? Does more of everything mean better? Does economic growth mean progress? Why bother to work longer hours for a bigger pay cheque to buy things I don't need? Where is true happiness and self-fulfilment to be found? Self-realisation, self-discovery and sensation-seeking are all parts of our present and of our future. Where are we going? Does it really matter?

Drug use and spiritual hunger have always been linked. In ancient times drugs were used to heighten spiritual awareness, and in the 1960s many who took drugs like LSD did so in the hope of some spiritual enlightenment. Drug use can be a substitute for religious experience, and religious experience can replace the personal need for drugs.

We live in a time of a world obsession with spirituality, as all the major world religions continue to grow far faster than the population, and as hundreds of new belief systems emerge every year. It is no longer a question for most people of whether you believe but of what or who you believe in. Islam is growing at 2.9 per cent per year, Christianity by 2.7 per cent while the population increases at 1.7 per cent. Horoscopes, occult, Buddhism, Hinduism – wherever you look, the interest in spirituality is growing.

Touchy-feely Western industrialised society is turning away from the idea that all human life and thought can be reduced to random robotic impulses and neural instincts. The modernist emphasis on rational thought, logic, scientific order and analysis is crumbling in the face of a global movement which is holistic, inspirational, intuitive and spiritual, seeing life as more than the sum total of its constituent parts.

These factors will affect drug taking and patterns of legislation, as society becomes more polarised between those whose moral code is personally derived and who vote for maximum freedom, and those who have an 'ultimate source' for right and wrong. Expect therefore that the extremes of legalisation and prohibition will clash repeatedly in nation after nation. The consequences may be surprising, with rapid adjustment in public attitudes over twenty to thirty years.

The pendulum is swinging

In many countries several pendulums are swinging at once and at different speeds. For example, in the US and Britain on the one hand we see a swing towards total freedom to use whatever drugs people want, spearheaded by enthusiastic users and by worn-out law enforcement officers, overwhelmed by the large-scale violations. On the other hand we see a swing towards a new Puritanism, part of a questioning across a whole range of issues. Is this the world we want to live in? Are we going to land up in a world we regret helping to create?

Expect this new Puritanism to feature a growing confidence in moral absolutes, shunned for so long in the late twentieth century. Expect to hear more statements such as 'It's morally wrong to smoke in a home where the children have to breath your fumes', or 'It's wrong to take a stand against what others want to do.' The last statement is absurd nonsense since the speaker is already taking a stand, but it will become even more common.

Smoking will dominate the future

One thing is certain: the outcome of the debate over legalising cannabis and other drugs will be hugely influenced by the rethink of the whole of Western society about smoking.

The drugs problem today can be traced directly to tobacco, and is caused by it, at least in part. Two hundred years ago the only drug addiction in most countries was alcohol abuse, and that was relatively uncommon in most cultures. Subsistence farmers face a daily struggle to survive, growing enough food for good times and bad. They could not afford to use scarce food-growing land to satisfy all year round addiction.

But with the advent of the factory-produced cigarette and increasing wealth, nicotine addiction became a mass movement, directly laying the foundations for a new drugs culture today. Smoking made addiction acceptable, smart, chic, fashionable – as it still is, despite billions being spent on its prevention.

A new prohibition movement starts with smoking

Abstinence from both tobacco and alcohol use is growing. Seven per cent of men and 14 per cent of women never drink alcohol.[13] However, expect a new, wider and far more powerful prohibition movement by 2010, starting with tobacco and bringing alcohol use in its wake. It will be a counter trend to the growing clamour for legalisation of some or all psychoactive drugs. Smoking is becoming rapidly outlawed in the US, and we can expect other countries to follow.

A key issue will be the right not of smokers to damage their own health, but of non-smokers to remain well. For example, more than 90 per cent of Americans now favour restricting or banning smoking in public places.[14] This is a major shift in social sensitivity.

Hard evidence of passive smoking

But is there any real evidence that passive smoking causes harm? Two reports in the British Medical Journal found that non-smokers with sustained exposure to tobacco smoke had a 25 per cent increased chance of lung cancer and heart disease. Other reports have estimated that the risk of lung cancer from passive smoking is 10–30 per cent greater than normal. That translates into around several hundred deaths a year out of 40,000 from all lung cancers.[16] Passive smoking has also been linked with other lung illnesses such as asthma, bronchitis, pneumonia and middle ear infection – all in the children of smokers.[17]

A more recent report has found links between environmental tobacco smoke and:[18]

- Sudden infant death syndrome
- Asthma in children
- Nasal sinus cancer
- Acute and chronic heart disease

Possible but weak associations were also found for:

- Miscarriage
- Cervical cancer
- Added problems for those with cystic fibrosis

These results have been questioned – by the tobacco industry and by a number of scientists, many of whom appear to have some connection with the industry. It is quite true that these kind of large-scale studies are notorious for flaws, when subtle differences are missed between different groups. For example, one study on passive smoking failed to take account of different kinds of lung cancers in non-smokers, some of which are known not to be tobacco-related. However the results need to be seen in the context of other research on atmospheric pollution.

It is now well recognised that the quality of the air we breathe has a small but significant effect on the lungs and heart in particular. Mega-cities like Mumbai, Calcutta and Beijing have atmospheres which cause early death in those with existing lung or heart conditions, yet the outside air in these places is far cleaner than that inside the home or car of a heavy smoker in London or New York with the windows shut. It is a fact that every clutch of research findings tends to be contradicted by another. The objective truth is found in the overwhelming consensus created by large numbers of carefully designed trials. In the case of passive smoking, most experts accept the case against smokers as thoroughly and convincingly proven.

The row today over passive smoking is just the beginning. There is already a legal case being fought where a parent could lose the right to see his own children because the other parent says his smoking could place them at risk. And there have also been attempts in America to take legal steps against pregnant women who smoke, drink or take drugs, for placing an unborn baby in danger. These sanctions have already succeeded against drug-abusing mothers. Expect excessive alcohol consumption to be next, together with smoking. Opinion is gradually shifting from seeing the unborn deserving few or no rights, as part of the pro-choice abortion movement, to seeing the unborn as having absolute rights not to be abused physically by deliberate acts of parental neglect.

So then, attitudes are becoming quite negative towards a wide variety of drug, alcohol and tobacco consumers. As far as tobacco is concerned, this is no repeat of the old temperance movement, backed by laws, but a mass movement controlling millions of people through minor inconveniences and regulations. Hence a new rule imposed by US state employers that no person may smoke inside or outside their buildings in some cases, even on their land in the open air, whether a pavement, or courtyard.[19] The original draft banned smoking within 50 feet of any public building but has since been watered down. Even offices and clubs have become smoke-free zones. Private employers are often just as strict, encouraged by lawsuits blaming passive smoking for ill health.[20]

Britain is going the same way, with a recent ban of smoking on buses and underground trains and severe restrictions on main-line trains; a ban in half of Britain's hotel restaurants and at several football clubs. Some of London's high profile finance houses and banks have bans inside their offices and strong discouragement from smoking *outside* because of a negative image problem.

Smoking lawsuits

As in other areas the pattern is not so much new draconian laws but a groundswell of public actions. Hence the avalanche of civil litigation swamping the American legal system, forcing tobacco manufacturers to set aside contingencies of $300 billion or more to pay for smoking illnesses over the next twenty-five years.[21] Manufacturers struggled in 1997 to reach agreement with the US government for massive one-off lump sum payments. The settlement collapsed in early 1998 leaving them wide open to an onslaught of case by case compensation claims by 'victims' and their families.

It's not just people who want a cut in this mega deal. Whole states want to be repaid for the costs of looking after all their people with smoking-related conditions. Florida won $11.3 billion from five companies over twenty-five years.[22] The recent 'buyoff' proposal between the industry and forty States was for tobacco manufacturers to pay $368.5 billion over twenty-five years in order to get immunity from prosecution in health-related lawsuits. The industry also agreed to accept severe restrictions on marketing and advertising practices, to place much stronger health warnings on cigarette packets, and to incur financial penalties if smoking rates in minors did not drop sharply in five years.[23,24]

The industry has not helped itself: it was strange to argue to a congressional committee that nicotine was not addictive.[25] In August 1997 the tobacco industry's chief spokesperson said that nicotine addiction was overblown and unfounded as a big problem, that links between smoking and illness were unproven and that second-hand smoke was safe to breathe.[26]

Their plight was made worse by leaks of documents from several company archives showing clearly that nicotine addiction was well recognised by the industry for decades, together with the hazards from smoking. One document even argued that a corporate aim was to increase the numbers addicted.

As is happening over drug testing at work, the market rather than morals is going to cause a revolution in the smoking industry.

Take advertising. Seriously large compensation deals will force a rethink on cigarette promotion far more effectively than bills in Congress seeking to ban adverts. In a world lighting up *15 billion cigarettes a day* the compensation packages could be unthinkably large if America becomes a trendsetter elsewhere.[27]

China cracks down on tobacco

Emerging economies are the fastest growing markets for cigarettes and are the focus of intense marketing efforts by huge tobacco multinationals whose profits are being squeezed in the northern hemisphere. Many governments of southern hemisphere countries have been slow to address the health issues but this is changing.

China, for example, burns 1.6 trillion cigarettes a year (25 per cent smoke) making it the world's largest producer and consumer. Most smokers are male and smoking kills 500,000 a year, expected to rise to 2 million a year by 2025. However, the industry has been the largest source of state revenues for 10 years.[28] China has banned cigarette advertising and smoking in public places in seventy-one cities. It has also banned smoking on trains. Fines are small and the measures are widely ignored at present but expect that to change.

Clash between new abstinence and drug culture

So there is a growing conflict between these two extremes of libertarians and proscribers. It is hard to predict which will dominate in each country and by when. These are issues we look at further in the chapter on legalisation. But before that we need to look far more closely at how drugs work, in order to decide where the line of the law should fall.

4

Caffeine, Alcohol and Tobacco

Caffeine, alcohol and tobacco are used almost universally, with exceptions in countries or areas with strict religious restrictions, for example, the ban on alcohol in most Islamic states. These substances set the stage for all drug abuse and so require the closest examination.

CAFFEINE

Caffeine is a mild stimulant. High doses can make someone feel jittery or on edge and may prevent sleep. Very large doses may cause flashes of light or odd noises. As with other stimulants, the greater the high, the greater the fall. It also can increase heart rate and blood pressure, is a weak diuretic (encourages urine formation) and increases the respiratory rate.

Coffee is drunk in every country of the world and is a mainstay of most offices in Europe and the US. The standard dose needed for stimulant effects is 200 mg, the equivalent of two cups of strong coffee or three cans of soft drink. As many as 30 per cent of coffee drinkers say they 'couldn't do without it' and are probably mildly addicted. Tolerance can develop rapidly.

Death from caffeine has been known, but only after doses of around 10 grams, the same as 100 cups of coffee. High doses of caffeine may affect the size of babies at birth. The foetus is especially likely to be harmed in the last three months of pregnancy, when the mother's ability to get rid of caffeine is reduced. Low birth weight, miscarriage and withdrawal symptoms in babies (breathing difficulties) have all been described.[1]

Mothers who are heavy drinkers of coffee or cola drinks in pregnancy have twice the risk of their babies dying suddenly, even when other factors are allowed for such as age at motherhood, smoking and bottle feeding. Heavy caffeine intake also increases the risk of a baby's sudden death after birth. Large doses of tea, coffee and cola should therefore be avoided in pregnancy.

Caffeine increases the effect on the unborn of other substances, such as tobacco and alcohol, shutting down the blood supply to the placenta, starving the foetus of oxygen and increasing the risk of low birth weight or malformations. However caffeine is harmless to the human foetus when intake is moderate and spread out over the day.[2]

A possible reason for increased cot death in babies of heavy caffeine consuming mothers is that caffeine stimulates respiration, and when this is removed, the baby has less drive to breathe. That may make all the difference when it comes to fighting off infection or other problems.

Coffee addicts

'I'm dying for a cup of coffee,' is a very familiar refrain, repeated perhaps a million times a day in Britain alone – usually half in jest. But what is the reality? Someone used to drinking six or seven cups of strong coffee a day will begin to experience withdrawal symptoms on waking and then every two to three hours after the last coffee drink. Caffeine withdrawal results in headaches and a range of other mildly unpleasant symptoms including drowsiness and lethargy.

So then, tea, coffee and cola can't be given a completely clean bill of health. What about alcohol?

ALCOHOL

It is impossible to read through the list of links between alcohol and accidents, violence, murder or other criminal behaviour in Chapter 2 without concluding that alcohol abuse is one of the greatest threats to civilised life in many cities. The sheer scale of destruction of life, property, relationships and communities by this drug is hard to comprehend. Alcohol abuse is a major epidemic. It is therefore bizarre that the cost of alcohol has become progressively cheaper over twenty years as consumption has soared, further encouraged by ever longer licensing hours and growing numbers of places where alcohol can be bought.

Indeed, the continued acceptance of alcohol abuse as normal, despite the havoc that results, is one of the strongest arguments in favour of the legalisation of cannabis. After all, in contrast cannabis (at first) appears a friend not an enemy. What is better? Relaxed and stoned, or violently drunk?

The biggest problem with alcohol use is where to draw the line with this substance, which appears naturally in all fermenting liquids, and which in small to moderate doses is not only a relaxant and a social lubricator, but also a health tonic.

Alcohol is the most widely accepted drug in the world, and is part of many social settings. It changes a person's mood, reduces inhibitions, helps us feel more confident and less anxious. It is often a part of celebrations and can be used to drown out unpleasant feelings.

Alcohol abuse often begins when a person feels that without alcohol he or she will not be able to enjoy the occasion or will be less able to cope with an unchanging situation. Dependency follows when the body becomes used to a certain level of blood alcohol. Withdrawal in someone who is heavily dependent should not be undertaken without medical supervision.

THE TRUTH ABOUT DRUGS

What is it?

Alcohol is a carbohydrate, a relative of sugar, and is therefore a potent source of energy for drinkers, supplying up to half of a heavy drinker's energy requirements in a day. It is created by yeasts which in the absence of oxygen get the energy *they* need by converting sugar to alcohol.

Alcohol is absorbed rapidly from the stomach – in five to ten minutes without food. The effects last several hours, related to body weight, which is why many women are more affected by the same dose than men.

Effects of alcohol

One unit is 8 grams of alcohol – equivalent to half a pint of normal beer, cider or lager, a standard glass of wine or a pub measure of spirits. After four or five units, most people feel relaxed and comfortable. Eight units cause slurred speech and clumsiness, with exaggerated emotions. Higher doses cause double vision, dizziness, staggering, loss of balance, nausea, vomiting. Beyond that alcohol can cause blindness, loss of consciousness, and loss of memory for events at the time.

The biggest danger is from injury caused by intoxication. In 1990, 15 per cent of all road accidents were alcohol-related, and 32 per cent of all pedestrians killed on the road were under the influence of alcohol. Drinkers may also choke on their own vomit while unconscious. Although such sudden deaths are uncommon, this is a real hazard in police cells or in a side room in an emergency ward.

A hangover may follow, caused by dehydration and toxic metabolites. Mixing alcohol with other depressant drugs such as barbiturates or heroin is particularly dangerous as the effects are additive.

Alcohol has many other effects on the body:

• Stomach irritation – can cause ulcers

- Liver damage – alcohol is destroyed by the liver but liver cells are also casualties (see below)
- Mouth and throat – cancers are more common in heavy drinkers
- Nutritional damage caused by neglect of a proper diet
- Brain damage caused directly by alcohol in the blood – in severe cases causing Korsakoff's psychosis, a permanent memory loss

Liver cirrhosis is common and deadly, killing more than 23,000 a year in the US. It is the third commonest cause of death in men in their fifth decade. The commonest cause of liver cirrhosis is alcohol abuse. There is probably a genetic reason why only 15 per cent of heavy drinkers develop the problem, but once cirrhosis is diagnosed it is often too late to prevent death and 30 per cent die within a year.

As the liver becomes progressively damaged it is no longer able to do its job as a food store, as a maker of digestive enzymes, and as a waste-disposal unit for toxins. The result is that the liver becomes enlarged with fatty tissue, the person becomes ill and jaundiced (yellow), and blood pressure rises in blood vessels draining into the liver, causing for example life-threatening bleeds of veins lining the gullet. This happens in 40 per cent of those with cirrhosis. These bleeds cause sudden, violent, catastrophic vomiting. Death follows in minutes in almost half of those who are unfortunate enough to have such a bleed.

Defining use and abuse

Is there a safe limit?

The World Health Organisation and governments have recently revised their guidelines about so-called safe limits for alcohol consumption in both men and women. The current accepted weekly limits vary from expert to expert but are around 21 units for men and 14 units for women. The problem is that these are general guides and do not tell us what the actual damage to an individual's health will be.

Alcohol can be good for you

Evidence is growing that alcohol in moderate doses increases life expectancy. This discovery was made following a series of large-scale studies comparing, for example, the health of teetotallers with moderate and heavy drinkers. One of the protective effects appears to be on the heart and blood supply, with a reduction in strokes and heart attacks. At first the beneficial effect was attributed to some mysterious ingredients in red wine, but we now know that the therapeutic action is related to alcohol itself, independent of the method of production.

The discovery that drinking alcohol can be good for health brought alarm calls from those concerned that the news would encourage abuse. It certainly undermined the case for absolute abstention.

Classic features of abuse

There are two main patterns of alcohol abuse: regular and binge. The regular abuser drinks every day or most days. The binge drinker rarely sees himself as an alcoholic because he often goes for days or weeks without touching alcohol. However, once he starts, he cannot stop.

A habit may start with social drinking over a meal, before progressing into higher consumption. As the liver gets used to destroying alcohol, the person needs more to achieve the same level of intoxication. Typically the next step may be private drinking, in secret, drinking alone at any time of the day or night.

In advanced cases the person wakes feeling jittery and vulnerable, and has alcohol instead of breakfast 'to calm the nerves'. A classic sign of a deteriorating situation can be when the person stops eating breakfast, partly because the stomach is often so raw from alcohol-induced irritation the night before.

Sudden withdrawal in a heavy drinker can cause sweating, anxiety and trembling or in extreme cases fits and delirium. Complete withdrawal in a very heavy drinker is therefore dangerous without medical help.

Special issues

Problems of acknowledgment

Getting someone to admit they have a drinking problem can be extremely difficult, and presents one of the greatest challenges. Alcoholism is made far more difficult to treat because social drinking is found almost everywhere. For someone with a past addiction, even the smell of alcohol can induce an intense craving, which can become almost irresistible.

Workplace epidemic

Alcohol is the most widely abused drug at work and the commonest cause of drug-related sickness and lost productivity. It is surprising therefore that so few companies address the issue directly. We look elsewhere at the issue of using urine and hair samples for drug testing, but electronic breathalysers are cheap to buy, fast, and cost nothing per test. Random tests at work, with instant discipline for any worker over the legal driving limit, could be a powerful disincentive. Part of the discipline process should be an offer of counselling and treatment, in cases where addiction is suspected.

Other alcohol issues

As with any other addiction, breaking it may require several attempts. Support and help are vital as a problem drinker begins to rebuild a normal life. As the addiction is laid to one side, some of the precipitating problems may come to the surface and need dealing with. A key step is releasing the person to be fully responsible and in control of their own life again.

In summary then, alcohol abuse is a scourge on society. It needs to be tackled far more seriously than in the past, with comprehensive measures which are outlined later. Failure to deal with alcohol as a problem will lead without doubt to cannabis being legalised. How can one possibly justify an aggressive stand against cannabis at the same time as the enthusiastic promotion of alcohol to a nation already reeling from excess? These two issues are linked, and those who seek to hold them apart play into the hands of those who want no restrictions at all.

TOBACCO

Nicotine is probably as addictive as heroin and on a national scale far more dangerous to health. It kills 120,000 every year in Britain alone, and if tobacco were reaching the market today for the first time would without question be banned outright as a highly dangerous, addictive substance.

In America tobacco use is the leading preventable cause of death, killing 400,000 a year at a cost of $50 billion in direct medical bills. Smoking kills more people than AIDS, alcohol, drug abuse, car crashes, murders, suicides and fires combined.

The medical effects of tobacco are far wider than could possibly be covered in a book of this size. Most people need no convincing of the dangers. The problem is that the addiction is even more powerful than their fears of illness or early death. And teenage smokers are usually particularly relaxed in the knowledge that any health problems will take years to emerge.

Nicotine is both a stimulant and a sedative. Nicotine reduces anxiety and makes users feel calm. It is physically and psychologically addictive. Smoking causes an almost immediate kick due to triggering adrenaline release and other hormones. Nicotine takes only seconds to reach the brain from the lungs and affects the body for around half an hour. Repeated stimulation leads to depression and fatigue so the user needs more. Research shows that nicotine users regulate their blood levels of nicotine so that they rarely fall below a certain point – even if it means waking for a cigarette in the night.

Cigarette smoke consists of a dozen gases, mainly carbon monoxide, as well as nicotine and tar – which varies from 7 to 15 mg. The tar causes cancer, emphysema and other lung disease, while carbon monoxide damages the cardiovascular system and heart. Nicotine also affects both heart and lungs. Tar from tobacco causes cancers of the lung, oesophagus, mouth, lips, and larynx.

Pregnant smokers have a greater risk of underweight babies at birth, stillbirths and premature labour as well as of sudden infant deaths. Every time a pregnant woman smokes a cigarette it reduces the blood supply to the developing baby, hence smaller birth weight.

Women who smoke also suffer more from strokes and heart attacks when using the pill, especially if over thirty. Nicotine gum and patches can be helpful to replace tobacco when a person is seeking to change behaviour, but the nicotine addiction still needs to be broken.

So then, caffeine, alcohol and tobacco use are almost universal. Abuse of alcohol and nicotine addiction have made it much harder to take an absolutely consistent line against all illegal drugs. As we will see later, society has a clear choice: either take a stronger line against alcohol and tobacco or relax the line on cannabis, Ecstasy and several other 'milder' illegal substances. The present situation is irrational and unsustainable for a new generation who view their parents' addictions, and their campaigns against cannabis, as both hypocritical and offensive.

5

Cannabis

Terms: *Dope, smoke, weed, draw, puff, blunts, blow, ganja*

Cannabis is at the centre of every debate about drugs. Pro-cannabis reformers argue that the drug is safe compared to tobacco and less unsocial in its effects than alcohol. Legalisation, we are told, will at a stroke deal with a huge problem of criminalisation, save money and make millions of people very happy. But what is the truth about cannabis? Using the latest technology it is now possible to search through four million recent scientific papers and pull out all those relating to cannabis, crunching down the results into a digest of the most important facts. Here are the results of that process.

PATTERN OF USE

Cannabis (cannabis, marijuana or cannabis sativa) is grown widely world-wide. Cannabis is smoked in a cigarette or a pipe on its own or rolled into tobacco. Cannabis is by far the most popular illegal drug. It varies in potency, according to the content of the active ingredient Tetrahydrocannabinol (THC), from 2–9 per cent in imported material to 8–14 per cent in home-grown flowering heads. Sixty-five to seventy per cent of domestic consumption is resin from North Africa or India, while herbal cannabis accounts for 25–30 per cent, and 'Skunk' or other high potency strains 5–10 per cent.[1]

New strains of cannabis are now available, designed to be grown indoors, with short bushy plants and high quality flowering tops. Cannabis is now being grown using the very latest, most modern agricultural techniques. This is a high value crop. Dried marijuana looks similar to tobacco and is compressed into a block the size of a brick, weighing around a kilogram.

EFFECTS OF CANNABIS

Smoking cannabis produces almost instant effects, lasting one to four hours. Cannabis makes people relaxed and talkative, but is a depressant, which can make people who are sad feel worse. Sound and colours also become more intense. Users typically report that cannabis improves self-awareness, relationships with others and makes them more 'easy going', tolerant and understanding. Some users say that it helps them to be creative.

One hundred and forty thousand admitted to hospitals every year in US after cannabis

In the short term, cannabis hinders concentration and slows reaction times, so is a dangerous drug when using machinery or driving. High doses can cause hallucinations and other sensory problems. Nausea and vomiting can occur, especially if inexperienced users take too much. The effects the following day are often less than after heavy drinking – no headaches or nausea, just a 'woolly head'.

Death is unknown except from accidents. However, 140,000 people are admitted to US hospitals every year because of cannabis abuse, mainly with mental health problems.[2] That's one in every 140 users. Physical dependency does not occur, but smoking it in tobacco will of course result in nicotine addiction.

How does it work in the brain?

Some brain cell surfaces have receptors that fit THC, which mimics a naturally occurring brain substance called anandamide.[3] Within minutes of taking cannabis, these receptors fire up, sending an urgent message to the nucleus of each cell, switching on the genes which tell the cell how to make more receptors. So the first dose may not produce much effect, with few receptors to be activated, but the following ones may be very different.

Now we can see why twins are often similar in their preference for a drug like cannabis – enjoyment is partly in the genes. Other important factors include the mental state of the person before they take the drug, their expectations and the setting in which the drug is taken.

It is too early to be certain about the long-term toxic effects of cannabis in humans but there are growing grounds for concern. As we have seen with tobacco, opium and other drugs, the history of drug use is that it often takes thirty to fifty years to evaluate impact and risk to health. Even today, almost a century after the first factory-produced cigarettes hit the market, some are still arguing that smoking does not cause cancer. Sir Richard Doll's famous studies which first indicated a link are only thirty years old. The question then is what science may conclude about cannabis by 2050.

We do know already that high dose exposure of rats to THC causes damage and destruction of nerve cells, and structural changes to the hippocampus region of the brain. This area is important for memory, learning, and the integration of sensory experiences with emotions and motivation. THC alters the way in which sensory information is interpreted.[4]

Brain activity is reduced in the cerebellum in regular cannabis users when intoxicated, while the orbitofrontal cortex and basal ganglia are stimulated. These effects do not occur in first time users, and explain the clumsiness, together with psychologically addictive effects, of regular cannabis use.[5]

Cannabis causes an acute and, with regular heavy use, a subacute encephalopathy (damage to brain cells – some viruses do the same). There is no evidence (yet) of irreversible cerebral damage resulting from its use, although impairment of information processing may be a long-term consequence of prolonged use.[6]

Long-term effect on the brain

There have been a number of studies on the longer-term effects of cannabis, some find significant differences, others do not.[7] The trouble is it all depends on what you are looking for. The truth is that long-term cannabis effects are subtle and easily missed – but they are there all the same. In view of the very large numbers of regular cannabis users, even subtle effects need to be taken seriously. After all, what is the effect of a single cigarette or of smoking for only a year? It is the possible cumulative effect, in a population of hundreds of thousands of young and older users, over a decade or more that requires the closest scrutiny.[8]

Scientists have studied electrical activity in the frontal lobes of the brain in cannabis users using event-related potential measurements (ERP). You can measure not only patterns of electrical activity in the brain using electrodes placed over the head, but also the speed of brain reactions to, say, a picture or a sound.

Research shows that with increased length of use, cannabis users are less able to focus attention and filter out irrelevant stimuli (frontal lobe activity). However, with increasing *frequency of use* there was a growing problem in the parietal area of the brain with slower speed of information processing.

For example, a thirty-four-year-old man who had been taking cannabis every day for eighteen years was monitored during six weeks of withdrawal. Brain event-related potential (ERP) measures of selective attention showed that he had problems filtering out complex irrelevant information. THC is fat soluble and stored widely in the body, taking several weeks to disappear completely. However, the changes persisted even when cannabis levels in the body were undetectable after six weeks of abstinence.

The man was allowed to take some more cannabis, and his ERP almost returned to normal. In other words, there is some evidence that people who are regularly stoned, *require* some THC levels in the brain for 'normal' function in some mental tasks. Some problems in thinking may actually improve when a chronic user is slightly under the influence. But effects of cannabis can last a very long time.[9]

This 'recovery' effect when intoxicated is not uncommon. Some musicians report that work they create when drunk or stoned can only be recovered fully when they perform in the same mental state that they were in originally.

Selective attention deficits

With so many school pupils using cannabis we need to look very closely at any possible effect on learning. The results are worrying. A study of college students found significant effects on a wide range of mental tasks more than 18 hours after using cannabis.[10] Heavy users made more errors and had greater difficulty in concentrating, in registering, processing and using information.[11] These are subtle effects that might not be noticed by the person or those around but are identified on formal psychometric assessment.[12] Another study also found long-term difficulties in focusing attention and filtering out irrelevant information, which got worse in those with longest exposure to cannabis.[13]

In summary then, cannabis is not physically addictive and there is no physical withdrawal, although there can be emotional problems. However, it produces profound changes in brain activity, activating genes and altering the way the brain functions – effects which can last months after a chronic user has given up. Cannabis is undoubtedly addictive psychologically, as seen in some who do not find it easy or pleasant to live without it.

The so-called *amotivational syndrome* has been well described in chronic users, who seem to have lost drive. Cannabis users can sometimes be convinced that this is a positive thing: an end to undisguised aggressive ambition, replaced by a gentler, more relaxed attitude to the whole of life.

But drive, the desire to succeed, to triumph over difficulties, to excel through a major challenge, these things are vital to the future of young people, who as we have seen are often the heaviest cannabis users. Stamina, staying power, determination, these are the substance of remarkable achievement, of developing one's true potential, of character development.

Indeed one could go further and say that the future of a community or a nation depends on motivating each generation to go out and make a difference, instead of sitting on their back-sides dreaming all day.

However, we need to return to the pressures created by the six faces of the future: fast, urban, tribal, universal, radical and ethical. Teenagers and young adults leaning towards a radical, ethical and tribal society, and against one that is 'power hungry' fast, urban and universal, can easily embrace a cannabis culture as part of a protest. For them, the answer to life may not be more, but mildness, not massive but micro, not mighty but meek.

There have been many suggestions that *schizophrenia* could be triggered by use of cannabis. There is no evidence for this but good reason for the link in people's minds. Schizophrenia is a condition affecting around 1 per cent of the population in the course of a lifetime, and is usually chronic, treatable but relapsing. However, schizophrenia is often confused with drug-induced psychosis. By the law of probabilities the two events – psychosis and onset of schizophrenia – sometimes occur more or less at the same time, as one would expect when both drug taking and schizophrenia are relatively common.

Acute mental illness caused by cannabis is a common cause of hospital admission. In many cases it is hard to separate the effects of different drugs that the user has been taking. The combined effect is often an acute psychotic state indistinguishable from many other mental disorders. The diagnosis may only become clear when the person who is unwell reveals the full history of what they have tried and when. The difference from other diagnoses is that drug-induced hallucinations, delusions and distortions disappear with abstinence from drugs.

Cannabis use is implicated in other health issues. Cannabis use in pregnancy carries similar risks to smoking tobacco – again from the tobacco used. It can also affect male sexual development in some cases (though this is unusual). Cannabis has a depressant effect on the immune system through direct effects on white cells. It can also slow healing. Regular cannabis smoking is linked to bronchitis and other chest problems, and possibly lung cancer. One to three marijuana joints a day can cause as much lung damage as smoking five times as many cigarettes. The way smokers inhale increases the effects on the lungs.[14]

Cannabis in combination with cocaine causes a particularly high rise in blood pressure and heart rate – typically a rise of 49 beats per minute combined compared to around 30 with either alone. Users taking both before exercising are placing an additional strain on their hearts.[15]

Special issues

The ladder or gateway – the facts

As we have seen, both tobacco and alcohol use in teenagers make use of other drugs more likely, and the same is true for cannabis.[16] Most people who use other illegal drugs started off using cannabis. A study by Columbia University's Centre on Addiction and Substance Abuse found that *children who smoke marijuana are 85 times more likely to use cocaine* than peers who have never tried it.[17] People who use cannabis do not necessarily go on to use other illegal drugs, although they may be open to other health risks such as unwanted pregnancy or sexually transmitted diseases.

The fact that there is a link does not prove cause. Studies show that people using crack or heroin have almost without exception used cannabis first. Chance association or real culprit? Some say that there is no real link. Whilst it is true that people who use heroin usually started with cannabis, they say there could be other reasons:

- Perhaps some common factor in background or personality
- Perhaps the studies on possible links were done when cannabis was more freely available than heroin – so people may simply have come across it first
- It may be the illegality of cannabis that creates the link – exposing users to an underground network of dealers offering other drugs

The same kind of arguments exist over violent videos and violent crime. We know from research that those with certain types of personality are more likely to feel aggressive and commit violent acts if they have recently been watching violent films. So surely violent films are to blame? No, say the film-makers. 'It may just be that people who are violent like watching violent films and anyway the link is not strong. Violent crimes are committed by people who have not watched videos or films beforehand, and many watch them with no effects.'

Common sense tells us there is a link

However, common sense tells us that there is almost certainly a link. We know that media exposure influences behaviour. Indeed the advertising industry sells billions of pounds of TV time on that basis. A campaign starts in a town or city and sales soar. People can be influenced to part with money, change the way they use their spare time or which brand of alcohol they consume – so why not accept the likelihood that people can also be influenced in the way they treat other people?

The same arguments apply to cannabis. Here is a drug which is relatively harmless in itself but which is almost always a front-runner in those who later become addicted to drugs such as heroin. We know that once teenagers smoke tobacco it is easier for them to cross the next step and smoke cannabis.

Lowering the threshold

We also know that once someone starts using cannabis it is easier for them to try something else, and for the following reasons:

- Desensitisation: 'It was a big step at first, but cannabis didn't kill me – actually I can't see what all the fuss is about so why not try some other things?'
- Targeting by dealer: 'My mate offered me some free dope and also had some other stuff he was giving away so I tried both.'
- Knowledge of supply: 'I was thinking about trying something else and I already knew exactly who to ask.'
- Drug taking part of social life: 'My friends do things together. We all smoke dope. Someone had something else so for a bit of a laugh we all tried it.'

It is dangerous nonsense therefore to suggest that cannabis use does not significantly increase the risk of a serious drug addiction later on.

Some say that the risk would be *reduced* if legalised because the person would buy cannabis from a licensed and regulated source (a shop) rather than from an illicit dealer supplying a wide range of other drugs. That might be the case but there is no doubt in my mind that it would also lower the threshold for other experimentation, and increase the numbers of young people for whom cannabis becomes a completely accepted part of normal every-day life. This is unlike the situation at present in most countries, including the US and UK, where the majority of teenagers and adults have never used cannabis, and where a very small minority of any age use it regularly.

Does cannabis have a medical value?

For years there have been suggestions that cannabis can help the sick, especially those with multiple sclerosis or advanced cancer. Indeed, as we have seen, the drug has been used by doctors for centuries in many countries, and in Britain up to 1928. The big question is whether doctors should be given the same freedom that they enjoy with morphine and other opiates.

California recently passed a law allowing doctors to prescribe cannabis as a treatment, although that law is being contested.[18] The British Medical Association has also recommended legalisation for medical purposes and more research into pain-relieving effects.[19]

As a doctor I find it strange that very addictive drugs such as heroin and cocaine have been in medicine for decades, yet the use of cannabis in medicine is still illegal in many countries and frowned upon in others. We will discuss later the beneficial effects of heroin, morphine and other opiate-derived drugs in the relief of pain and other symptoms such as severe diarrhoea and terminal breathlessness, but what about cannabis?

Let doctors decide how to treat illness

My own view is that doctors should be free to prescribe whatever drugs the medical profession as a whole considers to be helpful in treatment, unhindered by law. Great fuss is made that doctors might be persuaded to prescribe cannabis simply because it makes seriously sick people happy and their suffering easier to bear. But even if that were the case, would that be so wrong?

Doctors in general practice spend their lives prescribing psycho-active drugs such as tranquillisers and anti-depressants to help people feel happier about life. If a particular individual reports that he or she finds a reefer of cannabis as or more effective than conventional medication, why not let it be used for that purpose? It might be more acceptable to prescribe THC in cake form or as tablets.

A precedent has been set for decades by doctors who prescribe a glass of sherry before an evening meal or whisky last thing at night for patients on the ward. 'Her usual tipple and it will do her good.' The main reason is for a sense of well-being, rather than to produce a very slight reduction in the risk of heart disease.

Of course, every cannabis user in the country might go banging on the door of their doctor's surgery saying they're depressed and want cut-price dope from the chemist, but prescribing could be reserved for those with a limited range of chronic conditions or for those who are dying. People who might benefit include those with advanced cancer, motor neurone disease, multiple sclerosis or AIDS.

The refusal to allow doctors to prescribe THC as a drug is a political one and needs to change. It is no more likely to undermine anti-drugs campaigns than the use of morphine for pain or steroids to increase a sense of well-being in the dying.

oOo

In summary then, cannabis is a powerful drug with long-term effects on the activity of the human brain, plus a host of separate actions on other organs and tissues. Expect more reports of subtle learning difficulties, especially in teenage users who so far have been very difficult to include in clinical studies, for obvious reasons.

Cannabis is not a drug that should be available to anyone in society except on a prescription basis for a limited number of serious medical conditions. Given what we now know, it is clear that cannabis is a particularly unsuitable drug for large numbers of teenagers and young adults to be taking at a critical time in their lives. That's clear from research on the brain alone, without even considering other health issues and the ladder effect. People who promote cannabis as 'safe' or 'harmless' are dangerously ignorant, dishonest or deluded. One suspects the majority are users or past users themselves, and hardly likely to be impartial.

In view of how hard it would be to de-legalise cannabis were it to be legalised today, legalisation would be particularly fool-hardy and irresponsible. We don't yet know what future research will show, and the data we have is disturbing enough. Legalisation would be very premature to say the least. I have no doubt that future generations would judge such a decision very severely.

6

Cocaine, Crack and Heroin

COCAINE/CRACK

Terms: *Coke (cocaine, charlie, wash, rock, base, stones, crack)*

The cocaine family of drugs are some of the most dangerously addictive drugs in the world.

Cocaine is a white powder refined from the coca plant which grows in South America. It is usually placed on a smooth surface such as glass and cut up with a razor blade, forming thin lines or trails which can then be sniffed up through a makeshift straw such as a banknote. 'Snorting' is the commonest form of consumption, although cocaine is sometimes injected. It is easily absorbed through the lining of the nose. Repeated snorting of cocaine damages the membranes of the nose and can perforate the nasal septum (the barrier between one side of the nose and the other.)

Cocaine and crack speed up the body in a similar way to amphetamines, but the effect is shorter and more intense – less than an hour for cocaine and as short as a few minutes for crack. As with amphetamines, cocaine releases an intense rush of energy, makes a person feel good, mentally sharp, talkative and confident. When blood levels begin to dive, the craving is often overwhelming to take more. As with all drugs and life experiences, the greater the high, the worse the fall.

The early euphoric experience disappears in heavy users, who can feel very restless, with nausea, excitability, extreme agitation, anxiety, paranoia and possible hallucinations. Very high doses can in rare cases cause heart failure, convulsions and death. Regular cocaine users often have interrupted sleep patterns. They feel unable to cope until they've had some charlie, stressed-out and irritable. Life for weekend users can become a process of trying to get through the week until Friday. Regular users may feel that they cannot have a 'good time' without the drug. Stopping the drug produces terrible headaches, tiredness, nausea, sleepiness and depression.

Free-basing (smoking) is done by mixing cocaine with other substances and sodium hydroxide. The salt base dissolves leaving granules of pure cocaine, which are smoked in a pipe. The vapours in the lung hit the brain in eight seconds, producing a massive high which lasts around ten minutes, after which it needs repeating. That is why some people can easily get through several hundred pounds of crack in an evening. Cocaine and crack are also used during sex, and cocaine can prolong sex in a man by acting as a local anaesthetic on the genitalia.

Crack babies have been a growing problem in the US. One NIDA study there found that 200,000 used illegal drugs in pregnancy, of whom 20 per cent used crack or cocaine. The effect on babies can be terrible. Risks are increased of premature labour, stillbirth, low birth weight, ectopic pregnancy, sudden infant death and small size at birth. Behind these words are tens of thousands of individual lifetime tragedies, for example children whose mental development has been permanently affected by what happened to them in the womb.

Sex trades for crack are a common occurrence, and this has led to sexual abuse of women in 'crack houses' by dealers and male users, especially in the US. These women are at exceptionally high risk not only of pregnancy, but also of sexually transmitted diseases including HIV.

Cocaine and alcohol are a hazardous combination. The human

liver combines coca and alcohol metabolites to form new cocktails which are toxic.

Big scares but what is the reality?

In 1989 there were many predictions in the press that America would be severely affected by crack and that Britain was also about to become engulfed. Part of this was based on the fact that the US cocaine market was already becoming saturated following a large rise in production in South America.

Almost a decade later those threats have yet to materialise. However it is true that by 1987 seizures of cocaine in Britain exceeded those of heroin for the first time, and by 1991 seizures had doubled. Cocaine was a high fashion drug in the 1980s, particularly in the city and the entertainment and media world. By 1995 large amounts of cocaine were being processed into crack so that in some areas cocaine was relatively hard to find, and crack distribution networks were well organised.

Crack-related violence

Crack has a bad reputation for extreme violence, probably for several reasons. First it is highly addictive and the habit is expensive so large amounts of money are needed to keep a user happy, and stakes are high for people seeking to control a distribution area. The drug itself can cause anxiety, fear and paranoia, and when knives or guns are around, murder can easily be the result.

Crack rehabilitation

Treating crack addiction can be hard – even attracting users into programmes can be a real challenge. Cocaine users are often very different culturally from heroin users and may prefer to keep well apart. Crack clients can be far more aggressive and instantly demanding than heroin users, and many drugs services find it hard to respond. Crack users are not offered substitute medication – the equivalent to methadone for heroin users. Many crack users are black and feel uncomfortable in a white-dominated support centre. Finally, paranoia itself can fuel natural suspicions of authority.[1]

So then, crack and cocaine are real threats even if their use is more limited than some feared it would be. Fashions in drug culture come and go. Expect further surges in crack consumption in particular groups over the next couple of decades, with decline in others. Each wave of experimentation leaves a hard core of chronic addicts. They are a small minority of those who have ever used the drug but are a large part of the market.

HEROIN AND OTHER OPIATES

Terms: *Smack, junk, skag, H, brown, shit, horse, harry, boy*

Heroin addiction makes headlines and raises the blood pressure of politicians yet nothing is what it seems. Heroin addiction is often a stage in a young adult's life, rather than the final chapter. And pure heroin addiction can be unusual. In many places the addiction is more to the lifestyle of the needle, and to whatever can be injected through it, including a wide range of opiates, part of the same family of drugs as heroin.

Heroin used to be an end-stage drug, the one someone used after all the others, but this is no longer true. With the huge fall in the street price of a wrap, heroin is becoming an experimental drug for large numbers of young people, who may not be injecting it. Deaths can be accidental from overdose, or from multiple medical problems caused by injecting infected material over a long time. But heroin can wipe out a large section of an entire community. Once addiction is established, heroin kills around 1.5 per cent of users a year.[2] But that's without the impact of AIDS.

I will never forget my first trip to India. After travelling over a thousand miles by air and land, our Land-rover screeched to a halt at the end of the dust track through the outskirts of a remote village. We were just a few miles from the Burmese border in territory dominated by continual tribal disputes and tension. We were invited into a simple wooden shack, where a woman was dying. Out of 40,000 adults in the village, 8,000 were injecting heroin and 4,000 had HIV. She could hardly move, was too weak to eat and had painful sores all over her body. We gave her some basic medication and her family some advice, and went on to the next home, and the next. All were young, and all were dying because of heroin addiction.

This is a huge proportion of the younger adults in that village. In another home we found both teenage sons of the local church leader were infected and ill, with one dying. The parents in the village were beside themselves with worry. What do you do when you know that six out of ten of the older pupils at school are using heroin every day? How do you keep your own children safe? Every street corner is a place of danger. Every home becomes a possible place of supply. Villagers were talking of setting up various clubs to keep teenagers occupied out of school. There was very little for them to do in the village in the evenings or weekends – apart from hang around with others and get into trouble.

This is what happens to communities which are in or close to major opium growing areas. Heroin is ultra cheap, and becomes as available as tobacco or beer. Taking heroin becomes a normal way of life.

It is far too easy to dismiss such terrible happenings in remote villages as unimportant to the rest of the country or beyond, but that is to misunderstand what is happening. The following day we flew to New Delhi, a huge sprawling city. In a drug rehab project there we met around thirty former heroin users, almost all of them from the same tribes as we had visited the previous day. The drugs problem in the north-east had travelled over a thousand miles to create a new crisis in India's capital. The same has been happening in other larger cities.

Heroin is an off-white or brown powder made from extracts of poppies, papaveretum somniferum. The raw opium is collected from the dried milky sap of the opium poppy, which forms a gum containing codeine, morphine and alkaloids. Heroin is made from the morphine and in weight terms is 50 per cent more powerful than morphine.

These poppies are now grown in many countries including Burma, Afghanistan and more recently in the former republics of the Soviet Union as well as in Colombia. Many synthetic opiates are also finding their way on to the street from pharmaceutical companies and the health service supply chain. These include pethidine, buprenorphine (Temgesic), dipipanone (Diconal) and methadone (Physeptone). Other milder opiate preparations are also abused including dihydrocodeine (DF118) and codeine.

Pattern of use

Heroin can be smoked, swallowed, sniffed or injected. Fumes from heated heroin can be inhaled ('chasing the dragon'). It makes the user feel relaxed and happy, 'wrapped up in cotton wool', dreamy and drowsy in larger doses. It slows reactions and damages concentration. Blood levels halve in three hours so the effect rarely lasts more than four or five hours. It causes nausea and vomiting, especially with first-time use.

Non-sterile injections cause abscesses, damaged veins and septicaemia, hepatitis and AIDS. Heroin, like all other opiates, also causes severe constipation. Sniffing heroin damages the nose. Heroin depresses the nervous system involving coughing, breathing and heart rate, dilating blood vessels so the person feels a warm glow, and dilating the pupils of the eyes.

Heroin is almost always cut with other substances, of which sugar is the most common, together with caffeine, talcum powder and flour. As we have seen, the normal price has been between £15 and £40 for a wrap, but prices have fallen by up to 90 per cent in some areas. Nevertheless, someone taking heroin can easily spend £25 to £100 a day, as consumption tends to rise when the drug is cheap. Mixing heroin with other depressant drugs like barbiturates or alcohol can cause additive effects, making an over-dose more likely.

Overdoses can also occur when a user who in the past has been supplied with impure heroin suddenly shoots up with very pure stock. The same can happen if a user has been off opiates for a while, and then uses the old dosage.

Revival after overdose in casualty

Heroin is reversible, often with spectacular and bizarre results. The antidote to heroin, morphine and other opiates is a drug called Naloxone, which targets exactly the same chemical receptors in brain cells that are excited by heroin, but has no effect. When the brain is flooded with Naloxone, the Naloxone fills these cell receptors and gets in the way of opiates and naturally occurring endorphins (see p. 122).

As a young doctor I was working in the emergency rooms one night when a man was brought in almost dead, having overdosed on heroin. He had stopped breathing before the ambulance arrived, but they kept him in the twilight zone between life and death with oxygen and a ventilator. We were all lined up ready and the moment he was brought in we located a vein and gave him a shot of Naloxone, but slowly.

In less than fifteen seconds this 'dead' man suddenly began to sit up, waving and thrashing his arms around, climbing out of bed very confused (not surprisingly). Three or four minutes later as he struggled to run out of the hospital he began to stagger around, collapsed and was quickly unconscious again. Naloxone acts quickly and ends quickly. He needed more and was fine the following day. Another minute or two of delay before the ambulance arrived and he would never have opened his eyes again. Many aren't so lucky.

Process of addiction

Once someone is addicted, the usual euphoria becomes replaced by a mere return to 'normality' after another shot. Heroin affects motivation, so users may neglect themselves and not eat properly. Addiction can lead to huge social and housing problems, as well as criminal activity to pay for the habit.

The truth about withdrawal

Much has been written about 'cold turkey' and the huge trauma of getting a heroin addict off the drug. Withdrawal can certainly be very difficult. 'Clucking' or 'cold turkey' is characterised by unpleasant symptoms such as cold sweats, nausea, confusion and intense craving. None of these symptoms in themselves are physically dangerous.

Withdrawal effects start around eight to twenty-four hours after the last dose, with symptoms similar to flu – aches, chills, sweating, sneezing, yawning and muscular spasms. These effects take a week or two to subside but the feeling of weakness and loss of well-being can last months. Psychological dependence can be even harder to overcome than physical dependence.

Despite all this, some people have successfully come off high doses of heroin without medication or massive withdrawal symptoms (this treatment is particularly common in some rehab units run as Christian foundations outside Europe). Many factors are involved, not least of all mental state. For example, a heroin user who injects regularly may experience a 'hit' even if he or she is injecting medical saline (salty water) so long as the person *believes* it to be heroin. This so-called placebo effect can be very powerful.

And there is far more to breaking a heroin habit than the drug. There is also for many people the love affair with the needle. Terry is a thin thirty-six-year-old father of three young boys who lives alone in a council flat near Dundee. He has used heroin for several years, but is also injecting a whole range of other drugs, crushed tablets, whatever comes his way. He sleeps at night cuddling his syringe, holding it in his hand on the pillow by his head. The needle is a symbol of comfort to him, a source of happiness, even of hope.

For others the ritual of passing the needle has a meaning: a sign of belonging, of being a part of the club. Much of that has changed in a post-AIDS world, with most injectors now using their own equipment, replenished from government-funded needle exchanges.

How does heroin work in the brain?

So how is it that such a dangerous and addictive drug can be so safely used in medicine? To answer this question we first need to understand how the body feels pain and how the brain adjusts to it.

Heroin mimics naturally occurring opiate-like substances in the brain called endorphins. These have been extensively studied and are well understood. Endorphins are released by a whole range of normal activities including exercise and sex as well as body massage and acupuncture. They affect our perception of pain and our sense of well-being.

If I were to inject a healthy person with heroin, he or she would experience a 'high', especially if the drug was injected direct into a vein rather than a muscle. However, if someone is rushed into hospital with a badly broken leg, a heroin injection does not produce a high, it just relieves pain. So what happens?

When someone is in pain, endorphin levels in the brain fall so that the person becomes endorphin deficient. Giving someone heroin or another opiate restores the normal balance of brain substances so the person is relatively comfortable but not euphoric or heavily sedated.

When the same drug is given to someone who is *not* in pain, the brain decides that the level of opiates is too high and shuts down endorphin production, trying to bring levels back to normal. Then when the drug level falls, the person becomes endorphin deficient, and experiences withdrawal. These changes do not occur with the first dose, but accumulate over time. Recovery from physical addiction to heroin is therefore linked directly to the time it takes for the brain to get going again with its own endorphin production.

We see the contrast in medicine when someone who has been in severe pain and on high doses of opiates is suddenly relieved of pain. I remember looking after a man with advanced lung cancer who had pain in his ribs for which he was given morphine. An anaesthetist came to the ward and gave him an injection to destroy some of the pain-carrying nerves. Because these nerve blocks are often only partly successful I left the morphine dose unchanged overnight to review in the morning.

The following day I returned to the ward and found him very contented but also very drowsy. The nerve block had worked, his own endorphin levels had returned to normal and the medication I had given him had now pushed him over the edge, so that he was experiencing a mild overdose. We stopped the morphine completely and he was soon alert and pain free, without suffering from withdrawal. This was despite having been on large doses for several months.

So heroin and other opiates are *not* addictive when used to relieve pain. There is some acclimatisation to the drug at first while the body gets used to it, during which time any associated nausea and drowsiness usually wear off, but no addiction. I have known patients with motor neurone disease who have been on the same dose of morphine to relieve pain at night, over a number of years.

Heroin does not shorten life when properly used. The only way it could do so would be by depressing the respiration rate, at its most extreme causing the person to die because he or she stopped breathing.

It is a common tragedy that people die in terrible pain because they, their relatives or their doctor are afraid of morphine or heroin. If only they knew the truth. Indeed, ignorance about heroin is probably one of the chief causes of uncontrolled pain in those with cancer.

Too many times morphine is withheld ('It will kill him') until the person is almost at death's door and in unbearable distress ('Now is the time to start the morphine and go on cranking it up until it's all over'). In my experience most people who ask for euthanasia do so because of the ignorance of their doctors, and most change their minds rapidly when correct symptom control gives them a new lease of life.

Heroin can also be very useful when someone is short of breath in the last days. I will never forget the first person I ever met who was dying with AIDS. Here was a young man, stuck in a glass-lined cubicle by the entrance to a busy ward, mask over his grey face, gasping for breath, tubes in every orifice, leads across his chest, struggling to survive, drowning in his own secretions. He was terrified, knuckles white as he gripped the sides of the bed.

I was shocked. Where was the morphine? 'It will kill him,' I was told. 'Nonsense,' I replied. 'It will relax him, take away the terrible feeling of suffocation and *help* him breath – and anyway, as you can see, he's almost at death's door.'

I told them if they were worried to check the level of oxygen in his blood with a skin monitor, and to reverse the drug with Naloxone if needed. When I returned to the ward a week later I asked about the young man. He had been given the opiates, had relaxed and perked up for a couple of days before dying very peacefully with his family at his side. They checked his blood gases. The oxygen level rose and the carbon dioxide level fell. As he relaxed he began to breathe more normally.

Worries in the US

One of the problems about pain relief in the US is the paranoia over heroin. This is foolish. Morphine is just as addictive but there is one vital difference which makes morphine almost useless for some people with severe cancer pain: solubility. A large dose of morphine needs a few ml of water before it can dissolve, whereas the equivalent dose of heroin dissolves instantly in a few drops. But if you are very ill, and thin, that's a very big difference in comfort when the nurse arrives to give the injection. So people dying with cancer across the US are suffering frequent large injections of morphine unnecessarily.

oOo

In summary then, crack, cocaine and heroin-related drugs are highly addictive and destructive drugs, which turn regular users' lives into a near permanent obsession about getting and paying for the next dose. These drugs can be a major threat to whole communities and to the forces of law and order. They are notorious for damaging the lives of whole families where there is an addict in the house, and injuring the health of the unborn through addiction acquired in the womb.

These drugs raise profound issues about human responsibility in law. If a cocaine addict who is otherwise a sensitive and gentle person kills someone in an intoxicated and paranoid rage, do we blame the drug or the criminal irresponsibility of the addict? Clearly we cannot tolerate a situation where an addict feels able to get away literally with murder by pleading addiction and diminished responsibility as a defence. However, the truth is that the murder would never have happened without the person being 'out of his mind' with drugs.

In most countries the courts recognise when someone is suffering from, say, paranoid schizophrenia, and murder charges are usually altered to allow the person to be committed to a secure unit for treatment. But should we offer some of the same kind of care to those whose minds are temporarily deranged through drugs? And if the addiction is dealt with, should the person still be punished?

One cannot make general rules but it is clear that these drugs profoundly alter the mind. After a bout of intensive drug taking many people are no longer in their right minds. Indeed as we have seen, a drug-induced psychosis can be indistinguishable in presentation from schizophrenia in the acute stage. This must be taken into

THE TRUTH ABOUT DRUGS

account in order to decide how mad or bad a person was at the time of the crime.

Unfortunately, public sympathy is often very low for drug addicts, who may be despised as the scum of the earth, parasites on society, weak-willed, immoral and feckless non-citizens unworthy of care or attention when they attack others.

The plight of the sobered up addict before the courts is made worse by the politically correct movement which has tried to rule out emotive terms altogether such as 'addict' with words like 'user'. But the trouble is that a 'user' is like anyone else who 'uses' a car or a bus or a knife and fork. A 'user' can never make a claim for special treatment. On the other hand an 'addict' can, especially when the reality of life as an addict at its worst is spelled out.

By definition an addict is someone who has lost control to a drug, and, what is even more important, has a brain which is profoundly altered by it. For an addict, being sober is not being normal. Being sober is the worst possible position to be in because it means that the person's body is drug-free, and therefore experiencing terrible withdrawal symptoms. A crime may be committed when a person is sober but withdrawing, but in such a state one could say he or she is still being greatly influenced by the drug. The brain chemistry is upset whether drugged or non-drugged.

These changes are true not just for heroin and cocaine but for other drugs like amphetamines.

7

Amphetamines, LSD, Ecstasy and the Rest

AMPHETAMINES

Terms: *Wizz, speed, sulph, billy, crystal, crank*

Amphetamines are widely abused, addictive drugs, usually sniffed as powder or injected. The effects begin with a very intense 'rush' and last around four to six hours. They make people hyper-alert and lively, hence the label 'speed'. In the short term they help concentration, but leave the user exhausted, typically staying awake for up to a day. During this time most users can neither eat nor sleep. Heart rate rises and pupils dilate, sweating increases with body tremors, dry mouth and lips, itchy nose and dizziness. High doses over a short period can cause delirium, panic, hallucinations and paranoia.

In the longer term, appetite falls and users become very anxious, jumpy and paranoid. Rebound depression, lethargy and intense hunger follow withdrawal. Amphetamines postpone the need for rest and food, replacing neither.

Pattern of use

Amphetamines can be prescribed for medical purposes but are illegal to sell or give away. Amphetamine sulphate powder is the second most common illegally used drug in Britain after cannabis. The drug is usually sniffed but may be swallowed with a drink. The usual dose for a beginner is less than half a gram, but heavy users may need up to eight grams a day. For many users, injecting is the preferable route of consumption.[1]

In one large survey, 10 per cent of fifteen- to twenty-nine-year-olds in Britain claimed that they had tried the drug at least once. A similar proportion of those asking for help with drugs problems said that amphetamine was the main drug they used. Over half this group were injectors, the highest percentage after heroin.

Those who like speed often use cycles of uppers (amphetamines) and downers (barbiturates or other depressants) to help them have a good day and then a good night. Tolerance develops rapidly.

Paranoia and other problems

One of the biggest problems doctors face among those using speed is paranoia. I have seen many people who have become acutely suspicious of those around them as a result of amphetamine abuse: 'The milkman is poisoning my milk' or 'My neighbour is a member of the MI5 secret intelligence services and is informing on me.' Since paranoia is a well recognised psychiatric condition it can be easy to miss the real cause. In serious cases, amphetamine users land up in hospital because of this, but the symptoms soon settle if the person is weaned off the drug.

The trouble is that paranoia and drugs affecting the brain, including alcohol, can be a heady mix. The result can be fights, attempted murders or worse as people respond to what they are convinced is the truth about those around them. The strains on neighbours and friends can be immense.

Judith is a warm, friendly and outgoing person – in her right mind.

With two daughters she lives in Birmingham in a new terrace of council housing. The trouble is that her neighbours get on with her when she is herself, but are terrified when she is taking drugs. She is unpredictable and can be extremely violent if she thinks someone is against her. On several occasions she has threatened one woman with an axe ('I'll kill you'), but it's a close community, and police have limited powers — and anyway what would happen to the children if they took Judith away? Worst of all, no one dares inform on her in case someone gets butchered.

Other effects

Amphetamines strain the heart and blood vessels, an added risk when linked with extreme exercise as in a club goer. Women can find amphetamines interfere with their menstrual cycle, and make contraceptive pills less effective.

BARBITURATES AND TRANQUILLISERS

Terms: *Tranx, temazies, barbs, Valium, temazepam, jellies and sekkies*

Barbiturates and tranquillisers are sedative and hypnotic, helping sleep and reducing anxiety. Many drugs are sedative at low doses and hypnotic at high doses.

Barbiturates and benzodiazepines

Barbiturates are widely misused and therefore prescribed less now. Pills are swallowed, often with alcohol although they are sometimes injected after crushing and mixing the pills in water. This often leaves very small undissolved particles which can damage veins.

Barbiturates depress the nervous system and last three to eight hours. A small dose makes someone relaxed as if they have had one or two drinks. Sedation occurs at larger doses, with slurred speech, lack of co-ordination, and sometimes confusion.

After several pills the user becomes clumsy and at risk of injury.

There can be extreme and unpredictable emotional reactions. Barbiturates are very dangerous in overdose, with loss of consciousness and death from arrest of breathing. The amount needed to kill is not much higher than the therapeutic dose, so death from a deliberate overdose is a constant danger, increased if alcohol is used at the same time.

Psychological and physical dependence occurs. Withdrawal causes irritability, nervousness, lack of sleep, faintness, nausea, twitching and fits. Sudden, complete withdrawal can kill. Heavy users are more susceptible to bronchitis and pneumonia, through suppression of coughing, and also to hypothermia. All these risks are far greater in those who inject.

Tranquillisers

Tranquillisers are also used to relieve anxiety and help sleep, benzodiazepines being the commonest, e.g. temazepam and Valium. They are the most commonly prescribed drugs in Britain, with one in seven adults taking them every year and 10 per cent on a regular basis. Sixty-six per cent of regular users are women and many are addicted.

Unfortunately medical mistakes have led to a generation of 'therapeutic addicts' – people who are semi-permanently dependent on their usual medication just to get through life. A significant element of psychiatric consultations has been trying to wean such people off and on to less addictive substances.

Temazepam

When abused, these drugs are usually swallowed but temazepam is often injected. Temazepam is a short-acting benzodiazepine, used medically as a sleeping tablet. The effects are similar to alcohol with drowsiness, but also increased talkativeness, over-excitement and even aggression. Judgment is affected, with over-confidence and sometimes feelings of invincibility.

Temazepam withdrawal causes lack of sleep, panic attacks, loss of appetite, nausea, tremors and sometimes hallucinations. Sudden withdrawal from high doses can induce fits and is dangerous. Overdosing is more frequent in combination with other depressants such as heroin, alcohol or Valium.

Injectable temazepam has become a popular drug in Scotland and elsewhere. Production of the gel-form capsules has been illegal since 1995 because of the injuries caused. It became an illegal drug in *any* form for non-medical use in 1996.

Injecting temazepam can cause serious problems. For example, the gel inside the capsules can resolidify causing blockage of veins or arteries. If the person injects into an artery by mistake the result can be thrombosis with gangrene of a hand, leg or foot.

Fatal doses of benzodiazepines alone are almost unknown, unless combined with alcohol. Tolerance and withdrawal occur even at medically prescribed doses. Withdrawal effects last a long time: inability to sleep, anxiety, nausea, mental confusion and, after high doses, even fits. Psychological dependence is very common.

Rohypnol

Terms: *roofies, roche and 'Quaalude of the 90s'*

Rohypnol is prescribed in 64 countries for insomnia and as a pre-operative anaesthetic, and is ten times as potent as Valium. It is popular in clubs and at parties for giving a drunken-like high. However, the serious problem is with rapists who spike the drinks of victims. The drug leaves the person helpless, and with little or no memory after the attack. To combat the problem, the manufacturer, Hoffman-La Roche has recently added a strong dye to the drug so that attempts to hide it in drinks are more obvious. Rohypnol abuse is a rapidly growing problem: in 1990 there were just five seizures of 207 tablets in the US, but the figures were 81 of 140,000 pills by 1995.[2]

THE TRUTH ABOUT DRUGS

Other drugs are also commonly used by rapists – for example alcohol, cannabis and cocaine.[3]

Ketamine

Terms: *K, special K, KitKat*

Ketamine is a powerful anaesthetic used mainly by vets on farm animals. The liquid or white powder costs $10 and is snorted or swallowed as a powder, or swallowed as a liquid. It can also be injected, usually into muscle.

Ketamine makes the person feel disconnected from the body, and can cause hallucinations. Because it kills pain, the user may hurt himself without realising. In large doses the heart rate falls. Ketamine can cause loss of consciousness, vomiting and death. Tolerance is common but there are few studies of dependence.

Steroids

Steroid use today is far commoner than most people realise. For example, the Drug Dependants Anonymous centre in Nottingham found recently that over half their drug injectors were using steroids.[4] These drugs can cause wild mood swings, including manic-like symptoms, and withdrawal often leads to depression. Users may develop paranoid jealousy, extreme irritability, delusions and impaired judgment with feelings of invincibility.

Two per cent of American high school seniors have tried using anabolic steroids at least once, 1.4 per cent in the last year, and almost 1 per cent in the last month.[5]

Anabolic steroids are widely abused by those training in competitive sport, despite strict bans and drug testing. One problem is that steroids are eliminated from the body long before the body-building effects wear off, so that athletes are able to train hard with drugs and then continue to train without them in the weeks up to a major event. Since 1996 the supply but not the possession of these drugs has been made a Class C offence.

Steroids are swallowed as pills or capsules or injected. Anabolic or androgenic steroids are almost identical to naturally occurring testosterone in the human body, with a wide range of properties, including the encouragement of muscle formation and increased aggression, persuading athletes to train hard.

They are very widely abused in the body-building world. Bodybuilders tend to use them in cycles of 4 to 12 weeks, with rest periods. Steroids as drugs have been around since the 1940s but took off in the sixties and seventies, followed by a backlash in the 1980s when many athletes who abused steroids were stripped of titles.

Steroids cause many long-term problems. They have androgenic-like effects, so that female users develop smaller breasts and deep voices and have disrupted menstrual cycles, with an enlarged clitoris. Men may suffer from impotence, shrunken testicles, swollen breasts and low sperm counts, due to the testicles shutting down their own testosterone production. Users may become bloated from water retention, develop acne and suffer hair loss.

These effects take weeks or months to develop. Androgenic body changes can be semi-permanent, and steroids can stunt adolescent growth. Long-term use can cause liver, heart and kidney damage. Liver damage may be less if steroids are injected, as oral doses pass straight to the liver after absorption. Heart damage is due to blocking of arteries and increased blood pressure. There are also all the usual risks from injecting, such as septicaemia and hepatitis.

This particular epidemic will never be controlled in major competitive sport until better testing regimes are introduced. Even that will not prevent mass-market adoption of steroids by teenagers and young adults keen to build up their physique in order to look good.

POPPERS

Terms: *poppers*

Sniffing nitrites makes the user light-headed, with a feeling of blood rushing to the head, a flush of heat and increased sensual awareness. The effects are extremely short, perhaps one to two minutes. Some users get a headache afterwards, or coughing, or feel sick or dizzy. No sudden deaths have been reported. Tolerance occurs but there is no evidence of physical addiction.

Poppers have been particularly popular among the gay community because they cause relaxation of smooth muscle, helpful before attempting anal intercourse.

SOLVENTS

A huge number of commonly available carbon-based products can produce a high when inhaled. A report recently described a youth club which had identified and locked away over thirty 'sniffable' items on the premises – only to find members sniffing other products the youth leaders were unaware of. Aerosols, adhesives, butane gas from cigarette lighters, paints, polishes, varnishes, fire extinguishers, dry cleaning fluids, petrol, cigarette lighter gas – the list goes on.

Some sniffers use a plastic bag placed over the head, which can easily cause death by suffocation as the vapour displaces normal air. This state of 'drunkenness' usually lasts about half an hour. In the short term an overdose can cause loss of consciousness, and death through vomiting. The fumes replace oxygen in the lungs and can cause suffocation and heart failure. They are also toxic to the liver in the longer term, as well as to the kidneys and brain.

Solvents are rapidly absorbed through the lungs and reach the brain in seconds. Breathing and heart rate slow. In small doses the user feels drunk. In larger doses there may be hallucinations, disorientation, loss of control and loss of consciousness. Most users recover rapidly, leaving a mild hangover, with headache, poor concentraion and nausea, lasting perhaps a day. Heavy solvent use over years can cause brain damage. Aerosols and cleaning fluid abuse can cause liver and kidney damage. Tolerance can develop, but physical dependence is rare. Psychological dependence is also very unusual.

Sudden death usually happens through choking on vomit, or suffocation. Some solvents directly damage the heart causing heart failure. Gases squirted straight into the back of the throat can cause severe cold damage and suffocation.

HALLUCINOGENS

Hallucinogens have been known since ancient times but became prominent in the 1960s. The commonest hallucinogens are PCP (angel dust), LSD, mescaline, peyote and psilocybin (mushrooms). PCP is phencyclidine.

LSD

Terms: *acid, trips*

LSD is a chemical derived from a parasitic fungus: d-lysergic acid diethylamide. It is usually sold as stamps or blotters, in squares a quarter the size of a postage stamp, made by wetting the paper with alcohol containing a solution of LSD. The paper is usually covered with a printed design, for example 'star wave', 'om', 'white dove' and 'strawberry'. Effects vary according to the situation and mood. They also vary according to dose, which is difficult to regulate accurately because such tiny amounts are needed to induce a trip.

About an hour after taking LSD the user begins to feel a change, perhaps becoming giggly or anxious. Perception is distorted in this trip inside the mind, so that sense of time, colour, taste or sound is changed. You can *see* sounds and *taste* colours. A million years become a moment. The world can look and feel very strange. There is a sense of depersonalisation. Self-awareness alters, and the user may have mystical or ecstatic experiences. Hallucinations are very common.

The effects last up to twelve hours, and are greatly shaped by what else is going on around the person. LSD exaggerates whatever the person might normally be feeling – for example, insecurity, fear, loneliness or comfort and safety. In the short term, normal mental processes are impossible and reactions are slowed. Crossing the road, driving, swimming or other activities can be dangerous. Accidents are common, including drowning, burns, falls, car crashes and other tragedies.

A 'bad trip' can be very upsetting, with reactions lasting days. Users may feel depressed, disorientated and anxious. LSD can trigger acute mental illness. Flashbacks can also occur years later, with a return of the altered mental state in the absence of the drug. Tolerance develops but not physical dependency. With larger doses there is a risk of convulsions, coma, heart failure and death (110 deaths from LSD in the US in 1991). Death can result from users misunderstanding what is going on – climbing out of a window to fly or 'swimming' across a busy road for example.

LSD fell out of fashion from 1970 to the early 1990s. However interest in it is growing again as part of the rave scene and as part of the quest for self-enlightenment in new age consciousness. National surveys suggest that 10–15 per cent of fifteen- to sixteen-year-olds have tried the drug

Ecstasy (MDMA)

Terms: *E, MDMA, MDA, MDEA, pills, X, and a wide variety of other terms depending on the appearance of the tablets or capsules (doves, birds, etc).*

Methylene-dioxymethamphetamine (MDMA) is just one of a large family of phenethylamines including MDA, MDEA and MDBD, all of which are abused. They lie halfway between LSD and amphetamines. However, much that passes for Ecstasy is not. Fake

Ecstasy is widely sold as a mixture of drugs such as ketamine, caffeine and ephedrine. In fact only one in four of Ecstasy tablets tested in one survey contained any MDMA.[6] Ecstasy is available under more than a hundred brand names including 'Dennis the Menace', 'Doves' and 'Apples'. They change with great rapidity.

Ecstasy use by tens of thousands of young people as part of the club/rave scene may have helped the acceptability of other drugs such as cannabis, LSD and amphetamines, as well as newer drugs such as ketamine, GHB and amyl nitrite.

Ecstasy is expensive: £7–20 a time compared to £2.50 for LSD or £1.80 for a pint of beer. It is swallowed as a pill or capsule. In small doses the effect is not unlike LSD, but in higher doses more like amphetamine.

In the short term, users lose inhibitions, feel euphoria, and are struck by an initial rush of energy, 'butterflies' in the stomach and tingling, followed by a warm euphoric glow with increased empathy towards others. Users feel 'in tune' with people around them and with what is going on. Early effects include sweating, with dry mouth and throat, dilated pupils and raised blood pressure. Later on sweating may fall. However, effects may be greatly altered by the combination of other drugs in the capsule, for example, ketamine.

Effects peak in two hours and last around three to four. In the longer term, Ecstasy may cause panic and confusion, anxiety and depression or paranoia, and there is some evidence that the liver may be damaged. It is hard to tell what is caused by Ecstasy and what is caused by additives which vary, however 'E' itself can inhibit orgasm and prevent erection in some men.

A small number of people have negative experiences, and flashbacks can occur. Psychological addiction can develop. Tolerance builds up very quickly with higher doses needed for the same effect.

Why people die from Ecstasy use

Since 1988 there have been around 70 reported deaths in the UK associated with the use of Ecstasy in the rave and club scene. These deaths have not been caused by toxic effects, but from three other factors: heat stroke, fluid overload and heart failure.

Most deaths have been from heat stroke. The drug induces hyperactivity so the user dances to the point of exhaustion without feeling tired, generating huge amounts of body heat in an atmosphere which may be very hot and humid, reducing the effectiveness of sweating as a cooling mechanism. Body temperature can rise above 40 degrees centigrade, resulting in convulsions, dilated pupils, a collapse in blood pressure and rapid heart rate. The drug triggers massive clotting reactions (disseminated intravascular coagulation) blocking blood vessels to vital organs, and the person dies.

Every self-respecting club in Britain has now introduced air conditioning, which is often set to very low levels, to help prevent overheating. In addition dancers have been encouraged by massive publicity to wear loose clothes, 'chill out' regularly and drink plenty. However, at least three people have died from severe metabolic disturbances caused by drinking litres of water, far more than the recommended half a litre an hour.

Over-drinking of water or other non-alcoholic beverages causes body fluids to become less salty. Water finds its way inside every cell, causing severe disturbances of normal cell activity. Ecstasy appears to make matters worse by telling the kidneys to stop making urine. Early symptoms of water poisoning include dizziness and disorientation before collapse and coma as the brain begins to swell.

Ecstasy is a stimulant and causes the heart rate to rise as well as the blood pressure. This can push an undiagnosed heart condition to the limits, resulting in a sudden but rare death. Deaths have occurred after between one and five tablets.

Special issues

The big issue with Ecstasy is whether to classify it as a relatively safe or a dangerous drug. The truth is that the number of serious problems from Ecstasy use are very small considering the number of people taking it every week. While tragic deaths have occurred, they are far less significant in numbers terms than, say, deaths in which alcohol is involved including drink-driving.

UK deaths per year:[7]

- Tobacco 0.9 per cent
- Alcohol 0.5 per cent
- Ecstasy 0.002 per cent

As the *Economist* recently remarked, 'flying in a civil airliner is 1.5 times as dangerous as dropping an "E".'[8] And most of those deaths are avoidable in users who are well educated about how to behave when taking it. However, as soon as someone says the drug is relatively safe, the message becomes whiter than white, giving the impression that the drug has an (almost) clean bill of health.

Unfortunately, one of the greatest hazards of Ecstasy is that, as with cannabis, it gets a young generation used to the idea of breaking the law to buy and use an illegal drug, which makes them feel good and causes very little harm. As with cannabis, it lowers the threshold for further experimentation. It is also still far too early to be sure about the longer-term side effects.

Magic mushrooms

Terms: *shrooms, liberty caps, fly-agaric*

Hallucinogenic mushrooms have been used for thousands of years. They can be eaten cooked, heated with water or added to tea, soup or some other dish just like any other ingredient. The usual 'dose' is around 25–50 small mushrooms. Effects begin after 10–40 minutes and last 6–12, with some disorientation the following day. The user can feel relaxed or 'stoned' as with cannabis, or may experience hallucinations. Physical effects are few apart from increase in blood pressure.

The commonest psychedelic mushroom in Britain is the psilocybe semilanceata. These mushrooms grow wild on well manured grassland and are often found on the grassy edges of bridle-paths, as well as in woods. They are gathered in the Autumn. However, mistakes can be made in picking poisonous mushrooms and the psilocybin content can vary. Other mushrooms can be extremely toxic, and mushroom poisoning can be a terrible way to die. Often the person is unwell and then recovers temporarily only to be rushed to hospital a couple of days later.

As with other drugs, mushrooms can amplify how you are feeling – up or down.

DESIGNER DRUGS OF THE FUTURE

There are already growing numbers of so-called designer drugs, produced in laboratories, similar to other compounds. An example is the synthetic opiate fentanyl which is 80–100 times as powerful as heroin. Fentanyl acts very fast (one to four minutes, and lasts 30–90 minutes. Another synthetic opiate is meperidine. There are also dozens of synthetic amphetamines.

We will see hundreds of new designer drugs in the next millennium, acting not only on the brain but also on other parts of the body. For example, they may prolong sexual prowess and pleasure, or block the symptoms of a hangover, or enhance memory and intelligence. Expect big controversy over memory-enhancing substances and their use in preparing students for exams, and a huge black market in prescription-only sex-drive enhancers.

All designer drugs will work by targeting known pleasure mechanisms in the brain, looking to maximise pleasure and minimise side effects. Of course, the drug company and the illegal drug manufacturer have very different aims. For example, their attitudes to addiction may be very different. Highly addictive properties may kill the health sector market but create a large illicit one.

oOo

So then, a very wide range of substances are being abused, with new kinds of drugs becoming available. Each has its own characteristics and cultural associations. While users tend to have their favourites, in practice many will take whatever is available. Hence there is often a mixed picture.

Having looked at the extent of addiction and abuse, the costs to society, the nature of addictive behaviour, and at particular drugs, we now need to look at solutions. Prevention is better than cure, but why are governments so scared of prevention?

8

Why Governments are Scared of Prevention

From all we have already seen it is clear that global mobilisation is failing against the menace of illegal drugs. The war is lost – or is it? America spends $17bn a year fighting the drugs war, Britain a mere £0.5m on domestic efforts and more through other international bodies.[1] But what is the result?

8

INTERNATIONAL RESPONSE

The international response to illegal drugs has been to tackle production, supply and demand. The lesson of history seems to be that the more drugs are available, the greater their use. The drug trade is an economic activity and requires full international co-operation. It is no good burning fields if farmers are left to starve, as they will be even keener to plant some more. But co-operation requires bilateral and multilateral agreements with governments to deal with international criminal activity.

- Crop destruction
- Alternative crop promotion
- Destruction of refineries
- Seizure of precursors including chemicals for production
- Demand reduction

8
142

- Law enforcement
- Seizure of illicit profits

The United Nations Drug Control Programme (UNDCP) plays a vital role in co-ordinating efforts with an annual budget of $100 million. However, despite all efforts, strategies such as intelligence gathering and drug seizures are failing.

Drug seizures don't work

Drug-producing networks are obvious targets, but drugs will always find ways through thousands of other smaller routes. Big deliveries are easier to track and seize. Less easy to track are the millions of people across the world who carry relatively small supplies to sell to friends. Thus the idea of a fixed distribution network is not a reality.

In 1995 police forces around the world seized 1,000 tonnes of cannabis resin and 3,000 tons of herbal cannabis. Cocaine seizures were 251 tons, and heroin and morphine together came to 44 tons. However, that is a tiny fraction of world production. For example global production of heroin has leapt 60 per cent in eight years to 360 metric tons.

The amounts seized have grown, and give a false illusion of success. Headlines proclaim '£20 million of heroin seized' – but what good is that in a British market worth £1.5 billion? The best test is whether the street price changes for more than days or a few weeks following a major seizure. Unfortunately the reality is that street prices of heroin have *fallen* steadily as the number of users has continued to grow. Of course, one could argue that prices would have been even lower without the seizures, which is true, but the point is that seizures alone are having a small effect on drug prices and consumption.

There were 115,000 individual drug seizures in Britain in 1995, up from 30,000 in 1985 and 70,000 in 1991.[2] In 1995 around 14,000 kilos of herbal cannabis was found, together with 94,200 plants and 44,600 kg of resin.

In total that's equivalent to around 58 tons of cannabis, out of a world total for cannabis seizures of around 4,000 tons. Yet for every ton seized in Britain, perhaps another five were not. If so, in 1995 around 350 tons of cannabis entered the UK of which almost 300 tons were used, the rest destroyed by the Home Office.[3] *That's enough to fill a large van for every one of 2,500 secondary schools in Britain every year.* Every improvement in transport adds further problems. For example, 1997 figures show an alarming rise in the volume of drugs travelling through the Channel Tunnel.[4]

Heroin and cocaine seizures

Heroin is low bulk, high value. A single person can carry several million dollars worth on a commercial flight by filling and swallowing condoms, and with other concealment methods. Thus global seizures were a mere 32 metric tons, of which just 1.3 tons was in the US. South American heroin is being sold more cheaply and at greater purity in the US market to win extra market share.

Heroin seizures were 1,400 kilos in 1995, the largest figure ever recorded. However, if we take a figure of around 200,000 heroin addicts, using an average of 250 mg a day,[5] then total heroin consumption of heroin in Britain is between 7,000 and 17,000 kilos a year.

At a price of £250,000 a kilogram the total retail value of 17,000 kilograms would be £4.25 billion. So heroin seizures only capture 8–20 per cent of the illegal trade – less effect than if the whole trade was legalised and taxed, about the same as adding VAT, of no real consequence whatever in dealing with the heroin problem.

Every year around 230 tons of cocaine is seized globally, leaving 500 tons for consumption, of which 112 tons is used in the US. The same issues apply here.

Crop destruction

So having failed to intercept more than a fifth of what has been grown, the next strategy has been to shift efforts up-line to the opium, coca and cannabis farms. Once a crop has been harvested, it will eventually find its way on to a market where it will be sold (at however high or low a price), unless destroyed at source. Even a one hundred per cent effective control on drug imports throughout the entire industrial world would have little effect globally on consumption of drugs already in circulation. The drugs would simply be sold at a lower price in poorer nations where there is also a huge and growing demand. It would, however, reduce the amount cultivated or manufactured because the economics would shift in favour of other activities.

The logic of crop destruction is compelling, but once again the reality is very disappointing, with some exceptions. Drug precursors are often grown in emerging nations in remote areas with difficult access for high-tech Westernised destruction teams. The value of the crops is so great that only small plots of land are needed to be devoted to, say, poppies in order to make a big difference to the income of a subsistence farmer. But these small plots, scattered in valleys and hillsides, are difficult to monitor. A farmer may be pleased at his annual profits if only a third of his acreage survives raids by the security forces. He is still likely to be better off than if he had stuck to conventional crops.

Helicopter teams have been used with some success, but usually against bigger production units, and in any case, monitoring needs to happen frequently, covering every area. The fact is that this is impossible and always will be, unless every drug-producing area is run more or less as a police state with informers in every village, in every group of fields.

Then there is the problem of corruption. Many drug-producing nations have governments that are less effective than in many industrialised nations. Their budgets are smaller and their control is inefficient outside major population areas. Some of these nations also have huge internal problems, with dictatorships and civil unrest. Many of them have a history of corruption, deeply rooted at every level in society.

Those wanting to grow, carry or sell drugs are often wealthy enough to buy freedom from harassment, whether paying area officials to mind their own business or suspicious border guards. And if money does not work, bullets, explosions and other methods of persuasion create a climate of fear.

One way or another, the drugs trade corrupts for two reasons. First, those who are themselves addicted become willing accomplices, taking many risks for a reward of regular personal supplies. Second, because those in industrialised nations are willing to pay such vast sums for the drugs in the first place – the market rules with its power.

An exception to this has been seen recently in Thailand where the government has taken aggressive action, pushing most of the old heroin factories out of the country across Burmese and Chinese borders. Many former poppy growers are now growing conventional crops. However, opium fields still abound in northern forest clearings, and drug barons continue to travel Bangkok streets protected by corrupt officials and their own carloads of armed guards.[6]

Cocaine destruction

Cocaine production has been a key target for US anti-drug policy because of the worries about crack and the proximity to the US border of the main growing areas. The aim has been to destroy the 215,000 hectares under coca cultivation in Bolivia, Colombia and Peru, enough to make 780 metric tons of cocaine. Eighty per cent of the US market is Peruvian in origin. But the effort required has been immense, the costs great and the gains only slight.

These countries have small economies. The three main official Colombian exports, coffee, oil products and coal earn only $4 billion a year – but what is that compared to cocaine? Peru's total official exports are $4.6 billion.

A big drive against small aircraft flights in and out of Peru by drug-runners resulted in Peru cocaine prices falling by 50 per cent, but where does it all go? Unless that cocaine is destroyed, someone else will pick up the loads and take them by boat, car or commercial flights to where people will pay much, much more. Alternatively the drugs remain in-country, encouraging domestic addiction. The level of co-operation with some major heroin producers such as Myanmar is non-existent compared to countries like Colombia and Peru.

Certification

The US government has tried to make anti-drugs policy a trade sanction issue, making it very difficult for US companies to import or export goods from or to renegade nations.

Official certification on an annual basis by the US President has been a key tool. Countries not meeting government criteria for anti-drugs policies are denied certification. With this comes a ban on multilateral development banks lending money as well as other sanctions. However certification has limited power, as recent events in Colombia have shown. The government has won a certificate, partly for allowing close co-operation with American anti-drugs teams, but trade continues. After all the identify and burn programmes it seems the total area used for cocaine has remained almost the same or are actually increased.

HUGE SPENDING ON EDUCATION – NOT ENOUGH

So if interception is failing and also attempts to stop these drugs from being made, then the truth is that the global trade in drugs will continue to grow – unless demand on the ground can be reduced by persuading users to give up and non-users to remain abstinent. If demand falls, the market becomes flooded. In the resultant glut, farmers and traffickers cannot get the prices they want and many go out of business, all of course on a global basis. Drug production and consumption then return into balance, reaching a new steady state at a lower level of annual production. That, at least, is the theory. So then, what about demand reduction through prevention campaigns?

Huge amounts are spent on prevention in wealthy nations but nothing like enough. The trouble is that while prevention saves money in the long run it requires cash up front. The savings from prevention can be vast, but governments tend to think short-term while savings are long-term. We see this with smoking. If the rate of smoking doubles over the next year, it could be that the full health impact only begins to be felt by 2025. Therefore a very successful (and expensive) anti-smoking campaign which halves the numbers smoking by 2000 will all be money spent now, paid for out of reduced health bills from 2025 onwards. Governments find these kinds of cash flow hurdles almost impossible to overcome.

Take drug-related AIDS: each person with HIV costs £11,000 a year for drug treatments alone if they are on the latest cocktails, which have been shown to be surprisingly effective. Therefore saving just one drug injector from getting infected could save, say, £50,000 in medicines and a further £15,000 of hospital, clinic and home care costs.

An educator costing £15,000 a year would only have to prevent one person every three years from becoming infected through a dirty needle, and the government would save that person's entire salary and more. What if an educator saves just one person a month? The saving would be £780,000 every year. Suppose a team of five educators were working intensively to reach a group of several hundred injectors, and saved twenty people a year each from infection. Their combined efforts would save £36.5 million for a total cost of less than £100,000, including all add-on costs. But of course, you cannot place a price on people's lives anyway. The total 'value' of their work to society must be immeasurably greater than health service savings alone.

If we went down this economic model we should add in the savings to the economy through a person not becoming infected, and being rehabilitated back to mainstream society in useful employment on an average wage of around £17,000 a year. If we did that, the total economic gain to the nation from one 'saved and rehabilitated' individual would be £65,000 treatment costs plus an average of thirty years at £17,000 or *over £0.5 million per person.*

That is a staggering yield from one educator who might therefore be benefiting the total economy with future savings of half a million pounds for every month he or she is educating drug users, assuming one infection prevented a month.

Drug addicts who never get AIDS are also very expensive to the state, through lost productivity if they cannot work (£17,000 a year) as well as social support costs, health care and costs of dealing with drug-related crime. The Substance Abuse and Mental Health Services Administration in the US has estimated other specific savings as follows:[7]

- Each person in prison $15,500 a year
- Each drug-affected baby $63,000 over five years
- Each liver transplant from alcohol abuse $250,000
- Foetal-alcohol syndrome baby: neonatal care $30,000 in first year

In that light, the sums spent on prevention are microscopic, even bearing in mind the cash flow arguments. Governments are afraid to spend. Take the US State Alcohol/Drug services which spent $3.4 billion in 1992 on local, State and Substance Abuse and Mental Health Services funding for all alcohol and drug services (AOD). However, only 15 per cent ($540 million) was spent on prevention, admittedly an increase on $128 million in 1983, but surely not enough.[8]

The lack of government commitment to serious spending on prevention is a scandal, and almost suggests that they don't believe that education works – or that they can't add up. After all, as we have seen, a worker's salary for four years is more than paid for by the first heroin addiction prevented or cured.

What about savings in practice? From 1981 to 1991 as a result of intensive prevention efforts in America, alcohol-related admissions to hospitals fell from 38 to 20 per 10,000 people. That meant annual savings of $1.9 billion – enough to pay the employers' share of health insurance premiums for 1.5 million workers.[9]

However, a fundamental problem is proving *why* mass behaviour has changed. As we have seen, 13 million fewer Americans used illegal drugs in 1993 than in 1979, a 50 per cent decline. But was that a result of prevention campaigns or just a reversal of other more deeply rooted social trends?

Another difficulty in answering sceptics is knowing what would have happened without an intervention. A country might be criticised for a feeble prevention campaign in the face of ever rising figures for drug-taking by the young, but perhaps they would have risen twice as fast without prevention campaigns. These things are hard to establish.

US PREVENTION TARGETS

In addition to crop destruction and interception of illegal drugs, the US government has ambitious domestic aims – so ambitious that many have heaped ridicule.

- Cut cocaine and marijuana use in previous 30 days by 50 per cent
- Increase to 95 per cent students who sense social disapproval in trying cocaine
- Reduce drug-related deaths by 21 per cent
- Increase high school disapproval of marijuana by 27 per cent
- Increase numbers perceiving psychological or physical harm from marijuana by 60 per cent
- Reduce alcohol-related motor death by 10 per cent
- Reduce liver cirrhosis deaths by 33 per cent
- Reduce heavy drinking in teenagers by 20 per cent
- Reduce alcohol consumption by 20 per cent

US youth prevention targets

President Clinton's administration aims to send educators into 6,500 schools.[10]

- Education of youth aimed at enabling them to say No to illegal drugs and under-age use of alcohol or tobacco
- Zero-tolerance policies for use in the family, school, workplace and community
- Using community organisations, clubs etc – public-private coalitions – (4,300 such coalitions already exist)
- Partnership with media and entertainment industry and professional sports organisations de-glamorise illegal drug use and under-age smoking or drinking

Research shows that if a young person abstains from illegal drugs, alcohol and tobacco until the age of twenty years, they will probably avoid abuse for the rest of their life. The question is how to achieve this. The US government began a new $195 million national campaign against drugs targeting teenagers in early 1998.[11] But how does one measure results?

Many children abstain from using illegal drugs because an adult they respect convinced them of the dangers – usually a teacher, coach or religious leader.[12] We also know that individual counselling of teenagers at risk and family interventions reduce long-term patterns of drug use. Cultural sensitivity is essential, as well as involvement of the whole community. Exaggerating dangers only destroys the credibility of the person giving the health message.

One of hundreds of anti-drug projects is PRIDE, which has launched a Tool Box to help combat teenage drug use. It contains a guidebook, compact disk, two-way family pledge, family bulletin board and information on drug testing kits. The interesting thing about a voluntary family pledge not to use drugs is that, being open, it can be checked on with hair testing.

BRITISH STRATEGY ON PREVENTION

British policy on alcohol and drug use has five priorities:

- Supply reduction
- Demand reduction
- Public health
- Treatment
- Community safety

The British government has also made drugs education for teenagers a priority area, but once again with very limited spending compared to what is needed:

- Drugs education as part of the National Schools Curriculum
- Publicity campaigns
- Home Office 'Drugs Prevention Initiative'
- Other special projects e.g. DARE (Drug Resistance Training)
- Health educators

In practice the current situation is totally inadequate. Many schools in Britain have next to no drugs prevention programme. And what there is can be broken by gross hypocrisy – for example, the adult who ends a session on the dangers of smoking and is herself spotted smoking behind a school building.[13]

Unfortunately, despite unprecedented amounts spent on prevention use, consumption has risen and attitudes have softened. Culture shifts are stronger than existing campaigns. More of the same is not going to get the job done. Something has to change.

Own goals and backfiring campaigns

A major problem facing teachers is knowing how to tackle drug issues in the classroom or outside it. Messages about how to do it are so conflicting that many schools feel hopelessly confused. Every school also has the views of governors and parents to consider, who may not agree with the latest fads, backed by the new politically correct research findings.

Research should by definition be an objective effort to get at the truth, but educational research projects on prevention are bedevilled by poor design, lack of proper controls and the bias of those carrying them out.

Government Ministers are rightly nervous about drugs programmes in schools as reports continue to arrive of backfiring campaigns, where anti-drugs efforts are said to have *increased* experimentation. Tell people the detail and you *may* increase their curiosity. Tell people the dangers and you *may* increase their rebellion. But you have to do something.

Unfazed by the controversy, the Health Education Authority spends the grand sum of £5 million a year on mass campaigns aimed at discouraging young people from using drugs – less than 10p per pupil in secondary school. Since this absurdly small budget has to cover young adults as well as those in school it is hardly surprising that the impact has been slight.

Methods have ranged from radio and press campaigns focusing on Ecstasy, LSD, magic mushrooms and amphetamines, through a leaflet for parents giving drugs information and advice on speaking to their children, to other local and national initiatives through independent agencies. Similar campaigns were launched by the Scotland Against Drugs Campaign. An additional £0.5 million is spent every year on campaigns in Northern Ireland.

There have also been unofficial campaigns such as the one against Ecstasy following the death of Leah Betts, a young woman at home on her eighteenth birthday, with her parents actually in the house. Huge publicity was generated after they later allowed a photograph to be taken as she lay dying in intensive care. Media coverage led to a billboard campaign and a video. Anecdotal evidence suggests that as a direct result, some were put off trying Ecstasy and others were more careful. TV soaps such as *Brookside* have also profiled the impact of drug taking on family and friends, and local radio and press have run their own awareness activities. However these efforts too are just playing at the edge of the problem.

Helplines have performed a useful role in prevention and treatment by providing expert advice whenever needed, in an anonymous, safe way. The UK National Drugs Helpline was set up in April 1995 and operates day and night, every day. Trained advisers give information on drugs and local services in a range of languages. A number of voluntary groups also run telephone advisory services. But the numbers reached by helplines are only a tiny minority, and the calls they deal with are impersonal. Many are from people worried about what they or others have taken, or from people who are thinking about taking drugs and want to know more information. Helplines are vital in giving out useful data such as the location of the nearest needle exchange but are no substitute for face-to-face ongoing prevention work in schools, colleges and elsewhere.

One problem is that many who already use drugs don't go to school or attend other organised activities, so other ways have to be found to reach them, bearing in mind that face-to-face contact has a far higher impact than poster or leaflet campaigns – and anyway, one in ten of the population has difficulty reading.

Outreach teams have been very successful in reaching hidden groups and networks. Detached work happens in streets, stations, pubs, bars, cafes and nightclubs. Domiciliary outreach works with people in their homes. Workers need to be comfortable with the culture of the group they are seeking to reach and to 'fit in', with similar ages and dress, speech and other things.

In practice the gap between different kinds of outreach activity is blurred. I arrived on a Dundee housing estate in an unmarked van with several detached workers from the agency ACET. As the vehicle drew to a halt a number of drug users began to gather round. Most were unregistered and anonymous, appearing on no government statistic. Many were technically homeless, sleeping on the floors of council flats rented to other drug users. They were cautious about contact with authorities, including social workers and hospitals, and most had therefore dropped through the net of state support and care.

Within minutes we had been escorted to a flat where several others were waiting. Inside was a friend who was sick. The team provided basic care, and also gave simple health messages, whether on sterilising needles to prevent HIV transmission or preventing dehydration when taking Ecstasy. In a small bag they also carried clean needles and syringes to be used on an exchange basis. The workers offered advice on rehab programmes for those wishing to stop using drugs, and on access to other services including medical help, clinics and housing agencies.

Women and ethnic minorities have been poorly represented in the past by those using existing services, and 'low threshold services' have been developed as a result. The aim is to encourage those who are reluctant to seek help. Services have targeted non-residents and ex-residents.

Women face a number of special issues: childcare, stigmatisation and sexual relationships (particularly prostitution). One example of a targeted approach has been Wirral Drug Service's HIV peer education project, which involved women in planning and delivering services, including advice on drugs. Similar outreach programmes have been very successful in other countries.

A particular problem is designing services suitable for so-called 'chaotic' drug users, who are very difficult to help because of the erratic nature of their lives. They may come and go, fail to keep appointments, turn up after long absences expecting instant attention, and be unwilling or unable to undertake any commitment to the future. Is this a prevention service or is it treatment – or just containment?

There are few low threshold services other than needle exchanges and drop-in advisory centres. For physical needs, low threshold care tends to be provided by accident and emergency departments. Those with overdoses and abscesses are treated there but users with a range of milder complaints are often sent away. Because health care teams sometimes resent what they see as the abuse of emergency services by drug users, when drug users do become seriously ill they are often treated less than sympathetically.

Day centres like the Hungerford Project in London are good examples of a low threshold service run by the voluntary sector. They offer a wide range of help in a very specialised and targeted way. Services can range from counselling, work with parents and young people, prisons and detached work, needle exchange, education and training, complimentary medicine, advice on welfare rights, benefits, legal and housing matters.

Schools, detached work, targeting of groups, low threshold services and the rest are all very praiseworthy but you still have to agree on the message or messages for each audience. For example, aiming for harm reduction (clean needle exchange) in injecting drug users requires a general approach which is completely unsuitable for twelve-year-olds at school.

The trouble is that these messages have may become muddled, so that in school the lessons often consist of little more than a lesson on what drugs can do for you, and how to have some with as little risk as possible. The only thing left out of the promotion is where to buy supplies – but even general guidelines on *that* can emerge in class discussions, from comments by other pupils.

So how did schools get bludgeoned into such a ridiculous state of affairs? The answer is that schools live in fear of 'own goals', where their efforts make things worse. The chorus telling them they will increase drug use by being too prescriptive is far louder than the chorus telling them they will do so by being too permissive.

Heroin Screws You Up campaign

One of the most spectacular own-goals followed the Heroin Screws You Up poster campaign. The picture of an emaciated, sick teenage lad became an instant 'must have' for teenage girls. Thousands of posters put up outside classrooms disappeared home, where they became pin-ups in girls' bedrooms. The thin boy had become an attractive, desirable, sensuous hero, or anti-hero.

Teachers found that they were in a no-win situation. If they warned against the dangers of drugs, they were criticised by 'experts' as misguided naïve fools likely to encourage abuse as a reaction against authority. If they tried to bring in a former user to explain why he or she deeply regretted using drugs, they risked severe censure from parents and governors concerned about copycat behaviour. After all, such a role-model may suggest to pupils that drug use is a phase and that stopping is not that difficult, even for very addictive drugs.

But that left only one option: a relatively sympathetic approach to drug use, neither negative nor positive, just 'informative'. The philosophy was that each person must make up his or her own mind. However, it is impossible to educate in a moral vacuum, and even saying that you are aiming to do so is in itself a *very* strong moral position. In practice the message becomes:

> You know these things are illegal so I can't (officially) encourage you to try these things, but you know as well as I do that many of these illegal things are relatively harmless, far less dangerous perhaps than smoking so let's have a mature chat about it all. And because no doubt many of you are using these things anyway or soon will, I am going to tell you how to do it all as safely as possible. And because we believe in learning through sharing, I am going to do most of this through open class discussion. Any of you are free to share whatever views or information you have on any aspect of drugs.

This is a very mixed message. On the one hand it is supposed to be abstention, on the other it is clearly aimed at harm reduction. But these two very different outcomes require two very different strategies. We need to decide: is drugs education for fourteen-year-olds about encouraging abstinence, or is it just encouraging people to be safer than they might be?

Harm reduction lessons on drugs for younger teenagers are entirely inappropriate on their own and can themselves promote harm. The primary, overwhelming priority should be to affirm the confidence of the majority who are non-users, to remain so, and actively to discourage users from continuing through negative peer pressure. In the context of prevention it is possible to provide some important information on risks – for example, the dangers of overheating after Ecstasy, or of getting HIV through sharing needles. But the basic approach should not be 'value free'.

The idea of 'value free' drugs prevention is pseudo-scientific nonsense, empty-headed 1990s psychobabble. 'Value free' slogans hide the truth, which is that 'value free' education is shot through with value statements, which can all be summed up in one phrase: 'Now you have some information, go and do whatever you like.' But this abdication of moral responsibility for providing direction is itself a strong moral position.

The greatest problem of all is that those giving out the information are often doing so in a way which encourages a liberal attitude in a world where rules, obligations, duty and self-control only matter if they matter to you. 'Value free' education is destined to produce self-obsessed, narcissistic, self-indulgent individuals, and is very short-sighted. Places without values commonly agreed become living hell. When every person makes up their own moral code, by definition law and order break down, communities collapse and companies can't trade. If you want to join the club, you have to keep the rules. Without rules there is no club and without values there are no rules worth believing in.

Another example of backfiring messages has been in prevention of alcohol abuse. Pupils are commonly warned that 'alcohol leads to risky sex' or 'drinking makes you do stupid things'. Both these statements are absolutely true in statistical terms, as we have seen, but a disturbing piece of research has suggested that messages like these make it *more* likely that the person will behave in that way. The power of suggestion can certainly be enormous. Researchers found that those who took the greatest sexual risks after drinking alcohol were those who *expected* alcohol to lead to a higher risk of doing so. Thus the statements become self-fulfilling prophecies.[14]

The demonisation of alcohol allows the person to excuse behaviour as not really under his or her control. But where does that leave us? Does it mean that by warning that cannabis often leads to experimentation with other drugs we are actually propelling teenager cannabis users into *doing* so?

You can't have it both ways. If this research *is* a true reflection of real life then at least it shows that there is indeed a *powerful* effect from education messages. The question is what the message should be to get the desired result. For example, this research suggests that it may be helpful to stress that while alcohol loosens inhibitions, you still have free choices and are responsible for your actions.

Exactly the same dilemmas have been faced over the last decade in HIV prevention and sex education, in regard to telling people what not to do or just helping them to reduce risk when they do it anyway. For example, do you place condom dispensers in schools as a harm reduction measure, or does that undermine the message that it is better for teenagers not to have multiple partners anyway?

The result of all this has been near paralysis in schools regarding drug abuse. The education paper *Tackling Drugs Together* asks schools to develop policies on managing drug-related incidents and prevention, but energetic application requires confident leadership and vision, something many head teachers do not feel qualified to provide in this area. Official school inspectors take a close look at drugs policies on regular visits, but thorough implementation at every level of school life is very hard to enforce.

Another key problem in all areas of health promotion in schools is the difficulty in measuring effectiveness. It is especially difficult where the outcomes may involve breaking the law or other codes of practice. How do you assess what pupils are actually doing?

As we have already seen, self-reporting surveys of illegal or disapproved-of behaviour are notoriously unreliable. Some pupils exaggerate and boast, while others are scared to own up, even in strictly anonymous conditions. Yet while absolute numbers of users may not always be known, changes in reported attitudes, intentions and behaviour can be very important indicators. For example, between 1991 and 1993, a pilot of a new programme called Project Charlie was launched in primary schools in the London Borough of Hackney. It was found that pupils exposed to the programme for a year, when compared to others:

- Had greater knowledge of the effects of drugs
- Were more confident in their ability to resist peer pressure to commit anti-social acts
- Produced better solutions to social dilemmas

However, proving that the programme actually reduced substance abuse in later years will be more difficult.

DOES GIVING FACTS INCREASE CURIOSITY?

Giving facts is *bound* to increase curiosity, but that does not mean we should stop doing it. It just means that without balance 'value free' education will simply increase drug-taking. Take me. I drink alcohol although I have never been drunk. I have puffed once or twice at the same cigarette once in my life, and have never tried any illegal drug. However, as a direct result of spending so much time studying what these drugs do, and in debating the issues, I confess I am now far more curious than I was to try, for example, cannabis. I have not done so for several reasons but there is no doubt that I am closer to doing so than I was.

I have decided not to because:

- It is illegal (but then my wife and I visited Amsterdam recently and even sat observing others in a Coffee House where cannabis was on sale legally).
- I am concerned that others who look to me, including my own children, would follow my example, even if only doing so in a country where no law was broken, and go far beyond my example with a risk of real danger to themselves.
- I am not sure, knowing what I do about the alterations in brain

function, that I want to have an altered mind in any way what-soever.

- Deep down inside I am concerned that I might like cannabis as much as others do, and become fascinated by the whole experience, and that having tried it once or twice, would find myself becoming a regular user.

- I am concerned that I would not logically be able to say no to, say, Ecstasy, having tried cannabis, and that the same thought processes would lead me to justify trying a wide range of other 'relatively harmless' drugs. Indeed I could easily argue to myself that such experimentation is vitally important if I am to form a view on how much of a hazard these 'milder' drugs really are. It would increase my understanding.

But as I say, despite the noblest of arguments in favour of continued abstention and all my knowledge of the risks to mind and body, increased knowledge has increased my curiosity. I cannot believe this will be any different for any teenager having just sat through three classes, one week apart, on what drugs are, how they work, how wonderful they make you feel and how unsuitable, foolish, or evil they are to use.

Perception of harm

Perception of harm is a key issue. It is no good pretending that cannabis is bad for your health when the person doing the drugs education slot is a chain smoker of cigarettes. On the relative risk scale, as we have seen, cannabis is near the bottom of the league. The same is true of Ecstasy. The truth is that a small number of deaths and other problems have created a frenzy of headlines, out of all proportion to the tiny number of problems in relation to the millions of doses taken. Ecstasy is unsafe. Ecstasy kills, but so do hundreds of other things young people do, of which one of the commonest and most dangerous is allowing themselves to be driven by a friend who has only recently learned to drive.

WHEN HEALTH RISKS BECOME GOOD NEWS

Another difficulty is that when talking of the dangers of, say, smoking, we are addressing people who may be starting to worry not about dying but about living too *long*. They may not care about getting lung cancer at the age of seventy-five. 'We've all got to die of something. Who wants to live to ninety anyway? Look at my own elderly grandparents. I hope I do die before then.'

Belief in immortality

It's an illogical paradox because the same teenagers can be neurotic-ally obsessed with health in some areas, indifferent in others. Teenagers usually have a strong belief in their own immortality (for the foreseeable future): 'It won't happen to me.' Young people find it very difficult to estimate real personal risk.

Add these effects together and we have a young person who may be chronically anxious about his body, yet who also thinks he is currently leading a charmed life where he can take all kinds of risks and get away with it, and where longer-term health problems seem either too far removed to be worth worrying about, or a positive way of making sure that life comes to an end when it is still worth living.

SO WHAT IS THE ANSWER?

In summary then, no single approach works for everyone. The most effective campaigns target particular groups, whether teenage girls about to start smoking or heroin users sharing needles. The best campaigns are also very specific in the behaviour they wish to change, as seen in Christmas drink-drive campaigns, when the aim is not to tackle alcoholism or drink-driving, but rather to persuade people to keep to the legal limits for blood alcohol when taking to the road.

Research shows that close friends and wives/girlfriends are most likely to prevent a man from drink-driving. The highest risk is male, white, 21–35, has a blue collar job, drinks in a bar once a week, has driven after five or more drinks in the last year, and believes that he is safe doing so. So then, health messages targeted at one group can affect behaviour in another.[15]

Life skills training in schools

One reason why young people land up in trouble is because they often feel very insecure and vulnerable. Anyone standing out from the crowd can quickly become a target for teasing and bullying, whether for wearing the wrong kind of trainers or for having the wrong shaped nose. Social pressures to conform are there all day, every day, to be accepted, to be liked, to be one of the crowd.

It takes a lot of self-confidence to risk earning respect by standing out from the crowd, going a different way, when you appear to be taking a position that adults approve of. It is easier to be different when rebelling, flouting authority, daring to go three steps further than anyone else. It's considered to be cool and it's a fast track to positive image building.

A key strategy therefore in all health promotion among the young is to help people feel secure in who they are and what they want to be, so that they can be themselves and walk away from trouble. Much research is needed to find the most effective methods of esteem-building.

Self-esteem building – what works in the classroom

These issues recur in sex education, AIDS and a host of other areas, including vandalism and other crime, not just drugs prevention. Practical sessions build round certain scenarios, helping pupils think through what their options are, giving them freedom.

Around 10 per cent of adults do not drink alcohol, and the majority of teenagers do not use any illegal drugs and never have done. These are important messages. As we have seen, the biggest weapon we have in prevention is *normalisation*, helping those under pressure to see the truth, which is that abstention from illegal drugs and tobacco is the norm at any age of childhood, adolescence or adulthood.

This is vitally important. Otherwise normality becomes defined by those with the loudest voices. That is a major problem in class discussions on drugs, alcohol and smoking. These activities are often carried out by pupils as part of bravado, and being loud and dominant in class discussions is part of that. Pupils rarely admit to a criminal activity in the classroom. Few pupils will risk disclosing publicly that they are regular users of illegal drugs in a situation where that information might later count against them. However, their attitudes in discussion can be very influential, with every word measured by the other pupils in the light of what they know (and perhaps the teacher does not) about what the speakers get up to.

It is the same with sex education. By the time they are seventeen years old, most boys in some schools can be under the delusion that they are almost the only virgins left, such is the level of bragging about sexual conquests. Yet the most authoritative British survey ever conducted found that 75 per cent of all those leaving school to go to college had been celibate throughout their lives.[16] You should see the wave of relief across the faces of sixth formers when they find out that probably the vast majority of their peers are also as sexually inexperienced as they are. It helps next time they feel under pressure to follow a non-existent crowd.

Difficulty with double standards

The faintest whiff of hypocrisy destroys credibility in school, and any teacher with a personal double standard regarding drug taking is in an impossibly weak position. Teachers or educators may not be current users but they are liable to be asked sharp questions like anyone else – and pupils can spot liars a thousand metres away. 'Sir, have you ever tried cannabis?' could be an embarrassing question to answer truthfully. If the answer is no, that is one thing but what if the answer is yes?

'So then, you survived.' Or 'You tried it as an experiment, now we want to. Can't blame us.' Or 'Hypocrite to lecture us – typical.' Or 'So you carried on using cannabis for a while which just goes to show that you can have lots of fun while you're young and still go on to get a decent job.'

And of course, alcohol abuse and smoking by teachers are the biggest double standards of all.

Youth programmes outside schools

Youth programmes outside schools also have an important role to play. Successful projects include the Youth Awareness Programme in north-east London, which has found that non-using pupils had more negative attitudes to drug use after participation, and that users were less likely to feel like extending and developing their use.[17] Similar programmes have been developed across the country.

Role of parents

Parents have a far more important role in drugs education than teachers. For a start, most drug use occurs out of school hours at home, in the homes of friends (who also have parents or guardians) or nearby. Second, parents have more opportunity. One-off classes are relatively ineffective compared to the ongoing discussions at home about all kinds of life issues that should take place ideally month by month, year by year, in pace with each individual child's personal and social development.

Home is the best place to build up a child's sense of self-confidence and self-worth. Home is the best place to help a child feel special, important and loved. Home is the place where younger children will most naturally ask questions. Attitudes towards smoking, for example, are influenced in the home from the age of two or three onwards, mainly by seeing people smoke or not smoke and by overhearing conversations about it. The same is true for use of alcohol. Children are great imitators and example is the most powerful influence on future behaviour. We will look at this whole area more fully in the final chapter.

Yet, as we have seen, despite all the publicity, the numbers of US parents often talking to their own children about drugs fell from 39 to 31 per cent in the years 1991–92 to 1996–97.[18]

PREVENTION AT WORK — BIG IMPACT

Seventy-one per cent of drug users in the US are in work, with a similar number in other countries such as Britain, so how should employers respond? Federal government is trying to get all companies to create drugs policies, with work contracts forbidding possession, use, and transfer or sale of illegal drugs, preferably with a ban on being under the influence of drugs or alcohol at work.

These measures go hand in hand with training supervisors and staff about drugs and how they affect safety, as well as people and families, how they affect productivity, product quality, absenteeism, health costs, accident rates and the profits. Staff also need to know exactly what will happen if they test positive, and what help is available.

Some companies think it saves money to sack drug users, but from commercial and personal points of view helping a valued employee to stay on the job makes sense. Employee assistance programmes (EAPs) not only reduce accidents, compensation claims, absenteeism and employee theft but also improve productivity and morale.

EAPs only work if they are seen to be confidential. Staff must be certain that information disclosed to EAPs will not affect their job. On the other hand, EAPs cannot shield them from disciplinary action for poor work performance or violations of company policy. Smaller companies cannot afford their own EAPs but can maintain a list of useful agencies.

Drug testing is a component part of a full programme – or should be. It should only be introduced after:

- A written substance abuse policy
- A supervisory training programme
- An employee education and awareness programme
- Access to an Employee Assistance Programme

Since 1988, employers in Department of Transport (DoT) regulated transport industries have been required to implement comprehensive drug programmes. These require drug testing of staff in safety-sensitive roles:

- Flight crew member, flight attendant, flight instructor or ground instructor, flight tester, aircraft dispatch. Aircraft maintenance or preventive maintenance, aviation security or screening, air traffic control for commercial flights
- Operating commercial motor vehicles travelling between states more than a certain size or with hazardous cargo. Drug testing has already created driver shortages and turnover problems for some of the 14,000 US trucking companies.[19]
- Work on a variety of railroad jobs.
- Operate, maintain or emergency call-out on pipelines or liquid natural gas facilities.
- Crew on US commercial vessels. The US Coast Guard now requires drug testing of workers on board US vessels in foreign waters – pre-employment, periodic, post-accident, reasonable cause and random testing are all required.[20]

As a result of these measures the Department of Transport has the largest drug testing programme in the world, involving 8 million US workers. Any worker in aviation, car, truck, bus, sea or rail sectors who tests positive is referred for professional help.[21]

By January 1996, 81 per cent of major US firms were conducting drug testing, representing 40 per cent of the work force, while 95 per cent of those with more than 2,500 employees had drugs policies, and 91 per cent had drug testing programmes.[22] US Federal policy is to increase this to include small businesses that employ 87 per cent of the work force.

A recent survey of 250 large and small companies found that a third viewed drugs and alcohol as significant problems, and half would sack a worker immediately if under the influence at work.[23]

Some industries are notorious for high levels of drug abuse among workers – construction, for example. In the US building industry up to one in four workers has a problem with substance abuse.[24]

Drug testing works – fast. A plastics company in the Midwest US decided to change the normal eight-hour shift to twelve hours to increase output. Some staff began taking stimulants to help them stay awake. Before long the factory was facing a serious amphetamine addiction problem. The safety manager became worried after finding powder residues and razor cut marks on equipment, and called in a substance abuse consultant.

The company estimated that 15–20 per cent were abusing drugs – mostly on the job – and began a strong drugs education and prevention programme with testing. Within a year drug taking had fallen to negligible levels.[25]

A cardboard factory in Wisconsin caught the attention of its insurance company after a high number of accident claims at a work site that seemed to have few hazards. In 1995 the company was asked to start a drugs education and prevention programme, with employees being required to undergo random drug testing, and tests being a condition of employment. As a result, claims fell by 72 per cent the following year, and there was an 80 per cent decrease in days lost due to job injuries.[26]

Compulsory drug testing in Britain

Compulsory drug testing was introduced for the armed forces in 1995, with a budget of £1.5 million a year. In April 1997 testers began visiting naval and marine units unannounced, with the names of computer-selected personnel. Eleven sailors failed the first batch – 0.1 per cent of the sample – mainly for traces of cannabis.[27] Equivalent figures for the US were under 1 per cent.[28] True figures are probably higher as there are often leaks about the dates of 'surprise visits'.

A signalman was recently sacked by Railtrack for having traces of cannabis in his body. An industrial tribunal upheld the decision despite worries that the drug could have been taken weeks before.[29] More than half the prisoners in the first compulsory drug check failed the test at Shotts prison. Prisoners faced stiff punishment.[30] Drug testing has also been introduced in one police force.[31]

Cost of drug use at work in Britain

Drug- and alcohol-related problems at work cost Britain up to £2 billion a year and cause 11 per cent of workplace injuries.[32] A third of Britain's top fifty companies already has some kind of drug testing policy, introduced to increase productivity rather than because of any legal requirement.[33]

Other countries talk of testing

Other nations are also talking seriously about drug testing. The head of Narcotics Command in the Philippines called recently for compulsory drug testing and rehabilitation as a matter of drug policy, with 1.7 million drug users up from only 20,000 in 1992.[34] Thailand is testing tens of thousands of students and other groups.[35]

Is compulsory testing lawful?

US courts have upheld the legality of random drug screening of prisoners but there has been no firm decision yet about the screening of all prisoners.[36] In the meantime, British prisoners are campaigning to have the whole process declared illegal.

Questions to answer on testing

There are important questions that every business has to answer before testing. The aim should be to rid the workplace of drugs – not employees.

- Who will you test? Job seekers? All staff? Employees doing certain tasks?
- When? After accidents or only after some? On suspicion of drug use? As part of routine medicals? At random?
- What substances are you testing for? Many Federal government agencies require testing for marijuana, opiates, amphetamines, cocaine and PCP. What about alcohol or prescription drugs that may affect work performance?
- What do staff or job seekers face if they test positive?
- Who will carry out the programme?

Approaches to testing a particular employee

So how do you react if you think there is a problem with a member of staff? The Utah Council for Crime Prevention guidelines are helpful:[37]

1. Make sure there is a real problem, not just a personality conflict
2. Is the problem causing a real threat? If so, send the person home. If not, don't rush into a heavy-handed response
3. Get the employee's side of the story

4. Document problem behaviour
5. Check how other employees have been treated in similar situations in the past
6. Check your own responsibilities in the situation
7. Decide on a response
8. Get help
9. Take action. Define the new behaviour pattern expected in future, evaluate, follow up
10. Maintain confidentiality
11. Reduce risks of it happening again by communicating clearly understood corporate policy

If you get it wrong you could land up in court for violating human rights issues or under employee protection rules. For example, Imperial Oil in Canada had a policy that all past drug abuse had to be disclosed. Someone who had abused alcohol found that the result of being open was that he was moved to a worse job. The Ontario Human Rights Board of Inquiry declared that pre-employment drug testing that made offers of work conditional on a negative test were illegal, because the company failed to show why it would affect job performance. It also rejected random drug testing. The Board did support testing after an accident or a 'near miss' or where there were other grounds for suspicion of abuse.[38]

Impact of drug testing

Market pressures are increasing for wide curbs, more likely to be effective than just passing laws. Most people are far more worried about losing their jobs as a result of a positive random drug test, than about being arrested for possession of illegal substances in a public place.

The Ohio Bureau of Workers' Compensation is cutting employers' premiums by 6–20 per cent if they enrol in the Agency's new Drug-Free Workplace programme. This voluntary programme includes drug testing for employees and treatment for substance abuse. Different levels of premium apply depending on how much the employer does to curb abuse.[39]

The highest discounts require half of all workers to have random drug tests each year, including tests for all job applicants, and for all those involved in accidents. These kinds of programmes have resulted in a steady decline in positive drug test results at work to a ten year low in 1997.[40] In 1987, 18 per cent of the work force tested positive for illegal drugs, but by 1994 it was only 7.8 per cent.[8]

Workers with the lowest rates of participation in drug testing schemes have the highest levels of drug abuse. The food sector industry has a participation rate of 7.6 per cent and a past month use rate for illegal drugs of 16.5 per cent. The armed forces have a 100 per cent participation rate and a past month use rate of 2 per cent.[41]

It is often said that the difference between alcohol tests and drug tests is that alcohol tests detect intoxication today rather than previous use, whereas drug tests tend to pick up previous use, saying little about intoxication. However there are ways round this. Future technology will allow us to be far more precise about the drug levels needed to produce measurable effects on performance, while longer-term alcohol abuse can also be detected in sober employees with a battery of ten commonly used blood tests from a single sample. Results need confirmation using more reliable methods but it is a useful screening device.[42]

Methods of drug testing

There are four main ways to test whether someone has used illegal drugs: blood, urine, saliva or hair analysis. Urine, saliva and hair tests are simpler and less invasive, and urine is mainly used. Although the test is reasonably straightforward, in practice the results can have such devastating effects on an individual's career that a huge number of steps need to be taken to ensure that there is no interference by the person being tested.

For example, SmithKline Beecham carried out five million employee tests in the US during 1997. They have recently become worried about workers cheating the test by adding nitrites to their urine samples as an adulterant, although a separate test can detect nitrites.[43] Vigilance is necessary.

Their national survey shows positive US worker rates vary from 3 per cent in Miami to 4–6 per cent in New York, Chicago and Los Angeles. Of these 60 per cent are for cannabis. These results are all lower than they were a decade ago when the national average was 18 per cent.[44] Part of the reason for the fall is undoubtedly the impact of testing itself.

However, drug testing may actually *encourage* the use of *hard* drugs such as heroin and cocaine that do not linger as long in the body. Those working in prison are convinced that this is already happening in Britain. Prisoners have found a variety of ways to beat the system, such as carrying urine samples from abstaining prisoners in their pockets on a daily basis just in case there is a random check.[45] But even when allowing for cheating, positive tests in British prisons have fallen significantly by more than 2 per cent for cannabis and 1 per cent for heroin.[46]

As well as being tricked into false negative results by substitution, dilution and adulteration, drug tests can also give false *positives* – for example, some tests confuse heroin use with poppy seeds eaten as the outer coating of a roll. As a result the US Department of Health and Human Sciences has proposed making the test six times *less* sensitive for opiates. The same is true of cocaine testing, which is so sensitive that a milligram ingested accidentally from environmental contamination can be enough to trigger a positive result. This sort of thing can happen to a flatmate of a cocaine user or to a member of the police force who arrests a cocaine addict.

Therefore drug tests need to be regarded with a degree of caution, and should be conducted with the utmost care, taking many factors into account. Expect to see large numbers of court room challenges by those claiming that correct procedures were not followed, ranging from mixing up two samples, to failure to wash hair clean of environmental contaminants, or deliberate contamination of a result by a police officer or member of the prison service.

Taking a urine sample is a complex process fraught with dangers for the inexperienced.

- The person's identity is checked, for example with a passport or some other photo card document
- The seal on the test is broken in the presence of the person to be tested so that no tampering is possible by a third party
- The person being tested has to empty his or her pockets and remove outer clothing, as well as surrender cases or handbags
- The person is led into a washroom to wash their hands and then into another where there is no source of tap water that could be used to dilute the sample
- The toilet bowl is filled with strongly coloured water to prevent it being used
- The water cistern above the toilet is also sealed and tamper-proof
- Flushing of the toilet is forbidden (being a source of water)
- When the sample is produced it is checked for temperature. The sample has to be between 90 and 100 degrees Fahrenheit to satisfy the tester that the entire sample has just come from the body. If outside the range, a second sample is requested, perhaps with someone of the same sex watching
- The sample is then sealed in front of the person being tested, and placed in a container with a tamper-proof seal

Hair testing is becoming widespread, partly because it is far simpler. When drugs are taken they circulate in the bloodstream and are built by hair follicles into the structure of the hair. No amount of washing or hair care will remove these traces, which are different from outer environmental contamination – for example in a smoky room. Contamination is dealt with by washing with chemicals before testing.

The traces inside the hair remain there until the hair grows out, at a rate of half an inch a month. Standard hair tests use the inch and a half closest to the scalp, but testing much longer strands gives a more complete record of use over the past few months. In comparison, urine only gives reliable results about use over the last few days, and cheating is easier. Retesting is also difficult with urine. By the time the test comes back, it is often too late to ask for a second sample, whereas hair tests can be repeated as often as necessary if a result is questioned.

Hair cut from the scalp cannot provide information about use in the last five days because this is below the level of the skin. However, plucked hair that provides the root could do so.

So then, urine or blood testing is the only way to measure recent blood levels, although data is still lacking to enable us to say with confidence what the level was at a particular time before the sample was given, and to correlate level with performance limitations. Hair testing gives a full picture of the past, but not the present.

PDT-90 is a personal drug-testing service for personal use, using human hair. It's an example of a coming flood of 'consumer' products for drug detecting. It costs $60 a kit and is widely available in the US. It tests for use of any of five drug groups: marijuana, cocaine, opiates, methamphetamine and PCP in the previous 90 days, which is useful for long-range monitoring but not for determining whether someone is currently 'under the influence'. However, it is easy to use, and less embarrassing than asking for a urine sample. These kinds of kits can act as a powerful deterrent to a teenager, knowing that people will find out if they have used drugs at all over the last three months. It can also in theory be a help to a teenager who wants to use long-term testing as a reason why they cannot risk taking drugs.

PDT-90 is being marketed heavily to parents of teenagers in the US, who have to collect hairs and send them off to get the results. The person sending in the samples has to sign a form declaring that they are the custodial parent or legal guardian of the minor child. However, there are many ethical issues raised by home testing, especially of someone without his or her knowledge or consent – and what do you do with the information?

Hair testing has to be able to tell the difference between environmental contamination by smoke for example, from actual bodily ingestion, injection or inhalation. As we have seen, this requires rigorous testing methodology, and is not always reliable. In addition, hair testing may pose equality issues since blond hair does not retain traces of drugs as well as dark hair. For these reasons the Society of Forensic Toxicologists does not yet endorse hair testing for employee programmes.[47] Hair testing remains unusual and expensive. Testing accuracy can vary with the company used.

Saliva testing is becoming cheaper and more reliable with one-stop tests for alcohol as well as a range of illegal substances. Collection and test results take around five minutes.[48] Skin testing is also undergoing trials – for example the Drugwipe system. This takes a specimen of sweat from the forehead and gives an instant colour change on a strip. Drugwipe devices are drug-specific, available for cannabis, amphetamines (including Ecstasy), cocaine, opiates and benzodiazepines such as Valium.[49] Drugwipe products are being tested at the roadside in Britain, with Australia expected to follow.[50]

One compromise is to use non-invasive disposable tests like Drugwipe for situations such as road-side testing, with blood or urine tests back at a Police station when a result appears to be positive. It would be hazardous at present to rely on skin tests alone to support, say, a ban on driving or a pupil expulsion.

Ethical questions relating to drug testing

All these testing measures are controversial, especially random testing, with worries that some companies have used positive results to compromise privacy, harass and intimidate employees. Accuracy will undoubtedly improve as unit costs fall and testers become more experienced, but even if the results are always 100 per cent accurate, there are other questions to be dealt with.

How is the information to be used? Are those testing positive to be given counselling about voluntary treatment programmes or be threatened with the sack, or sacked on the spot? What about the difference between, say, hair testing which might show use in the last 90 days, and blood or urine testing which might indicate far more recent use or actual intoxication in the work place? Is it right to penalise job applicants when a hair test might show positive despite the fact that the person has not used any illegal substance for half a year?

The real question is this: how serious are we as a society about wanting to tackle the drugs problem? And what alternatives are there, given that many other measures seem to have failed? If we conclude that the drugs menace is a real threat, and that drug testing is one of the only practical measures proven to have a significant impact on the problem, then we may conclude that we have little choice but to welcome a measure which would have been unthinkable in the past.

Almost all major steps against drug abuse involve *some* degree of compromise over personal privacy and other freedoms. For example, tight customs checks require opening people's luggage at airports between aircraft and collection areas, as well as thorough random checks on all those entering and leaving the country. It also involves stop and search at any point where police have reasonable grounds for suspicion. Anti-drugs teams are allowed to bug phones, intercept mail, follow people, open packages, break into warehouses and homes and inspect bank accounts. We accept all this as a normal part of maintaining law and order.

Yet at a time when drug use is soaring, borders completely opened with Europe, and the numbers of customs officers have been reduced, random road-side testing for intoxication of any kind is very unusual, and in Britain random testing for drugs or alcohol use at work is almost unheard of. There are hard choices to be made, which require clear evidence that the invasion of personal freedoms is worthwhile in terms of lives saved, injuries prevented, crimes curtailed.

Civil liberties groups are gearing up for a big fight, which they will lose because there are so few alternatives to controlling a growing problem, and because as we have seen, market forces will have the ultimate say. Because of this, the counter-arguments being used are now economic ones as well. The language of the market is being used by *both sides*. For example, the American Civil Liberties Union says companies are wasting millions of dollars a year on a urine testing industry with an annual turnover of $340 million.[51]

They argue that 80 per cent of their members with urine testing programmes have never worked out the cost benefits. They go on to say that if positive results are only 3 per cent of the total then the cost of identifying each person could be as high as $10,000. However, the testing process itself keeps the numbers of users low – indeed it has contributed to a fall at a time when other trends would have led many people to expect a rise.[52]

PREVENTION WORKS FOR DRINK-DRIVING

Drug testing does in fact have a long history with widespread acceptance in Britain, for alcohol abuse. The best studied example of anti-alcohol abuse campaigns is drink-driving. Many countries have run these high profile advertising campaigns and the outcomes have been easy to measure: numbers of drink-driving accidents down, numbers over the limit down at kerb-side random testing sites.

My own view is that drug testing is inevitable and necessary whether in the workplace or at school or at college. It should be part of a package of comprehensive prevention methods aiming to inhibit use and to channel care to those who need it. Drug testing has only recently emerged as a realistic large scale-option because the technology has only recently improved. We still have a long way to go before drug testing can be applied with the same precision as alcohol testing of breath, blood or urine, but that should not dissuade us from applying the technology we have wherever we can, within the limits of its accuracy.

Drug testing is not an expensive option because it can be limited to cases where there is suspicion, and to random samples. These together are a strong disincentive. As we have seen, for a small investment in training and technology there can be a great increase in productivity, and in the well-being of the work force. There are ethical challenges to be faced, all of which can be worked through with clear guidelines, consistently and fairly applied, introduced after a proper period of consultation and after pilot testing.

Society will have to take a view on whether workers such as train drivers and pilots should continue to be disciplined or dismissed if they are found to have traces of illegal drugs in their bodies. Few would question the need for immediate sanctions if such a person were drunk on duty or obviously 'out of it' because of recent drug taking. My own view is that in the absence of a sophisticated measure of drug intoxication, it is far better to err on the side of caution. If someone has traces of cannabis in their body that is sufficient for me. If I have a choice I would rather that person did not fly my plane or drive my bus. I would also rather they kept out of the operating theatre or the cab of the crane. Those who feel comfortable about positive tests for cannabis may draw the line at a positive cocaine or heroin test.

A strict line on drug testing would fill a yawning gap in current anti-drugs law, a gap that laws are not suited to fill. At present there is an inconsistency. If three teenagers are given Ecstasy at a party, and two swallow the tablet while the third declines and leaves it in his pocket, two may land up in hospital while the third could land up in prison. So long as the drug is inside your stomach, you can't be charged. The only exception is in the case of the courier who has filled his stomach with sealed condoms containing drugs.

In contrast to the letter of the law, drug testing disciplines the *user* rather than the *carrier*. Since use is just as relevant as possession, if not more so, there is a strong moral argument in favour of drug testing rather than just relying on searching and finding supplies *before* they have been used.

I am not proposing a change in law making it a crime to have taken drugs in the past, but I am in favour of employers being able to choose to take action where staff are found to test positive for drug use, if they work in situations where the health or safety of others could be compromised. The same argument can be used to justify pre-employment testing for those in these kinds of jobs. In practice, as we have seen, very large numbers of jobs could be said to fall into these categories. To be consistent, such measures should go together with a drive against alcohol intoxication.

So then, as we have seen, that prevention can work. Seizures alone are ineffective, as are attacks on farmers or drug factories. It is vital to reduce demand. Face to face education is effective and cost-efficient when backed by mass campaigns and set in a values framework, and where everyone pulls together, whether parents, teachers, youth workers or others who influence image such as those in the media. Workplace testing is also very effective as part of a range of interventions, with the option to extend what is already happening in the US more widely in countries such as Britain, and to encompass places of education. Testing is the one measure most likely to have the greatest impact on behaviour, and if introduced sensitively, with compassion, should become a central part of government, industry and community prevention efforts.

However, some will always use drugs and we face an enormous challenge in helping those already addicted to break free. But does treatment work? What kinds of treatment programmes are most effective? And how can we help ensure that those who beat addiction manage to stay free of it for the rest of their lives? Is enough being done?

9

Treatment Works

If preventing production is hard and interception almost impossible, and if stopping teenagers and young adults from trying illegal drugs is only partly successful, then it is of the utmost importance to ensure that those who become addicted are helped as quickly as possible to break the habit.

The biggest barrier to treatment is the person who needs it. You cannot help someone who is happy to stay as things are. Often it takes a personal crisis of some kind to bring a person to the point of recognising the need for help and being motivated enough to take it. It might be a wife threatening to leave home, or losing a job, or major debts, or a life-threatening illness caused by addiction. Drug testing may assist that process by helping to identify those with dependency and encouraging them to see the habit as something that is unhelpful to their future.

TREATMENT GETS RESULTS

Treatment not only rehabilitates a user back into normal life, but is also a key strategy in demand reduction, since, as we have seen, a relatively small number of heavy users are responsible for a significant proportion of the total spending on drugs purchases. Yet treatment can be hard to find – effective treatment, that is, and offered in a way that the person needing it feels able to accept.

Let us look first at the US situation. Almost four million

Americans need help with addiction.[1] However, only a million a year get help, with big regional variations. A key aim is to focus on chronic drug users, helping identify them and offering treatment.[2] For example, two thirds of US cocaine consumption is by 20 per cent of users, who are being targeted aggressively with rehab programmes.[3] Drug testing is part of this identification process.

Treatment locations are:[4]

- 54 per cent clinics
- 16 per cent community health centres
- 10 per cent general hospitals
- 7 per cent free-standing residential
- 13 per cent other

Outpatients cover 87 per cent of clients, of which 75 per cent are expected to be drug-free and 12 per cent are being given methadone. There has been a steady decline in residential care as a proportion, from 16 per cent to 13 per cent from 1980 to 1992.[5]

The lack of treatment is appalling. It is particularly shocking in the light of some very encouraging results. A recent US survey found that substance abuse treatment:[6]

- Cut drug use by half
- Reduced criminal activity by up to 80 per cent
- Increased employment
- Decreased homelessness
- Improved physical and mental health
- Reduced medical costs
- Reduced risky sexual behaviour
- Reduced drug injecting/needle sharing

Treatment has proven and lasting benefits. Significant reductions in drug and alcohol use are found a full year after the end of treatment (averaging 50 per cent of former level).

In a large national study, use of a primary drug (the one which led to their treatment) fell from 73 per cent of the whole group to 38 per cent a year after treatment ended.

- Cocaine use fell from 40 per cent to 18 per cent
- Heroin use fell from 24 per cent to 13 per cent
- Crack use fell from 50 per cent to 25 per cent

These are great achievements, hard facts, and behind each statistic is a life totally changed and others greatly improved. This impacts not only those addicted, but also those who love them and the communities in which they live. It shatters the cruel myth that heroin and crack addiction are one-way tickets to oblivion and personal destruction. Breaking free is hard. It is a huge, almost insurmountable personal challenge, yet every year significant numbers manage to do so, with and without help. But the right kind of intensive long-term help makes a successful outcome far more likely.

Some cynics may choose to believe that release from addiction is only temporary but this is untrue. Over the years I have worked alongside a number of people who have been addicted to heroin or other drugs but who have been completely set free, and have walked clear of all addiction for many years, now holding down long-term jobs with stability and responsibilities. I would defy anyone to guess at their past on meeting them.

These spectacular success figures face us with a direct challenge to come up with the resources for everyone who needs help to benefit. No longer does society have any excuse to marginalise the problem, deriding a 'bunch of junkies' for every possible evil, and casting them out of circulation or putting them in prison. Here in front of our eyes is clear evidence that addiction can be a phase through which someone can grow to a place of wholeness and maturity.

We cannot and must not abandon those directly affected, nor their families, their children, neighbours and friends. As we have seen, addiction can become a curse on a whole community, and it requires a compassionate, caring response from us all. This may seem at odds from what has been said about testing in the previous chapter, but we must keep in mind that the primary purpose of testing is to identify those with a problem, for the protection of others and so that help can be given.

And if compassion does not sway the argument enough for some, then let the economic reality speak for itself. The cost/benefit ratio for treatment programmes shows a one-to-seven ratio: ten dollars in treatment saves seventy dollars in other costs. One California study found:[7]

- $209 million spent
- 150,000 drug addicts treated
- $1.5 billion saved – mainly in reduced crime.
- Hospital use fell by 33 per cent
- Illegal drug use fell by 33 per cent
- Criminal activity fell by 66 per cent

These effects were greatest where the treatment was longest.

So how do different methods compare? Another study found that *all* treatment options cut abuse, whether methadone replacement therapy, residential or community based programmes, and non-methadone clinic support.[8]

- Reports of 'beating someone up' fell from 50 per cent to 11 per cent
- Arrests fell from 48 per cent to 17 per cent
- Substance abuse hospital visits fell by 50 per cent
- Mental health admissions fell by 25 per cent

So then, what about the effectiveness of prevention programmes in Britain? Less data is available because far less has been spent on research (which in itself is an indicator of previous government policy). However, a recent British study showed that shoplifting fell by between 40 per cent and 85 per cent in heroin users following treatment.[9] There is no reason to think that any of the other US findings will be different in other countries with regard to the effectiveness of long-term treatment programmes in getting people back to a drug-free, non-dependent life.

US figures showed:

- Selling of drugs fell 78 per cent
- Shoplifting fell 82 per cent
- Violence against another person fell 78 per cent
- Arrest rates for any offence fell 62 per cent
- Numbers supporting themselves through illegal activity fell by 48 per cent. Welfare support costs also fell
- Employment increased from 51 per cent to 60 per cent
- Welfare recipients fell from 40 per cent to 35 per cent
- Those reporting they were homeless fell from 19 per cent to 11 per cent

Health costs were reduced:

- Alcohol or drug-related medical visits fell 53 per cent
- Mental health problems fell 35 per cent
- Those needing mental health hospital care fell 28 per cent

What more evidence do we need? The fact is that any medical intervention programme or community action project would be delighted with this scale of achievement. Outcomes are often notoriously hard to measure – for example, levels of independence of elderly chronic sick men and women in the community following extra provision of home care. Most health care workers would be content with a 15 per cent improvement in such a situation, but here we are seeing improvement greatly in excess of this – of 50 per cent or more in some measures. The outcomes are both clear and convincing, often based on objective data rather than self-reported levels of drug taking. Arrest figures and admission rates to hospital, for example, are both verifiable.

Treatment has a far wider impact than just on the person with dependency. Children settle down at school as a parent returns to his normal self, truancy and petty crime fall – both often expressions of distress at home. Marriages recover, friendships and relationships with neighbours are restored. Other risks are reduced. For example, a major concern has been that the sexual partners of drug users may be exposed to HIV if the users are carriers. Rehabilitation is also a very effective way of reducing sexual risk taking among drug users. In the US study:

- Numbers of people trading sex for money or drugs fell 56 per cent
- Numbers having sex with an intravenous drug injector were reduced 51 per cent
- Those having vaginal sex without a condom fell 35 per cent

COSTS OF TREATMENT

So then, we have seen that treatment works and that the cost/ benefit ratio can be as good as one to seven. But how are those figures broken down? And how do the costs of keeping people in hospital, at home or in residential care compare?

Treatment costs varied from $1,800 to $6,800 per person, compared to the cost of keeping someone in prison of more than $20,000 a year.

- Methadone clinics cost $13 a day per person for average of 300 days – total cost $3,900
- Non-methadone clinics cost $15 a day per person for average of 120 days – total cost $1,800
- Long-term residential care costs $49 a day for average of 140 days – total cost $6,860
- Short-term residential care costs $130 a day for average of 30 days – total cost $4,000.
- Treatment in prison – additional costs $24 a day for an average of 75 days – total cost $1,800

★ ★ ★

So there are very significant differences in costs per person treated. It would be easy to assume in the light of current research that one should go for the lowest cost option if all outcomes are effective. The trouble is that even in the US there is insufficient evidence yet to be able to compare different options with confidence, and there is even less in other countries such as Britain. Anecdotal experience suggests that for very obvious reasons the residential care option is likely to be the most effective for most people.

There are three patterns of residential rehabilitation:

- Therapeutic communities
- 'Twelve step' Minnesota model houses, largely in the non-state sector
- General houses, including those with a Christian philosophy

There are also a variety of community approaches. The problem is that many different addiction patterns and social groups tend to get muddled together, when they require separate solutions. Indeed, every person is unique. As we have seen, the stereotypical heroin or cocaine user may be hard to find. Many people are using a wide variety of different drugs, or have done in the past. Their personalities and support structures are different. For example, one man may recognise, with others, that remaining at home in his own locality will be an impossibly difficult temptation, when he sees drug-taking friends in the pub and on the street corner. He may come to the conclusion that nothing will work as well as going into a long-stay, residential, therapeutic community several hundred miles away.

On the other hand, another person may be in a situation with a very supportive partner and several children who do not want to be separated from him or her for six months or more, nor do they want to live next door to a residential unit. Every person is unique, which is why a comprehensive range of options is needed. One of those options has to be treatment in prison.

Culture is also important. A support group mainly consisting of former heroin users may not have much to offer one or two others who have problems with binge alcohol drinking. The philosophy of the residential unit may also vary – for example, some may be strongly Christian and others aggressively secular. People have their own preferences, which must be respected if the therapy is to have the greatest chance of success.

The antabuse programme for alcoholics is a good example of how alcohol and illegal drug abuse often need very different approaches. Antabuse (disulphiram) is a drug with no therapeutic action inside someone who is fit and well. However, it prevents the normal destruction of alcohol in the body causing very unpleasant reactions such as flushing, low blood pressure (faintness), sweating, nausea and weakness. Antabuse lasts up to four days, and so is a useful psychological barrier for someone who knows they might be tempted to do something on impulse that they might later regret. However, the reactions can be extremely severe.

Christian organisations have always been at the forefront of rehabilitation. Indeed the Christian community has been responsible for building hospitals and care centres in more than a hundred nations over the last century and a half, following a tradition expressed in countries like Britain and America. The philosophy of Christian care historically has been unconditional love to all, regardless of how they come to need help, and the offering of spiritual support as an optional part of a comprehensive package of care, designed around each individual according to their own preferences.

Large numbers of rehab projects in Britain, America and other nations have a Christian basis, and attribute their success to the fact that many who pass through the door leave with a new spiritual certainty or faith. Indeed so many have religious roots that a secular drugs association has been created in America to help provide wider choices for those who want a completely secular approach.[11] An excellent example of secular residential rehab is Phoenix House, a network of residential projects, such as the one based in Glasgow.

Links Project in Edinburgh provides a similar service.

One prominent US religious group is the Prison Fellowship Ministries, founded by Charles Colson. Christian organisations also have a long track record in prison visiting, primarily through chaplaincies and the work of religious orders, influenced by the command of Jesus to visit the imprisoned as well as the sick. They also have been successful in helping motivate those who have lost hope to find new ways of living. There is far more to prison rehab than withdrawing the drug. Aftercare, counselling, literacy skills and job training are vital. Support needs to be well organised before, during and after release.

All too often in Britain a drug user is pitched out on to the street on leaving gaol, with unresolved issues from the past and an active addiction. The first problem can be housing, where there are large rent debts and the local authority is unhelpful. The next problem is often persuading an employer to take on a former convict, who possibly is still an active drug user. So within a couple of days the person may be living on the floor of a flat belonging to drug-taking friends, short of cash, ready for offers, and back into the previous lifestyle, which includes stealing or pimping to make enough money to get by.

Almost all residential abstinence programmes for drug users follow a very traditional pattern, whether religious or secular. The ideal is to take the user away, out of their usual environment, far from friends and all known networks of supply.

Once there the user is rapidly weaned off all drugs (usually with the exception of tobacco, which is generally the most difficult addiction of all to break), and then integrated into a supportive community of former drug users under staff supervision. Those with alcohol addiction are treated in a similar way. Once again tobacco addiction often remains. Numbers who smoke are usually the same regardless of whether or not they have been through an alcohol rehab programme.[12]

Community duties help give the person a sense of worth and bring in the normal disciplines of non-addicted day-to-day living.

Group sessions help explore some of the reasons why the addiction developed in the first place, and begin to tackle underlying behaviour patterns which put the person at risk of relapse once the treatment period is over.

People stay variable lengths of time and are usually free to opt out of the programme at any stage. They may also be thrown out if they insist on breaking rules, for example, by bringing drugs into the site.

Rebuilding a whole way of life takes a long time – many months in most cases. There are no short cuts. This is nothing short of a complete mental and emotional refit. That is why it is hard to be convinced that community care can really deliver what is needed, the depth of transformation, the total turn-around. We are talking more about personal growth than about weaning a body off physical dependency. If the person has been addicted for some time, she will have created for herself a world where every action, every conscious thought is influenced and shaped by the need to satisfy a craving that keeps on returning.

When a person leaves rehab she will need to find new friends. A drink in a familiar pub could be all that is necessary to lead back into drug use, when surrounded by people who themselves are quite keen for the person to indulge again. Some will encourage it because it makes them feel better about their own addiction. Others will make money out of it.

Then there is the job to consider for someone who may have been virtually unemployable for years, and a home to find. And there are issues of self-esteem, self-confidence, relationship skills and other matters.

To be strong it is helpful for a former addict to come to an understanding of the psychological pressures that helped lead him or her into an addiction, and how to cope with those same pressures in a different way in the future. These units are non-judgmental about the person's past, yet communicate strong values about the future.

The aim is to help the former user to reach his own judgment of his past, which may take some time. It can be a painful realisation, for example, for a former alcoholic to bring himself face to face with the pain and suffering his drunkenness caused his wife and children. Yet it is only through the pain that truth comes and the way ahead emerges. Without the pain it would be too easy to go back. 'I know now what hell I put them through. I had no idea at the time. I was a real xxxxx. I was completely blind to it – and for quite a while after I stopped drinking. I was blind to how it was killing me too.'

Track record

Residential communities have remarkable track records although obviously they are expensive individual solutions. But then addiction is expensive for society in terms of social costs and crime. It is scandalous that many people in Britain who want to give up addictive drugs are unable to find suitable residential units. There are not enough places. It is also a shameful reflection of bad priorities that residential facilities for treating chronic alcohol abuse are even fewer.

Society seems to have the view that someone addicted to heroin needs intense, long-term professional help, while someone with alcoholism can somehow manage on his own at home with just a weekly support group. Who are they kidding? This is blatant discrimination of the worst kind against those with alcohol-related problems. And it's not just the alcoholic man or woman who suffers. It also means that for families with an addicted member there is little or no help to put their own lives back together again. As we have seen, alcohol addiction is an appalling burden on families and those in the workplace as well as a major cause of stress and ill health to those addicted. In statistical terms it is far more an issue for society, and therefore a correspondingly large budget should be devoted to supporting those whose daily lives are dominated by it.

Community-based support

An alternative to residential rehab is community support. Whilst it is undoubtedly true that someone can withdraw from drugs or alcohol safely in a community setting, it requires close supervision which can also turn out to be more costly than one might imagine. For these reasons community care is not necessarily cheaper. And if the poorer outcome means that there is a relapse followed by a second period of rehabilitation then whatever potential savings there might have been are immediately vaporised.

Community teams in Britain usually consist of a social worker, a community psychiatric nurse and administrative staff, working with a consultant psychiatrist, often with a link to a local family doctor. GPs are increasingly involved in seeing drug users and this trend is likely to increase.

Team roles can include assessment and counselling, detoxification and prescribing, advocacy, child protection, complementary therapy, writing of court reports and liaison with the criminal justice system, with clinics, probation officers and referrals to other services. However, most teams emphasise harm reduction, with abstinence as the ideal eventual goal. This could hardly be more different than the residential option which is based on absolute abstention from illegal drugs and (usually) all alcohol, with discipline and possible expulsion for those who break the rules.

The fact is that supervision is almost impossible in the community. This is quite different from the rehab unit. In a residential placement the inmate may be faced at any time with close monitoring by staff, and by other community members who may also be very effective in policing the abstention policy. Alcohol can be smelled on the breath, pupils may be narrowed, mental awareness may be changed. Those who are experienced and have a high index of suspicion quickly pick up the signs, especially when they follow an unexplained absence from the grounds without permission, or gossip in the corridors.

Living at home carries a daily risk that the person will wander out down the road and come back intoxicated or with fresh supplies. Who is ever going to know? Drug testing will pick up illegal substances, but a binge on alcohol? These are serious risks if the community support is based in the area where the drug user has lived in the recent past. However, community settings are an excellent half-way house between the formal disciplines of residential care and the totally exposed full integration back into normal life.

Long climb up to full rehab

In summary then, full rehab is a long climb back up. It takes time and energy, and relapses are common. It is not unusual for a user to need two or three attempts at residential rehab before kicking free for the long term. Despite this, success rates are excellent and the impact is very significant from every person who is fully recovered.

THE TRUTH ABOUT DRUGS IN PRISON

We need now to return to the vexed issue of drug taking in prison. As we have seen, a high proportion of heavy drug users commit multiple crimes to pay for their habit, and of those, large numbers inevitably are arrested, charged and gaoled. But what happens then? In many cases the prison service has become nothing more than a temporary holding ground between one conviction and another, bulging at the seams, tens of thousands of addicts or former addicts jammed together, very little in the way of effective life-building, yet ideally placed to become the biggest rehabilitation programme in the nation.

However, the whole system militates against what should be happening. No amount of tinkering at the edges will produce results while the old-style institutional incarceration remains. Staff attitudes are entrenched in many prisons, not helped by chronic overcrowding, low staffing, poor morale, high sickness absence, tension among stressed prisoners from appalling conditions, violence against staff, periodic riots and the rest. This then is the background to the daily flow of drugs on a breath-taking scale into every prison in Britain. The same is true of most other nations in the world.

> 'Ah yes, what have we here?' said the prison officer to me, lifting an upturned flowerpot in the greenhouse area of Holloway women's prison in London. 'This is where they pass it on.' She tried another couple of pots. 'So then, none today. We tried stamping it out but there was a lot of trouble so now we turn a blind eye.'[13]
>
> Later we visited a number of women in cells, unlocked to allow them to wander in and out of the corridors for several hours a day. Many had young babies. Some had been convicted for offences relating to prostitution, others also had HIV, and drug addiction was common. 'Sex is how they pay for the drugs when they get out. It's the only way they can find to survive.'

A great number may be addicted on arrival, and their addiction led to the crimes for which they were convicted. But others begin a drug habit once inside, or they relapse.

Prisons are a school house for drug taking

Needles are hard to come by and sharing can be the normal pattern. One might imagine therefore that an elementary step in protection would be to issue clean needles – particularly following the disturbing reports recently that fourteen prisoners were using a single needle in one British prison. Such stories could be repeated in the prison service almost every day.

However, issuing needles is a major risk. One of the biggest nightmares for a warden is the thought of being threatened by a prisoner holding a needle and syringe, contaminated with HIV-infected blood. As an offensive weapon, whether as a dagger or thrown, it is terrifying. Such a weapon is more than enough to persuade a gaolor to hand over keys. That is why prisons have never supplied needles, even on an exchange basis. But injecting continues just the same – ten or twenty prisoners sharing the same needle on a daily basis. *One lad in Perth prison (Scotland) was so desperate for a needle that he sharpened the plastic shaft of a biro and used it to inject into veins in his neck. Then he shared it.*[14]

Desperate situations call for desperate measures. Just as we have seen over the issue of drug testing, normal sensitivities have to be cast aside. Hence the extraordinary statement by a British Minister in Spring 1998 that the government was in fact seriously considering issuing needles to prisoners.

What makes such a proposal even harder to live with is that the very people who want the needles are by definition far more likely to be those whose blood may be carrying hazardous viruses. In fact the risk of HIV transmission from a carrier who is symptom-free by a single needle stick injury is now recognised to be less than one in two hundred. We know this from the very large number of such accidents among health care workers world-wide over the last decade which have been carefully followed up. Nevertheless, it would be a very brave man or woman who would tackle a drug user with such a weapon. The risk to *them* could be far greater than after a typical hospital accident if the needle and syringe are heavily contaminated or full of fresh blood and the aim is to inject rather than merely to stab.

This single issue of needles in prison illustrates the complexity of prison-based addiction, a problem which would be greatly eased by separating those who agree to be drug-free from hardened drug users with no desire to change. Once again, there is no doubt whatever that drug testing could have a huge impact on the pattern of abuse, if consistently applied with a well-defined set of sanctions such as loss of early release possibilities. On the other hand, if sanctions are applied too severely, there are no rewards left that a prisoner feels are worth the effort. The greatest reward is of course the promise of a shorter sentence.

The problem of drugs supply in prisons is just a mirror of the rest of society. One might suppose that prison should be the one place on earth where drugs should by definition be easiest to control. No one comes in or goes out except on a semi-permanent basis, and those who arrive are searched, there is limited contact with visitors, and the staff one might assume are trustworthy.

Compare this highly controlled environment to the open gates of a local school. Prisoners have little or no money to trade with – in theory. Contrast that to the free flow of cash to pupils from parents or small-scale theft to users, and then to dealers just outside the school gate. The drive to find fresh supplies inside a prison can become a compulsive obsession.

Keep the prison happy

It is a well known fact that the harsher the prison regime, the more disgruntled and angry the inmates become, and the greater the risk of disturbances. Drug supplies keep some prisoners quiet, but keep others in a simmering furnace of increasing dependency and loss of self-control.

Just stopping prisoners from using drugs – even if you succeed – does nothing to help them after release.

- 75 per cent of those released on parole with previous heroin or cocaine addiction return to their old patterns of use within 90 days[15]
- 66 per cent are re-arrested within 18 months[16]
- 75 per cent of those who receive treatment in prison and good support after discharge are 75 per cent drug-free after 18 months
- 70 per cent are arrest-free

These figures are compelling and are the reason for the huge growth in US prison drug rehabilitation programmes. In a growing number of prisons the inmates can chose to be moved to a 'drug-free' wing where they enjoy privileges and access to extra support, therapy and care. If they break the rules and test positive they risk being transferred back.

They also risk other sanctions such as 'closed visits' where all physical contact with friends and family is barred.[17] As these programmes are being rolled out nationally it seems that with the right approach, a skilled team and a decent budget, a very significant proportion of convicts are willing to take part in such a programme. Of course, there is always a danger with any incentive-based system. If the rewards become big enough, people will take risks to take part, even perhaps taking heroin for the first time in gaol just to qualify for rehab privileges.

In Britain there have already been cases where drug injectors have deliberately shared needles with others they knew had HIV in order to get themselves a positive HIV test, which would qualify them for immediate priority housing and other benefits.

Now the British government has plans to create a drug-free wing in every prison, costing £7 million a year. The new deal will also cost an additional £40 million for drug testing and compulsory treatment schemes.[18]

The AIDS factor

AIDS caused a complete rethink about the goals of prevention. For a start, what is the point of someone struggling to beat a heroin addiction when they are likely to die soon anyway? That was the new theory.

Giving free needles and syringes to addicts seemed outrageous at first to many in Britain, and still remains highly controversial in the US. People were worried that it would appear to officially encourage injecting, and that it might prolong the injecting career of the user. However, if users are going to inject anyway, then there is a public health need to prevent the spread of illnesses, which will inevitably also affect a wider community through sexual relations and child-bearing. A key worry has been also that, for some at least, the sight of injecting equipment itself arouses a desire, and there is clear evidence that needle exchanges have been targeted by people looking for equipment.

Needle exchanges have to operate as:

- Friendly and non-judgmental
- Anonymous
- Free from police watchers as people come and go

Their dominant purpose is to change needle-sharing behaviour, therefore attracting and retaining a large number of active users is essential. Needle exchanges can also be a vital avenue for other health information and support – for example on sexual health or contraception.

There are over 300 specific needle exchange projects in the UK, and needle exchange is a part of many other programmes. In addition, over 2,000 pharmacies participate in needle exchange schemes. These schemes have been very successful in containing HIV among drug users, which has remained as low as 1 per cent outside London and 7 per cent in London by 1995. This is very modest compared to other European nations. In Edinburgh HIV rates of 55 per cent 1985 had fallen to 19 per cent by 1994.

oOo

In conclusion, there is no doubt that well run treatment programmes have excellent success rates in curing people of addiction long term, whether addicted to heroin, crack, cocaine, alcohol, or other drugs. Spending on these programmes should be an urgent priority area, with very little cost in total society terms because of the enormous benefits from dealing with addiction. Alcohol addiction is much neglected and the prison service will need a cultural revolution to turn around from a greenhouse for addictions to an effective rehabilitation service.

Having seen the size of the drugs problem, counted the cost, looked at different drugs, seen how effective prevention and treatment can be, and how little governments are actually devoting to dealing with the problem, we now need to turn to the most

vexing question of all: legalisation. If it is true that drug using now
has such a hold on society at every level, should we not stop turning
users into criminals? Should we not at the very least seriously
consider decriminalising cannabis and perhaps Ecstasy, seeing that
both are far less harmful than tobacco?

Legalisation and Decriminalisation – The Arguments over Cannabis

In the light of all that has gone before perhaps it is surprising that we still need to address the question of legalisation. After all, we have already seen overwhelming evidence of the menace of illegal drug use, the enormous cost to society, and that prevention and treatment are both highly effective, if resources are applied in the right way. So why consider a *relaxation* of law, making it *easier* to obtain drugs, at a time when, as we have seen, the facts push us clearly the other way, to tightening up on alcohol and tobacco as well as on other drug use?

Yet, despite all the evidence we have seen (or in ignorance of it) every day the calls for legalisation of some or all drugs grow louder. the *Economist*, for example, believes the benefits to us all would be enormous: police and customs would have far less to do, saving £500m a year. The British prison population would be cut by 10 per cent. It would reduce, they say, crime and violence, as well as force drug barons out of business. If licensed sellers were taxed it would raise £1bn a year. But at what price to our way of life, to the youth of the nation, to the welfare of an entire people?

As we have seen, the law in many cases is confusing. In countries such as Britain it is not strictly illegal to take drugs but only to possess them or supply them to others. This inconsistency is at the heart of the debate over drug testing. Is it fair to take action against people who are completely sober because ultra-sensitive tests show that they have used an illegal drug months ago, when an alcoholic gets away undetected simply because he has not had a drink for sixteen hours?

WHAT SORT OF SOCIETY DO WE WANT?

We can easily become caught up in heated arguments over the rights and wrongs of laws on cannabis, and lose sight of the bigger issues. I remember some years ago working at a hospital in the Transkei, South Africa, in a Xhosa tribal area. Cannabis use in remote rural areas was widespread, there was no policing of the situation and there was a cultural tolerance. However, the result was that many men in particular were wiped out for long periods, incapable of sustained work. Happy perhaps, but unable to contribute to the welfare of the community. What sort of society do you want?

Dangers of fatalism and pragmatism

There are dangers both in fatalism and pragmatism. Fatalism says that everyone will want to take drugs anyway, the battle is lost, just go with the flow. Pragmatism says that while it may not be desirable to legalise cannabis and possibly other drugs, it would deal practically with a number of problems.

THE PROBLEM OF CONSISTENCY

We cannot sort out a rational approach to dope until society's attitudes to alcohol and tobacco are re-examined. If tobacco was being developed today as a new consumer product, it would be banned. Knowing what we know today, tobacco companies would be hounded into the ground as immoral profiteers who deserved public damnation. However, the biggest weapon in the tobacco company armoury is history: the fact that millions of people have smoked as a 'smart' way of life for over a hundred years.

Every 1950s film, every war movie from the 1940s, every authentic reconstruction of a 1930s drama requires cigarettes as props: long ones, short ones, smelly ones, mild ones, with filters, without filters or sucked on the end of long elegant holders. To renounce tobacco *en masse* is to spit on our past, turning our backs in contempt on an era for whom a daily courtesy was to offer a light. But that is exactly what we have to do.

If this is so for tobacco then it is a thousand times more so for alcohol. Thirty years ago teetotalism was treated as a joke by a large section of society. A sign of being a man was being able to 'hold your drink', to drink heavily without losing the ability to conduct a normal conversation or be outwardly affected in any other untoward way. Today a sign of greatness in many circles is still, for men, having a head for alcohol. Attitudes have changed and saying No to alcohol is more acceptable, but the cultural memory still lives, whether in the gin and tonic brigade or the beer drinkers down at the local pub.

As attitudes have begun to turn against tobacco and become more tolerant of the low or no drinker, they have warmed to legalisation of cannabis – 35 per cent in favour in Britain compared to 17 per cent in 1989.[1] But that is an average across the generations. Sixty-six per cent of people under 25 years old want cannabis legalised. Yet as we have seen, there is a profound shift under way among employers for simple economic reasons, with a hardening of resolve against the recreational drug user as well as the addict.

Argument of naturalness

Almost all drugs are naturally occurring and so, an argument goes, people should be allowed to consume them in a process no more unnatural than drinking tea. Exploration itself is not the issue, so much as the personal danger from psychological or physical dependency and other subtle changes to health, emotions and mental well-being through indulgence. Sensation seeking on its own is not a moral issue. Roller coaster enthusiasts, bungie jumpers, white water rafters and food connoisseurs are all sensation seekers. Without sensation seeking our natural curiosity would die, we would be mere automatons, programmed to wake, eat, work and sleep without any sense of pleasure. The problem comes when sensation leads to excessive risk to self or others.

DRUGS AND THE LAW — CURRENT UK SITUATION

Laws applying to alcohol have been proposed as models for legalisation of cannabis: treat them both the same, or in a similar way, with licensed outlets and controls on the limits of intoxication, especially for drivers. But are alcohol laws a good model anyway? As we have seen, they have failed to curb an epidemic of alcoholism, a major scourge on society today.

Alcohol regulation has focused on:

- Licensing of premises to sell alcohol
- Age restrictions on purchases
- Limited opening hours
- Heavy taxes to increase price

Research shows that price control is an effective way to reduce demand. These controls have been undermined by a combination of factors including duty free sales and cross-channel shopping, where there is almost no limit in practice to the amount of cheap alcohol that can be bought in France and imported to Britain, for personal use.

However, price controls are a blunt instrument which discriminates against the poor. All control measures will become harder with further European integration. As it is, the real price of alcohol has fallen towards levels in the rest of Europe while consumption has soared from 5.7 litres per person a year in 1960 to 9.1 litres a year in 1992.[2]

Legalisation by the back door

As far as illegal drugs are concerned, the application of the law is far from clear. Some drugs are already effectively legalised, in practice. For example, heroin addicts get replacement therapy free, plus needles and syringes, while those using cannabis are largely ignored. It's hard to reconcile the reality with some of the tough anti-drugs rhetoric of government ministers. Very few would want to close down units providing replacement therapy (methadone) or needle exchanges, but the relaxation of law enforcement over cannabis is significant.

As we have seen, almost 90 per cent of drug offences in the UK are for possession, and 55 per cent of all offenders are let off with a caution – up from only 13 per cent in 1985. Therefore one may conclude that because of the way the *practice* of law has changed, over the last ten years, the personal possession of cannabis has become accepted as within the law in many parts of the country.

The watershed came in 1991 when for the first time cautions became more common than prosecutions. Indeed, there has been a nine-fold increase in cautioning in the ten years to 1995 while prosecutions have (only) doubled at a time of rapidly growing use.

In 1995 for cannabis offences (all kinds and amounts):[3]

- 40,391 were let off with a caution
- 24,000 were prosecuted
- 12,000 were fined
- Fewer than 1,000 were sent to prison
- There are big differences in sentencing patterns from area to area, ranging from a caution to prison for identical offences. The maximum penalty for possession of cannabis is five years in gaol
- The proportion fined has dropped from 48 per cent of offenders in 1985 to a mere 22 per cent in 1995, varying with area

★ ★ ★

These area inconsistencies are very unfair. Depending on who you are, where you are and who arrests you, if you are carrying cannabis you could either be let off with a warning or land up with a criminal record.

The *real* caution figures are even more startling, since official records only record *formal* cautions. Thousands of others each year are let off with an informal caution, just a warning. This is different from a formal caution where admission of guilt leads to arrest and charges but no court case. And of course the vast majority of drugs offences are unreported because those in a position to report them were themselves involved.

Even import or export offences resulted in only 40 per cent going to prison.[4] Seventy-five per cent of the 7,100 prison sentences for drug offences in 1995 were for less than two years.

Crime arrest statistics can be very misleading. For example, the British Crime Survey suggested that in 1993 at least 4 million people in Britain misused a drug but only 70,000 were cautioned or sentenced – less than 2 per cent of offenders. This means that higher detection rates could easily double the number of arrests from 2 to 4 per cent of users, giving the false impression that use has doubled, when it has actually fallen.

THE CASE FOR AND AGAINST FORMAL LEGALISATION

My own views on the legalisation question have changed considerably in the writing of this book. I started with the view that the drugs war was all but lost, that law was a blunt instrument with which to regulate private behaviour, and that in view of the numbers of users of illegal drugs, we should at least decriminalise cannabis. Let us look one by one at the main arguments in favour of legalisation.

People say that drug laws create greater evils than drugs themselves. They say that it would be better to put all the funds spent on policing drug laws into education and treatment. But what would happen in a world where buying Ecstasy becomes as easy as buying a packet of cigarettes?

People say that young people are now being placed the wrong side of the law, for no good purpose. It is true that society is sending out a very stark message about right and wrong regarding drugs, but is that such a bad thing?

People say that teenagers are being exposed to dealers and the risk of being persuaded to go up the ladder towards more dangerous drugs. That is true but will always be the case so long as some drugs are legalised and others are not. Say, for example, that the law is relaxed on cannabis and Ecstasy – what about the tens of thousands using LSD, amphetamines and steroids? The ladder argument will always be there so long as there is a ladder to climb.

People say that it would be better to have dope shops on every corner (carefully regulated of course) so that all those wanting cannabis can get as much as they like, whenever they like. But laws strictly limiting sales of tobacco to over eighteens have completely failed to prevent a free flow to almost all younger teenagers who want to smoke. The biggest suppliers are irresponsible older brothers, sisters and friends, closely followed by disreputable retail outlets.

Exactly the same pattern will develop with cannabis or Ecstasy. It is inevitable. Whatever is in the local corner shop will be in every local school and in every youth club. Limiting the age to over eighteens would make the flow slightly less, but not a lot. The irresponsible sixteen- and seventeen-year-olds who currently supply under-agers with tobacco would simply get their Ecstasy or cannabis from friends a year or two older. Drugs will find their way down the age groups, with each feeling comfortable in giving supplies to the year or two below. And people lie about their age. Photo cards are already forged by those at school, so even that solution will not be watertight. And even if it were, those old enough to buy legally will supply those who are not.

People say that making drugs legal will not increase demand. They say that by taking away the forbidden element it may even *reduce* the elusive attraction of taking drugs. This is nonsense. We know that drug use is price sensitive: as price rises consumption falls. But legalisation would *have* to result in a price *fall* – why else would people bother to buy from a licensed outlet? Officially sanctioned drugs shops will need to undercut the dealer network on the street to survive. If government prices for cannabis are set too high, the black market will step in with illegal supplies at the real market value.

The State would then be in competition with every dealer in the country, with a slight advantage for the few who prefer to buy from the corner shop rather than discreetly from a friend. But the inescapable fact is that legalisation will mean drugs cost less and consumption will rise, addictive habits will become cheaper to acquire.

Some people say that lower prices will be a good thing. They say it will mean less crime and prostitution for a start. But the way to deal with that is to provide replacement therapy on the State for proven addicts – less easy, admittedly, for cocaine addicts than for those addicted to heroin. The other way is to provide easy access at short notice to a comprehensive range of treatment facilities, which, as we have seen, have an excellent success record. No, all illegal drugs should be kept as expensive and difficult to obtain as possible, except for officially registered addicts receiving treatment, for whom supplies should be free. In addition, taxes should be raised further on tobacco and alcohol – within the confines of European laws.

People say that you can't go on enforcing a law against 'soft' drugs, because it has turned a majority in some age groups into criminals. But this is nonsense and based on myth rather than fact. For a start, current laws on smoking turn every smoker under sixteen into a criminal, yet there are no howls of protest over *that*. Are these same people proposing that we should abolish all laws about sale of cigarettes to minors because we have turned a generation of twelve-year-olds into criminals? It is exactly the same argument and hardly bears serious consideration.

And who dares to suggest that we are talking about a majority in *any* age group? The fact is that figures for drug taking are serious enough without being deliberately overblown by those seeking to argue the case 'on behalf of the majority who are users'. As we have seen over and over again, an element in the pro-legalisation lobby has tirelessly seized every possible opportunity to overstate the numbers of drug users – *current* users, not those who tried it once. One-time users are largely irrelevant and should be trimmed out of many statistics about use in certain age groups.

If we look at smoking we might find that almost all adults at one time or another tried a puff of a cigarette, but that is hardly important when looking at the impact of regulations on smoking across a whole community. What is more significant is the numbers that will be affected by smoking in a given month or year. In the case of smoking it is a large minority, with cannabis a fraction of even that number.

It is interesting that the pro-legalisation lobby often tries to distort the same figures towards both extremes, as it suits them. Whenever people challenge them about the serious scale of national addiction, many say the official figures are far too high, fearful of a backlash and stricter anti-drug measures. Whenever others challenge them about the fact that the typical teenager is *not* a drug user, the same lobby has been known to pronounce the official statistics as far too low. The truth is that we have a serious problem requiring urgent action, which involves a significant minority.

People say that international control has completely broken down. It is true that international controls are ineffective, incomplete, weak and have negligible impact on the global drug flow, but they do send out a powerful moral message that global society condemns drug trafficking. If we made global drug trafficking legal, we would be saying that trading drugs for a living is just as acceptable as trading copper, cotton or sugar. Instead we have a situation (quite rightly) where drug traffickers are almost universally despised as international pariahs, objects of universal contempt. And that same revulsion is reserved for the actions of everyone involved in the mega supply chain. Of course, many do so because they are addicted themselves, and in such situations we need to have a measure of compassion and understanding for the person while still taking the toughest measures to curb the activity.

Do we really want to live in a world where a local teacher can drive from London to Paris to fill up a car with £20,000 of cannabis resin which he can then sell perfectly legitimately to an authorised retailer? That sort of scenario will be the consequence of legalisation. Or is the government going to run the whole process, from commissioning farmers to growing cannabis, to processing factories and distribution networks?

We are told that now cautioning is the rule, with few arrests for possession, the law has become a mockery and should be revised. People ask what the point is of having a law which is not applied – or worse is used in an arbitrary and unfair manner. But many other laws are not applied with consistent discretion. That does not mean that they should be abolished. It is said sometimes that laws are made to be broken and this is true in the sense that laws are often set in place to allow steps to be taken if necessary.

One example might be laws on the age of consent for sex between men and women. It is very rare for two children attempting sex together to be prosecuted if both are willing parties. It is also very unusual for, say, a sixteen-year-old boy to be charged for having sex with a fourteen-year-old girl. Yet the law has several purposes. It helps define the limits of expected behaviour, and also can be used where necessary at the discretion of the authorities to protect a child who is being taken advantage of.

Laws against possession of cannabis are therefore very important, and should not be set aside simply because in practice minor offences are overlooked. And in any case, with shifts in attitudes it may well be that prosecutions will rise again as a proportion of outcomes. While inconsistencies between areas can be undesirable, in another sense they may be important if they reflect local feeling. For example, why should those who live in the Highlands of Scotland be the same as those in London when it comes to their views on sentencing drug users? Why should Newcastle be the same as Belfast? What is important is that there are clear, locally agreed sentencing guidelines, rather than the current situation which is still far too arbitrary.

People say that legalising some or all drugs will deal with corruption, reduce law and order costs, empty crowded courts, gaols and prisons – and no doubt flood hospital wards, GP consulting rooms and social workers' caseloads. We know that high rates of drug taking are linked to huge losses in productivity and other costs. One set of evils will be more than replaced with another. It is perverse to call something that is bad good, simply because calling it for what it is has become hard work.

People say that it would be excellent for the State to control and tax drug production and distribution. They say it would save lives by guaranteeing drug purity. It would save health costs, HIV infection and the rest. It is true that buying from the State will always be safer than buying from a bunch of criminals, but you can carry that argument to a nonsense position.

Take a terrorist group committed to economic sabotage, blowing up empty buildings in key areas. Should the government supply fail-safe detonators to them so that they don't land up accidentally killing themselves and members of the public with premature detonations? It's the same moral issue. An undesirable act is about to be committed. The State could help reduce risks to people by supplying what is necessary, but in so doing could give a bad example, seeming to encourage deviant behaviour. The right compromise is the current position with needle exchanges and replacement therapy – we should go no further.

People say that State control of the drugs trade would mean billions in extra tax revenues to pay for the consequences of addiction. That may be true but why start down this route at all when, as we have seen, the *only* way you could *raise* those taxes would be by setting taxes so low that drugs shops were undercutting the current street prices. In itself this would directly encourage buying from official outlets and increase consumption.

Raising money from taxing drugs would also have another very harmful effect: drug users would be dangerously comforted by the thought that far from doing others harm, their use of drugs actually does society *good*. Thus the perceived tax benefits would be a further encouragement for drug use.

The same thing has happened over the lottery. In Britain there is an epidemic of lottery addiction among teenagers, as many as 6 per cent of whom have stolen to pay for tickets. One of the key justifications people make for the lottery is that it raises money for good causes. Some charities (especially Christian ones) have refused on principle to apply for lottery funds because they know the organisers will (ab)use the publicity of lottery grants to justify an activity to which many low income people are now addicted.

THE CASE *AGAINST* LEGALISATION IS OVERWHELMING

So then, each of the arguments in favour of legalisation is flawed, not just slightly, but seriously. Each point made by the pro-drugs lobby is based on a partial truth, but with no proper accounting for the consequences.

Drug laws help contain a huge social evil which, if they were swept away, would spread unchecked through every layer of society. The truth is that no one can possibly be sure what the impact would be, but one thing is certain: it would be almost impossible to reverse the tide in the short to medium term by tightening laws again. Even if it turned out that legalisation created fewer problems than feared, we have no means of knowing for certain today, and the stakes are far too high to abandon caution.

It is sobering to look at what has happened in Amsterdam, where relaxation over the personal use of cannabis has led to problems. Technically it is illegal to buy and sell cannabis but official policy is one of toleration. At licensed house parties, a government-funded testing service checks the purity of Ecstasy tablets, but people are not encouraged to use the drug and the police have powers to arrest anyone carrying drugs in. The Netherlands has fewer drug-related deaths and a lower rate of experimental use among school pupils than many other European countries.

All this sounds very promising, positive steps towards formal legalisation with few social costs. But that is just the surface. Many people are beginning to question the experiment. Walking around Amsterdam recently I saw some of the most blatant drug dealing on the street, and drug taking, that I have ever witnessed in any city. Right in front of the main station, for example, a crowd from nowhere gathered in a few seconds around a man with a plastic bag, bustling around as eager as a flock of hungry pigeons. Within a couple of minutes they were facing walls, on the ground, sitting, standing, taking what they were taking. Other tourists have been approached aggressively by dealers.

Amsterdam is a magnet for every man and woman in Europe who wants to be able to sit in a public café and get stoned, or worse. People say that if every city was run like Amsterdam, the novelty would wear off. However, unless it was the case in every city in the world we would still be likely to see drugs-related tourism. Something has gone very wrong with this experiment. What normal parent of teenage children wants to live in a street where cannabis is openly on sale?

Holland is now clamping down on marijuana growers with a new Act of Parliament. At the same time new powers have been given to town mayors to close the cannabis coffee shops if hard drugs are sold, delivered, supplied or found on the premises.[5]

The Swiss also made an experiment of their own. A particular park in down-town Zurich was designated a protected area where drug users could go and use drugs without arrest. This was Zurich's answer to the growing drugs menace. Don't harass, just embrace. Don't make things difficult for drug users, make them easy. Instead of hounding them from street corner to street corner, welcome them into a nice open space. No doubt some thought it would mean that scenes like those outside Amsterdam station would move off the streets altogether.

However, the park quickly became famous among drug injectors across Switzerland and in other nations. It became a drug injector's paradise, a safe haven for the largest dealers. Non-users felt intimidated, afraid to enter the park or even to go near it. Eventually it all became too much for the city to cope with and the freedoms were removed.

The questions no one wants to answer

The biggest hole in the legalisation argument is law itself, which can only work within precise definitions and boundaries – but what does the pro-drug lobby say they should be? Their answers are very confused. Many complex legal questions arise. Here are just a few examples:

- What drugs do you legalise?
- Can that position be justified logically?
- What potency levels should be permitted?
- What should be the age limit(s) for such drugs?
- Should sales of some drugs be limited to addicts?
- Where should they be sold?
- Is mail order allowable?
- What about vending machines?
- Which drugs should be prescription only for addicts?
- Which drugs should be available for medicinal purposes on prescription only and for what medical conditions?
- Where and by whom is cultivation or home manufacture allowed?
- What about advertising?
- If there is a complete ban on advertising, how strictly is it applied?
- Restrictions on use – e.g. pilots, drivers? If so, what blood levels are permitted?
- Licensing for drug pubs, drug cafés etc.?
- What about use by under-age children in the home under adult supervision?
- Which government department should supervise?

oOo

In conclusion then, there are many reasons given for decriminalising cannabis and possibly Ecstasy, but far more compelling reasons not to. We have troubles enough dealing with a legalised tobacco industry and with widespread addiction to alcohol without adding another group of hazardous substances.

We have seen that cannabis is far from being an 'innocent' drug, with profound short- and long-term effects which are still only partly understood. Ecstasy is also a drug which is becoming more rather than less worrying as time goes by. Both are gateway drugs which make other drug use far more likely, and that is likely to continue to be the case even if they were legalised.

It is illogical and irrational as well as unscientific to propose a law change for cannabis without also including Ecstasy, which raises a further challenge. With every year the number of psycho-active drugs increases, and this will continue at an accelerating rate with new generations of designer drugs. Many of these will turn out to be similar to cannabis and Ecstasy in risk profile, so a decision to legalise cannabis could lead to a situation where ten, fifteen, twenty or a hundred different drugs would have to be given the green light, following exactly the same arguments.

And all the time the counter-trend is gathering speed, with anti-tobacco campaigns and increasing concerns about the future impact of long-term drug taking on a significant proportion of the community.

The law should stay the same, but many other things must change. There are many steps that governments, organisations and individuals should take without delay. So then, what should we all do?

Conclusions – What We Must Do

TEN-POINT PLAN FOR THE GOVERNMENT

The battle against drugs is far from lost. There are many cost effective, practical, hard-hitting steps that governments can make, drawing together many of the issues raised in earlier chapters.

1. Toughen penalties against all those making profits from the drug trade

While it is true that law enforcement against producers and traffickers has only a marginal effect on total availability, it is important that a powerful message is sent out from every government in the world that drug profiteering is an international crime that will be severely punished. This also reinforces a prevention message. Every time the media report another seizure of cocaine, heroin or LSD it strengthens the public perception that involvement in the drugs business is a crime of which almost the whole world disapproves. Fortunately, there is close agreement on these principles in almost all countries.

Further investment in intelligence/arrests

Border controls are the weakest form of law enforcement on drug traffickers because the volumes of traded goods are now so overwhelming. The future lies in highly sophisticated intelligence gathering and this is where money should be spent. Every trick learned in cold war espionage needs to be used, including covert surveillance, infiltration and sting operations where government agencies run groups who look to buy large amounts of drugs and capture whole networks. These operations by definition will invade privacy and personal freedoms, but are essential if the war against drugs is to be waged as effectively as possible.

This trade-off of loss of privacy and personal 'rights' versus fighting the drugs menace is a recurring issue. The drugs war cannot be won by the same sort of approach as fighting car crime or burglaries. A different scale of intervention is required altogether.

Further international co-operation

Drugs operations at present are severely hampered by lack of international co-operation. One reason for this, as in every other area of intelligence work, is trust. Even within nations different agencies are often extremely reluctant to work together. As a result operation after operation is all but destroyed. For example, British intelligence may hear that a container lorry full of cannabis is due to arrive on the Eurotunnel shuttle in three days' time. They would be foolish to intercept it on arrival. The aim is always to observe and follow, leaving interception as late as possible so that an entire drugs ring can be smashed.

Yet all too often trigger-happy police forces have got wind of the deal and swooped in, either in France or in Britain. Their reward was high profile publicity from a big haul, but at the same time their haste blew months or even years of undercover work, and may even have exposed an agent on the inside.

Then there is inter-agency competition. Intense rivalry damages drugs operations. Agencies are too secretive, too slow to ask for help. An example might be a surveillance operation run by a drugs squad, which is spiralling upwards into a highly complex operation requiring ten times as many observers. Instead of calling in the intelligence services, the chiefs decide to make arrests, and boost their own success ratings. All these issues need sorting out urgently. Leak-proof co-operation is vital at every level.

Crop destruction also requires international co-operation, between producing nations and nations which have the intelligence including satellite data, the equipment, personnel and the funding to deal with it.

New funding for replacement industries/crops in emerging economies

Crop destruction programmes are necessary and should be expanded, with extensions of the certification process for countries agreeing to co-operate. As many nations as possible should agree sanctions against countries which are known to be major production sources, and where the government is taking little or no action to deal with the situation.

However, such programmes will fail unless coupled with crop replacement programmes and development funding for new industries. If a subsistence farmer can quadruple his annual income by growing poppies it's no good destroying the poppies and telling him to grow wheat or rice instead. The problem is that subsidies are expensive and further distort the local economy. For example, some farmers who might have drifted away from the land to seek work in the cities may, with subsidies, decide to stay where they can grow crops the market does not need at grossly inflated prices. Nevertheless this is a route which must be followed, in parallel with other measures.

Seizure of assets

Too many drug traffickers are sent to prison with their fortunes intact. Although countries like Britain have passed new laws enabling assets to be seized from criminals, all too often the gap between the first warning of an arrest, conviction and taking assets away allows the criminal to move assets beyond the reach of a British court. The only way to seize assets effectively in a digital age is to do so *minutes* before a formal arrest is made. This would obviously require a court order, which should only be given if in the Judge's view there is a very high index of suspicion – someone acquitted or not formally charged would no doubt wish to press for substantial compensation. Once again, rights are lost if the aim is to be achieved.

Seizure after an arrest is far too late. The moment an arrest is made, others can switch funds from one country to another, or load smart cards with electronic cash or whatever, using a few mouse clicks on a computer connected on-line. Just one phone call could be enough.

2. Schools and parents – new campaign

Spending on drugs prevention in schools is one of the most effective things a government can do. After all, there is no other place in society where you have such a captive and well organised audience. Each year some 650,000 pupils enter British high schools and a campaign targeted at those between twelve and seventeen will reach a rising generation very effectively. It also reaches them at their time of greatest openness to using drugs, and at the time when the majority of people start smoking.

Face-to-face education is proved to be most effective in changing behaviour, when backed by mass campaigns. However, once pupils have left school this becomes extremely difficult to achieve on a large scale. College students tend not to turn up to health lectures, and adults at work or in the community are also notoriously difficult to reach.

CONCLUSIONS – WHAT WE MUST DO

The emphasis on use of illegal drugs in schools must be broadened to deal more fully with alcohol and tobacco. This requires a separate educational approach – alcohol and tobacco are more available, widely used by parents, legal for some pupils but not for others, widely advertised and big funders of sport or other leisure activities attractive to the young.

Normalising abstention

The most important part of any schools prevention programme is normalising abstention: helping pupils understand that when they say No to all illegal drugs, they are in the large majority. This is *the* best way of all to reduce peer pressure, because it deals with the lie that they are being left out. Accurate surveys of drug use for different areas are therefore very important, for use in normalisation efforts.

We have a duty to teenagers to feed them the truth instead of the daily distortions peddled in much of the media they consume. All too often sensational surveys are published and widely quoted, that suggest drug use is far higher than it really is. But these studies are usually based on small samples, sometimes of readers who volunteer to send in questionnaires. They lack the proper scientific methods which are vitally important to eliminate bias, yet are touted as the facts.

It is almost criminal to write a headline suggesting that most pupils are using illegal drugs by the time they leave school, or that most have tried Ecstasy or cannabis. Both assertions are incorrect, yet they are believed. As a result many, perhaps the majority, of those in schools feel under pressure from a peer group that exists only in their imaginations.

School teachers can be just as foolish. A teacher may try to win 'street cred' by coming out with statements like: 'I know most of you have probably tried it anyway, but . . .' By trying hard not to be accused of being naïve, the teacher has dropped a bomb under their own prevention efforts. That single phrase, more than anything

THE TRUTH ABOUT DRUGS

else that could be said, will convince some that they really are out on a limb by holding out against the drugs culture.

Assertiveness training

Assertiveness training is at the centre of all effective prevention, helping pupils stand up for their own values without feeling intimidated. What is the point of winning the argument in pupils' minds if that night they are in a pressured situation where they can't find a way to say what they think? Skills they learn here will help them throughout their lives, whether in the workplace, or when facing other pressures at school, for example to have sex before they want to or to do other things that may risk getting them into serious trouble. More research is needed into methods.

Severe sanctions for trade/consumption in school grounds

Schools need to take a tough anti-drugs stance, making it absolutely clear in their prospectus information that parents and children choosing that school are choosing one with a strong line on drugs. Government policy should encourage this.

Schools need to spell out clearly what this means: an absolute ban on any illegal drugs in the school grounds, and especially in dealing. It also means severe sanctions for pupils bringing drugs on to the premises or turning up intoxicated from alcohol or illegal drugs including solvents.

Drug testing – random in school

Schools that wish to could go a stage further and create a 'drug-free zone', a voluntary contract with pupils, parents and teachers. This has already been proposed by some in the US, where parents and governors agree, and with results being given only to parents of tests taken by their children on a voluntary basis.[1] British independent schools are already testing pupils they suspect of taking drugs, including Eton, St Paul's, Harrow and Rugby. State schools are beginning to follow, including at least one which is experimenting with random testing.[2]

Pupils can be given special privileges if they agree to sign up to a drug-free agreement. Part of the deal is that they agree that hairs can be taken at any time for drug testing, with immediate loss of privileges if the test is positive (indicating use in the last few weeks or months). Special privileges might include permission to go on extra school trips, for example.

Fee-paying schools could make it an absolute rule that all pupils test negative throughout their time at school on random testing, as a condition of remaining there. There could be warnings before expulsion. State-funded schools could do the same. The trouble is that many schools are under pressure *not* to expel pupils, from those who point out that the majority of those expelled never return to any other school. It can be hard to persuade school to take on a pupil who has already been thrown out of another one.

In the vast majority of cases pupils are only expelled as a last resort, after a long pattern of disruptive behaviour which threatens to undermine education for the rest. Head teachers must have the authority to take tough action, and with the abolition of corporal punishment, there is little else they can do at the most serious end. Keeping pupils behind after school or setting homework are both ineffective measures in the case of an extremely rebellious and uncooperative student. Some schools operate an instant suspension policy for first drugs offence, and expulsion for the second.

Random drug testing in school may seem draconian, but it is a ridiculous situation when many pupils in America are allowed to turn up to classes despite taking drugs on a daily basis, with no action at all being taken. The same pupils would fail routine pre-employment drug tests and would have difficulty getting a job. One could argue therefore that for the sake of the pupil and others in the school random screening should be introduced in all schools. This would not be expensive. It would be scary enough to take pupils from each class every couple of weeks and remove hairs for testing even if they knew that only one in twenty samples would be sent away. Spot checks can also be made where there is cause for worry.

The big question is what to do with the results. The answer is that this is a matter for each school to decide, in consultation with pupils and parents. The options are:

- Pupils only see the result (given in sealed envelope)
- Parents only see the result
- Teachers see the result

The options taken could vary according to the drug. For example, a school may wish to take different action in the case of a pupil whose hairs show clear evidence of heroin and cocaine use over a continuous period of several months, than in that of a pupil who shows traces of cannabis.

If teachers are allowed the information, it then gives them the chance to take action which could be, depending on the information and school policy, one of more of the following:

- Informing pupil and parents
- Counselling on dangers of illegal drugs
- Offering access to treatment
- Warning of major disciplinary action if repeat tests show continued abuse

Whether or not schools introduce testing, teachers need training in spotting signs of addiction and intoxication. If pupils are drunk in school they are sent home to recover and steps may be taken the following day. The same should be true of drug use. It is intolerable for pupils to turn up to school stoned or otherwise intoxicated, or hung over or still slightly befuddled from drugs the previous night.

CONCLUSIONS – WHAT WE MUST DO

Parental education

Parents should be targeted with government action at a number of levels. Parents need help in how to tackle these issues at home. With drug testing kits for home use becoming widely available, many parents will need advice on how to handle a situation where a suspicion has suddenly been confirmed by a test done without the knowledge or consent of the child. Many may argue that it is very unwise to test in such circumstances in the first place. However, parents with a wayward twelve-year-old behaving in a bizarre way may welcome knowing that the real reason is cannabis and cocaine. At least the problem can then be tackled. The only alternative in the face of flat denials is to bury your head in the sand and hope the child will ask for help soon enough.

But testing at home is just one of a bewildering number of issues that parents of teenagers now face in a drugs age. Government programmes aimed at parents should emphasise that example is important. As Edmund Burke once said, 'Example is the school of mankind and they will learn at no other.' If that is so in general, it is even more so of children.

Getting drunk

Children who see their parents getting drunk cannot be expected to listen to sermons from mum or dad about keeping away from cannabis or about not getting drunk themselves.

Smoking

Children of smokers are facing an example which is dangerous to their health every hour of every day, not to mention the direct risks from passive smoking. Parents who smoke are telling their children that addiction is okay – and actions speak far more powerfully than any words.

Children of smokers are living with addiction every day.

THE TRUTH ABOUT DRUGS

Addiction becomes a part of normal, acceptable life. Smoking is okay, and so is alcohol abuse and so is cannabis and Ecstasy. Prevention is more difficult.

Communication at home

As we have seen, one of the best ways to protect children from addiction is to talk to them. Communication is vital and takes time. The trouble is that many parents only wake up when there is already a problem with deviant behaviour, insolent attitudes and unwillingness to talk. Communication does take time, on a regular basis. Time to listen, time to understand, time to be. Communication problems in teenage years can often be traced to an earlier stage in life.

Parents need help, support and advice on how to prevent communication problems and keep the channels open.

3. Drug-free workplace testing

Legislation should be passed enabling employers without difficulty to be able to test their staff randomly for drug use. It should be law that all workers in occupations where public safety could be at risk, or the safety of others at work, are subject to random testing and disciplinary action if testing is positive. This will cover a significant element of the work force. Car mechanics, drivers of cars, lorries, cabs, motorbikes, pilots, surgeons, doctors, dentists and nurses, train drivers, air traffic controllers, assembly line workers, chefs and catering workers are all just a few examples.

Performance

It should be made possible without difficulty to sack a worker who is intoxicated in the workplace on several occasions despite written warnings, on the basis that the person is unable to fulfil their contract of employment in such a condition, and might act in a way which damages the interests of the employer.

Therefore it should also be made possible for an employer to test for intoxication on suspicion at work, whether for alcohol or for drugs. As we have seen, to date urine and blood test results for drugs do not correlate accurately with impairment of mental state. Expect this to change but in the meantime every sizeable company should at least have an electronic breathalyser which has zero test costs, and be prepared to use it.

4. Child welfare

Many drug users are excellent parents living in fear every day that their children will be taken away. Yet some children are also at great risk, especially where they are young and the only adults in the home are struggling with cocaine or heroin addiction. Government policy needs to be tightened in this area.

Punitive measures push the problem underground

Child-centred support can have the reverse effect from that intended. Punitive measures just push the problem underground. If mothers think that asking for help will mean that their children are taken into care, then they will struggle on against addiction in secret and the children could land up in a far worse position. This is a real dilemma. For the sake of other children in future it may be right therefore to allow a fairly risky situation to continue.

We should also be under no illusions about what happens to many children in care. Far from being in a protective environment, many children land up among many others with severe emotional problems, in situations where those who are younger are corrupted by those who are older. Drug-taking and prostitution among fifteen-year-olds have been the result on several occasions, while the scandal of sex abuse by staff has been repeated many times.

Yet young children need monitoring

The answer is to strive in every way possible to keep children with their parents in the community, with every support possible. The key is regular monitoring. There does need to be an understanding that the ultimate sanction will be removal of the children.

One social worker told me recently of a mother who kept her crying baby quiet by breathing out cannabis smoke over her face as she cradled her in her arms. Abuse – yes. Serious enough to warrant taking her baby away? These are difficult questions. If you step in too hard and too frequently another generation of young drug-taking mothers will disappear, failing to report to clinics, social services or their own doctors because of the fear that people will take away their children.

Those involved in monitoring children at risk because of addicted adults should have the power to test for drugs and alcohol at any time, if a court decides as an absolute final warning that the children can remain only if the drug user agrees to keep to a rehabilitation programme.

5. Road safety

Expect roadside skin surface testing for illegal drugs to become common by the year 2000. Twenty-five per cent of all people killed in British road accidents carry traces of drugs, illegal in eight out of ten cases, the others being medication.[3]

619 DEATHS (DRIVERS, RIDERS, PASSENGERS, PEDESTRIANS)[4]

- 16 per cent illegal drugs – mainly cannabis
- 34 per cent alcohol – 23 per cent over 80 mg per 100 ml
- 6 per cent medicinal drugs

284 DEATHS OF DRIVERS ALONE[5]

- 18 per cent illegal drugs – mainly cannabis
- 30 per cent alcohol – 22 per cent over 80 mg per 100 ml
- 4 per cent medicinal drugs

However, cannabis figures represent use up to four weeks previously, not just being 'high' at the time of death.

Laws are in place to deal with drivers under the influence of drugs but there are almost no measures in place to detect them. Yet in Britain there are around 200,000 people addicted to controlled drugs and perhaps a million other users of other substances (excluding alcohol). How many of them drive?

While breath tests for alcohol have been used by police for 30 years there is still no parallel testing in wide use for illegal drugs. To make matters worse, while officers are well trained to recognise classic signs of alcohol intoxication, there is no structured programme of training to help officers recognise drug intoxication. In one recent example a man was stopped by police in Glasgow and breathalysed because of his erratic driving. He tested negative and was allowed to carry on his journey. He was later stopped a second time by other officers for dangerous driving and arrested. A blood test showed that he had been 'high' on cannabis.

Routine drug testing at roadside

In 1995, 25 per cent of drivers said that they had drunk alcohol before driving in the last week, while one in twenty-five said they had driven after drinking more than six units. Statistics show that selective targeting of younger male motorists with random roadside tests will be particularly effective in preventing deaths.

Stiff penalties for drug intoxication at the wheel

Penalties should be severe and consistently applied for drink-driving, with treatment for offenders where alcohol dependency is suspected or proved. In exchange for a shorter spell of disqualification, the offender should be permitted to pay for their own treatment programme. There needs to be more education given to help people understand that a given dose of alcohol can result in wide variations in blood levels depending on many different factors.

Lowering of blood alcohol limit

The legal limit for alcohol in drivers should be reduced to 50 mg for several reasons. First, many drivers have impaired reaction times at the level 50–80 mg, so the current limit is unsafe. Second, people tend to misjudge the limit and so a significant number may be driving with 90–120 mg levels. A 50 mg level will ensure that even in people who have made a misjudgment, the level they drive at is less dangerous. Third, it sends out a message that society is taking alcohol abuse (drinking and driving is a form of abuse) more seriously, rather than less.

But what about prescribed medicines which can also impair judgment? In Australia a new law has been passed covering 'driving while impaired', which also means driving under the influence of medicines. Expect fierce debate over how exactly one decides what the permitted blood levels should be of a wide variety of commonly prescribed substances. However, the issue will not go away.[6]

6. Expansion of residential treatment programmes

It is a disgrace that people who have addiction but have had the courage to seek help are being turned away because of the lack of residential rehabilitation units.

New national network

A greatly expanded national network of residential rehab pro-grammes is needed now. This is particularly the case for those with serious alcohol problems.

Different centres for addiction types

Different kinds of treatment centres are needed to reflect different kinds of addictions and the preferences of people for the type of programmes they want. It is unreasonable to expect a high-flying city executive with a severe alcohol problem to become an effective community member alongside a majority of crack addicts. It will be far more effective to bring him into a community of other business people drying out from alcohol.

Compulsory treatment for offenders

There should be more widespread random testing in prisons with rewards for those who stay drug-free. Whole prison wings should be set up as drug-free zones with extra privileges for those who live in them. New partnerships should be explored between the prison service and rehabilitation agencies.

Alcohol information and education as well as access to treatment should be available throughout the criminal justice system – from caution to prison. Therefore police, probation officers, magistrates, prison officers and others should all receive training in recognising and managing alcohol-related problems. The same approach should be taken for dependency on illegal drugs.

A condition of parole or probation orders should be agreement to participate in a rehabilitation programme. Exclusion orders should also be used, for example forbidding someone from going near a favourite pub or club.

7. Further investment in harm reduction schemes

Harm reduction schemes save lives and more are needed. America in particular needs to learn from British experience and create a national network of needle exchanges.

Opiate prescription

Opiate prescribing cuts out the racketeers, destroys drug-related crime and saves lives by providing heroin addicts with a constant source of pure methadone. Clinic access should be improved, especially for those from ethnic minorities who have their own cultural needs.

Caffeine

Pregnant mothers should be warned that heavy caffeine intake places the health of the unborn at risk. Tea, coffee and cola in large doses should be avoided.

8. Tighten up laws on selling/promoting/using tobacco and alcohol

The licensing laws for sale of tobacco and alcohol need tightening up.

Tobacco

There should be a complete *ban on all tobacco advertising* in Britain. In practice this will be extremely hard to achieve now that television has become a completely global medium. A few years ago governments were able to regulate what was shown on British television but those days have almost died.

Billboard hoardings, newspapers, magazines and most radio

stations are relatively easy to control and an absolute ban should be imposed on them without delay, as well as on domestic television stations. The difficulty is with satellite TV, which can originate in countries with whom there is no agreement on advertising.

One example is sport. Motor racing takes place in many different countries with relaxed advertising rules, that the images are broadcast by a satellite or cable company based in Britain or elsewhere in Europe. What is the company to do? The advertising breaks conform to the rules but the actual race coverage does not since drivers and cars carry banners promoting cigarettes. The only way to enforce a complete ban therefore is to censor all sports coverage in such situations, which is clearly unacceptable to most people.

And then many satellite companies are based in one country yet broadcast over a huge footprint from a single transmitter. So 40 million people in China receive Western TV, despite Communist Party policy to ensure that all broadcasts in China conform to Party standards on culture and decency.

Licensing laws for tobacco should be made far stricter, in line with a growing understanding of the dangers of this highly addictive habit. For a start, the legal age for buying cigarettes should be increased to eighteen. This will reduce the availability to those under the age of sixteen and discourage sixteen- to eighteen-year-olds. A less drastic measure would be to make it an offence to sell cigarettes to a sixteen- to eighteen-year-old without seeing an identity card with proof of age.

It should be a criminal offence to supply someone under age with tobacco, with very strict maximum penalties for supplying those under the age of sixteen. It is wicked to give cigarettes to a twelve-year-old, and those who do so should be severely punished. There is no point in having licensing laws if the law takes a blind eye to an army of older teenagers who take money from under sixteen-year-olds and use it to buy them cigarettes.

At the same time, nicotine treatment centres should be set up, especially aimed at teenagers. They should be licensed to issue limited numbers of cigarettes on a reducing basis to teenagers wanting to give up, perhaps refunding the tax-free purchase costs entirely to those who can show they have been nicotine-free for six months.

There is strong evidence that consumption of alcohol and cigarettes is influenced by retail cost, which effectively regulates availability. If the person can't afford a certain level of consumption they will be more likely to cut down or go without altogether.

Tobacco duty should be increased sharply in annual stages, aiming to double the cost of smoking in real terms over a five- to ten-year period. Agreement should be made to do the same in all European countries. In addition all duty-free allowances for tobacco should be abolished. Why should we reward those with money to travel by giving them cut price cigarettes? Regular business travellers can keep themselves constantly supplied with tax free stock. This is not right and should stop.

Alcohol

In 1996, £189.5 million was spent persuading people to drink alcohol, much of it linked to sport or sports personalities. This is an effective way to target the young and should be more strictly controlled. Sponsorship of sport by alcoholic drink companies should be banned. *Alcohol advertising* should be subject to a health tax used to fund all-year-round awareness raising of the problems alcohol can cause. Alcohol advertising should carry government health warnings.

Licensing laws for alcohol need urgent review. Many variations exist between areas according to local magistrates and the action they take. There is a need for consistently tough action.

Licences should be taken away from premises which are a regular focus for alcohol-related violence or other crimes. It should be made far riskier for someone to sell alcohol to anyone under eighteen, with tougher penalties, and more checks by teenagers working for law enforcement agencies. This double strategy has worked well with the tightening up of laws relating to adult video sales and hire. The same covert methods should be used against retailers who sell tobacco to minors.

Toughened drinking glasses would help prevent some of the 5,000 'glassings' a year, in which a broken glass is used as an offensive weapon. Their use should be insisted on as a condition of a licence.

As with tobacco, *alcohol duties should be increased* throughout Europe. Alcohol prices have fallen in real terms throughout the last twenty years. The price in real terms should be restored immediately, with further increases above the level of inflation. Duty-free allowances for drink should be abolished for the same reasons as for tobacco. If France and other nations insist on ridiculously low tax rates, then we should go it alone, blocking imports in lorries, vans or the cars of people who are currently crossing to France simply to avoid British tax on alcohol. Raising taxes will reduce consumption. That's why the French have campaigned so aggressively for low British tax on wine.

Of course, in current EC law it is almost impossible for a national government to vary tax rates on products such as wine or beer. The trend is to convergence with the aim of abolishing all trade barriers inside the EU. If the current EU trade structures survive, then the only way to achieve satisfactory price regulation will be by EU agreement.

9. Encourage a drug-free culture

Every possible means should be taken to encourage a drug-free culture. There has been a recent rash of films showing heroes smoking, sometimes in many shots. This is totally irresponsible, and directly undermines efforts to persuade teenagers that smoking is undesirable.

Not only should there be a complete ban on promotion of brands of tobacco in advertising, but also on the promotion of smoking itself. That means a ban on covert advertising such as photos in newspapers of supermodels on catwalks smoking, or characters in TV soaps smoking, except in exceptional circumstances when the habit is relevant to the plot – for example if the person develops smoking-related problems.

Media support

Active attempts should be made to enlist positive media support in the anti-abuse campaign, on a much greater scale than that seen until now. Anti-drug heroes should be developed.

Exceptions for medical use of illegal drugs

Doctors should be allowed to prescribe cannabis for a limited range of chronic and terminal conditions such as motor neurone disease, multiple sclerosis and advanced cancer on a five-year pilot basis.

10. Tackle other preventable risk factors

Drugs prevention programmes in isolation will never work without tackling some of the underlying factors which encourage abuse. These include the growing underclass, long-term unemployment and family breakdown. Each of these helps create a climate of hopelessness and depression where drug use and dealing becomes increasingly attractive. These are complex issues but must be addressed.

NEW GOVERNMENT PROPOSALS – ARE THEY ENOUGH?

So how does the recent UK government White Paper on drugs measure up against these ten action points? Much of the White Paper is couched in vague committee-speak with huge gaps whenever an important area is touched on. But there are other omissions too and serious mistakes.

For a start there is a worrying target given to shift money from treatment to prevention – but as we have seen, that would leave even more people without care. Treatment budgets need rapid expansion too.

Great play is made about finding ways to channel profits seized from dealers to drugs programmes. This is an irrelevance. The reason for seizing assets is to prevent drug dealers profiting further from past crime. In any case the total amounts seized are unlikely to be enough to fund what is needed. This is a fudge, designed to assure the Treasury that (a little) more can be spent without blasting a hole in government spending plans. It can't be done this way. Either society agrees this is a serious problem or it does not. If not, then legalise, but there'll be an even worse problem in the future. If so, then invest more now.

Much of the White Paper talks of structures, liaison and communication. All these things are important but difficult to measure and they do not in themselves deliver services or prevention programmes on the ground.

The decision to create a Drugs Tsar is a good one, a senior official deputed to keep attention focused on drugs, working closely with the Cabinet Office. Annual reviews of progress will be a useful part of this new function as well as ensuring that every government department is thinking about the implications of drug addiction.

The new emphasis on face-to-face prevention in schools is good, but starting at the age of five is a serious mistake, and shows how little consultation there was with schools and parents before the paper was written. Eight years is the right age to start and then the focus should be on smoking and alcohol. Drug information can be integrated into various areas of the curriculum between the ages of eight and ten, with more formal presentations from eleven onwards. As we have seen, there are real hazards in awakening curiosity too early.

The Paper is entirely silent on the most important issue in schools, which is the approach taken in prevention – value free information or a directive lesson on life for the future? As we have seen, 'value free' in practice delivers a pro-drug use message.

Targets like monitoring a fall in the number of exclusions for drugs issues in schools are unworkable since they are misleading. The drugs problem could fall as a result of other measures, while exclusions rise due to increasingly tough action being taken. Thus one could argue that exclusions are a vital statistic showing that schools are taking the drugs problem seriously. A school which has 1,300 pupils and has never suspended or expelled a pupil for drugs in the last five years is probably one with an uncontrolled drugs problem.

New plans to carry out extensive surveys and evaluations of treatment and prevention outcomes are to be welcomed. One of the reasons that so much of the statistical material in this book is derived from the US is because successive British governments have neglected this area. They should start by reading up on US research rather than reinventing wheels. One is soon confronted with drug testing as a serious option in many different settings, as well as the urgent need to spend more on prevention and treatment programme methods that we already know are very successful.

The new commitment to provide all problem drug users with proper access to appropriate services is a bold one, and will be far more expensive than the government appears to recognise.

There are plenty of strong words in the Paper about law and order, interception, international co-operation and the rest –

nothing controversial here. Similar grand statements are found in the drugs strategies of most countries of the world. However, there is deafening silence on the issue of drug testing, which as we have seen from experience in the US will be a dominant issue in Britain.

There is a one-line mention of drug testing for drivers, and another brief mention of testing for prisoners. Are they really the *only* kinds of people in our society who would benefit from testing? There is no comment on the growing use of testing in the US, backed by Federal law. There is not even a suggestion that there should be a consultation process about which groups (truck drivers, airline pilots, surgeons and others) might be ones among whom random testing could be encouraged or made compulsory. In other words, drug testing is almost completely outside current government thinking. Expect this to change.

There is very little about any aspect of the alcohol abuse epidemic and even less about, for example, using breathalysers more widely among those where public health and safety could be at risk. There are just general statements about helping those with any kind of addiction.

Just as there is a special chapter on the need to keep illegal drugs off our streets, there should have been an *entire chapter* devoted to tackling alcohol abuse in our society. None of the measures in the paper address alcohol-specific issues, of which as we have seen there are a great number.

While the White Paper sets imaginative targets such as 'Reduce levels of drug-related absenteeism/dismissals from work' it offers not a shred of practical detail about how to achieve this. As we have seen, random drug testing at work can have a very significant and immediate impact on abuse patterns. It costs the government nothing because it saves employers their own money so they are prepared to pay for it. Failure to mention this issue at all is serious and indicates an unwillingness to really deal with addiction.

In summary then, the British government's proposals are full of facts about addiction and bland suggestions for action, but with no commitment to invest the amount necessary, nor to implement less popular measures even where they are proven to be some of the most cost-effective.

Expect government action to sharpen up when what is proposed has been carried out and the problems have continued to get worse. Expect far greater emphasis on alcohol and tobacco as part of a larger struggle against all forms of chemical addiction. Expect pro-legalisation campaigners to raise their voices even louder, at the very time that the whole nation wakes from slumber at the way the curse of addiction has swept right across every area of society.

The choice is ours: either we take bold steps today to take control of the drugs problem or the drugs problem will take hold of us, and all we take for granted in a civilised society.

TEN-POINT PLAN FOR PARENTS

So what can parents do if they are worried about drugs? The time to worry is long before a problem starts. Here are some suggestions. In addition you may want to contact some of the organisations listed at the end of this book.

1. Invest in relationship

As we have seen, parents have a central role to play in raising a drug-free family. Research clearly shows that parental influence is powerful, especially through role models and boundary setting. Discipline and character formation in early years is important, as well as encouraging children so that they feel valued, loved and appreciated, with the self-confidence to be themselves in the face of conflicting peer pressures.

From the earliest years

Communication is vital. The trouble is that many parents only get serious about this when problems start developing: 'I hardly understand her any more.' By then it is often far too late to do anything but contain the situation. Parents who often spend time talking to their children have 30 per cent less risk of children who take illegal drugs (37 versus 26 per cent).[7]

Communication is more than an occasional intense heart-to-heart conversation at a time of crisis. Communication is an ongoing process, a part of a warm, open relationship, based on mutual respect. The rewards are not just more harmonious home life and reduced risk of drug abuse, but also reduced risk of teenage pregnancy and a whole host of other problem behaviours that are also associated with unhappiness at home.

Parents who take care over their *own* relationship will also find they are helping their children stay free of drugs. Teenagers who are traumatised by constant rows between their parents or by a messy divorce, or by other parental relationships starting and ending, are far more likely to stay out, to find other outlets for their unhappiness and to distance themselves emotionally from their parents.

2. Be a good example

It is very hard for a parent who used to smoke cannabis to make convincing arguments as to why their own children should not now do the same. It is even harder if the same parents are still abusing illegal drugs or alcohol or tobacco.

Smoking is an invitation to experiment

Nothing destroys trust and respect faster than double standards when it comes to older people encouraging teenagers to avoid risk. Parents who smoke can hardly blame their children for copying them. Example is the best possible way to teach.

As we have seen, teenagers who smoke are far more likely to go on to take cannabis and other drugs. Therefore one of the most effective steps parents can take in helping to build a drug-free future for their children is to give up smoking or other drug use, with the exception of moderate intake of alcohol. Children who see their parents get drunk find it particularly hard to listen to sermons from them about the dangers of cannabis or Ecstasy.

3. Encourage wide interests and activities

Parents can help keep their children out of trouble by encouraging active participation in a wide range of activities outside and inside school. Time spent fetching and carrying children and their friends is time well spent.

Research shows a strong relationship between involvement in school activities and illicit drug use. Forty-one per cent of those in US high schools who never participated took drugs compared to 23 per cent who did.[8] The same protective effect is seen from involvement in community activities. The rate of drug use was twice (40 per cent) in those not involved at all compared to those involved heavily.

4. Encourage self-esteem and self-worth

There has never been an age where the image of a young person has been so under pressure from high-level media advertising. The message is that without designer trainers and jeans, a fast car, the right kind of hair, the right shaped body, the right kind of friends, you're a freak, a loser. The pressures to conform are intense and follow teenagers throughout their school years and into adult life.

Child psychologists describe an epidemic of low self-worth, high numbers of depressed adolescents, many with eating disorders or other stress-related medical and emotional problems. What can be done to help?

Encouraging self-esteem and self-worth directly reduces the risk that a child will feel under pressure to follow the crowd. Praise, encouragement, turning up to the school concert or end of term play, taking time to help with homework, helping each child find his or her areas of interest and fulfilment – these kinds of things directly help the development of a well-rounded, balanced, self-confident individual.

A strong personal faith can be a real strength, especially when backed by a supportive peer group from a church. Those never attending church are two and a half times more likely to take drugs than those who do so often (45 versus 19 per cent).[9] And the stronger the commitment, the lower the risk of drug addiction.

5. Discourage smoking and overuse of alcohol

It's not enough just to present a good example when it comes to smoking and alcohol abuse. These things need to be talked about – often – as part of every-day life. So many parents are scared of making a position clear because they fear that their children will rebel – or worse still, perhaps stop talking to them altogether or even leave home. But this is pure defeatism. A family faced with such a situation is in serious problems, with a history probably going back several years. The time to address teenage drug taking is when children are pre-school, in the decisions we make then and every day following, the atmosphere in the home, the boundaries we set, the discipline we establish (and keep to), the love, care and affection we show. We reap what we sow.

It is near criminal nonsense to suggest that parental opinion can't be a positive influence. Most people looking back will admit that they were profoundly influenced by their upbringing, even if they rebelled against parts of it for a while. Children need to hear the arguments. For example, if a child comes home saying 'What *are* the reasons why I shouldn't smoke dope?' we do the child a great disservice by abandoning them to work it all out themselves. Far better for the child to be able to go back into the school the following morning armed with four or five strong arguments that you have talked through together, than with the impression that you don't seem to mind (or care).

6. Firm but fair boundaries for expected conduct

Setting boundaries for children is essential for their development and safety. We accept this for toddlers, but many parents cave in as soon as their children start getting as tall as they are, yet that can be the stage when they need boundaries most. Fifty per cent of teenagers who never have clear rules from their parents are likely to take illegal drugs compared to only 22 per cent of those whose parents have many clear rules.

Take the practical example of a party. One of our own younger teenage children was invited recently to a party in a church hall run by parents we knew, and whom we assumed would be present throughout. We discovered afterwards that no food and very little (non-alcoholic) drink had been provided.

The host's parents disappeared soon after the start, leaving the front doors open to gatecrashers and to guests piling in with their own alcohol, despite the fact that the majority were under age. Of course, drugs were not far away. Leaving the party unsupervised was in my view an act of gross irresponsibility. A similar event in a house unsupervised is a recipe not only for drunkenness and drug taking but also for unplanned pregnancies and sexually transmitted disease.

Dictatorship doesn't work for long, yet many teenagers respond well to agreeing their own ground rules with their parents, including their own self-imposed scale of sanctions, which can often turn out to be more severe than the parents would themselves have set.

Rules are made to be broken, but there is a difference between humane adjustments of rules, and inconsistency through laziness, neglect or impatience. Rules need to make sense to win respect.

7. Watch for signs of possible abuse[10]

The following should raise the possibility that a teenager is abusing drugs. However, they can also be a normal part of adolescent growing up or of depression or other personal problems. The key issue is change: in appearance, personality, attitude or behaviour.

- Loss of appetite, increase in appetite, changes in eating habits, unexplained weight loss or gain
- Slowed or staggering walk, poor co-ordination
- Inability to sleep, awake at night, unusual lethargy
- Red watery eyes, pupils larger or smaller than usual, blank stare
- Cold, sweaty or shaking hands, puffy face, blushing or pale
- Unusual smell on breath, body or clothes
- Extreme hyperactivity, excessive talkativeness
- Running nose, hacking cough
- Needlemarks on lower arms, leg
- Nausea, vomiting, excessive sweating
- Change in attitude or personality, in friends, sudden avoidance of old friends, won't talk about new friends, friends take drugs
- Changes in activities or hobbies, falling back at school academically, loss of interest in family or family activities
- Difficulty concentrating, forgetful, low self-esteem and apathetic
- Moodiness, irritability, silliness, paranoia, excessive need for privacy
- Withdrawn, secretive and stealing
- Car accidents, needing lots of money for unclear reasons, possession of needles and syringes

No one of the above proves anything but a combination may give rise to high suspicion. It may be tempting to carry out a secret test on hair but the big question is what are you going to do with the information? Are you sure you are going to be able to handle the result? Will your aim be to confront or is the information just for you alone? And if your child does find out that you have sneaked into their room and stolen hairs for testing, how is that going to affect your relationship? Whether one opts for a secret test or not, or one after a conversation with a child, will depend on many factors such as the age of the child and the seriousness of the situation.

One has to balance these things up. How would you feel if you missed the fact that for two vital years your adolescent son had been a cocaine and heroin addict, living under your roof, needing your help but unable to tell you the truth, while all the while you had been blaming his emotional ups and downs on growing up?

8. Keep in touch with the school about your concerns

Parents and teachers can and should work together. Home and school only see part of the picture, which is why co-operation is so essential.

Those getting good grades at school are far less likely to take drugs. Of course, drug use may damage academic performance, but commitment to studying is also strongly protective. This effect is also seen in sexual behaviour. A British survey of 19,000 people found that those dropping out of school early are far more likely to have multiple partners as teenagers. Only 25 per cent of those staying on to take final grades (A levels) at the age of eighteen had lost their virginity.[11] The reason seems to be that those committed to study are more likely to have a mature approach to their future.

9. Confront where necessary but in the context of commitment to working things out

Many parents are afraid of confrontation, but without it all we have are older people co-existing alongside younger people. Parenting by definition must involve guidance, rule setting, negotiation, persuasion and if necessary outright confrontation. However, confrontation will always be far more successful in the context of good communication and relationship.

There needs to be a commitment to working things out. The most destructive form of confrontation is one which constantly threatens to throw the child out of the house, or worse, never to see or speak to the child again. Such threats simply reinforce the idea in a child's mind that love is superficial and conditional – which is hardly love at all. Such an approach is a recipe for further conflict as an 'unloved' child hits back in an attempt to gain attention.

10. Don't let guilt destroy you when things go wrong

When we start out as parents on the very first day the baby is born we are acutely aware that in our hands is an impressionable, vulnerable being. As the baby grows into a child and into adolescence parents are reminded hundreds of times that they reap what they sow. Encourage a child in playing sports, and with some natural ability he or she will probably do well. Give the child music lessons, and with enthusiastic support so long as there is an interest there the child will probably become a real achiever in this area. Neglect a child and the child will neglect you.

However, while it is true that children are hugely influenced by their parents, and we can influence and shape the growing up process, at the end of the day each child is a unique personality and makes his or her own choices. While it is natural as parents for us to torture ourselves with self-doubts when things go wrong, the child also has to take responsibility. This is especially true in adolescent years.

Therefore when times are tough, we can only go forward. We did the best we could with what we had at the time. We made mistakes. All of us make mistakes, but now we have to go forward, learning what we can from the past to make the very best from the future.

Appendices

Appendices

Useful Organisations

UK

ADFAM National
0171 928 8900
Support for families and friends of drug users. Free phone call back
if phone bills are a problem for callers.

Drugs in Schools Helpline
0345 366666
Run by Release. Advice for drug incidents in school – open
10 a.m.–5 p.m. weekdays.

Families Anonymous
0171 498 4680
Self-help group for parents of drug users – local branches.

Home Office
(Central Drugs Prevention Unit)
Room 354, Horseferry House
Dean Ryle Street
London SW1P 2AW
0171 217 8631
Information and free illustrated wall chart to help parents and others
identify drugs and drug-taking equipment.

International Substance Abuse and Addiction Coalition
c/o Yeldall Manor
Blakes Lane
Hare Hatch
Reading
Berkshire RG10 9XR
01189 401 093

National Drugs Helpline
0800 776600
Free calls and advice about drugs – open all day and night every day.

National Drugs Prevention Alliance
PO Box 594
Slough SL1 1AA
01753 677 917
Range of useful resources.

Northern Ireland Drugs Information
Health Promotion Branch
DSS
Upper Newtownards Road
Belfast BT4 3SF
01232 524234
Drugs information for Northern Ireland.

Release
0171 603 8654
24-hour helpline on drug use and legal matters. Useful if someone is arrested for a drugs offence.

Scottish Drugs Forum
5th Floor
Shaftesbury House

5 Waterloo Street
Glasgow G2 6AY
0141 221 1175
Comprehensive information on Scottish drugs services.

Standing Conference on Drug Abuse (SCODA)
Waterbridge House
32–36 Loman Street
London SE1 OEE
0171 928 9500
Independent co-ordinating body for drug services and advice.

Welsh Office
Cathays Park
Cardiff CF1 3NQ
01222 825592
Drugs information for Wales.

Yeldall Manor Drug Rehabilitation
Blakes Lane
Hare Hatch
Reading
Berkshire RG10 9XR
01889 401 093
Residential unit.

USA

National Clearing House for Alcohol and Drug Information
PO Box 2345
Rockville MD 20852
1-800-729-6686 toll free
Information on all aspects of drug abuse and latest research. Many
free resources.

Useful Websites

With 600,000,000 megabytes of data added to the web daily, how do you find the latest resources?

1. Thousands of useful resources covering every country of the world can be accessed from the Yahoo search guide: just type the drug addiction and the country of interest if needed.
   http://www.yahoo.com

2. The author's own website has many useful links relating to drug addiction, prevention, treatment and government policy.
   http://www.globalchange.com

Notes

Chapter 1 The Size of the Drugs Problem

1   United Nations Drug Control Program (UNDCP) figures 1998
2   1997 Harvard School of Public Medicine Survey
3   Figures for use in last month when surveyed in 1996
4   Substance Abuse and Mental Health Services Administration, Preliminary Estimates from the 1995 National Household Survey on Drug Abuse
5   *Los Angeles Times*, (15 February 1998)
6   Luntz Research Companies, *National Survey of American Attitudes on Substance Abuse II, Teens and Their Parents* (New York, NY: Centre on Addiction and Substance Abuse, September 1996)
7   Substance Abuse and Mental Health Services Administration, Preliminary Estimates from the 1995 National Household Survey on Drug Abuse
8   Rand Corporation, *Modelling the Demand for Cocaine* (Santa Monica, Calif.: Rand Corporation, 1994
9   National Criminal Justice Reference (NCJR) Service US Government data
10 W. Rhodes, P. Scheiman, and K. Carlson, *What America's Users Spend on Illegal Drugs, 1988–1991* (Washington, DC: Abt Associates, Inc., under contract to the Office of National Drug Control Policy, 1993)

11 Office of National Drug Control Policy, *Pulse Check, National Trends in Drug Abuse* (Washington, DC: Executive Office of the President, Spring 1996)

12 National Narcotics Intelligence Consumers Committee, *The NNICC Report 1995: The Supply of Illicit Drugs to the United States* (Washington, DC: Drug Enforcement Administration, August 1996)

13 NCJR US Government data

14 Substance Abuse and Mental Health Services Administration, Preliminary Estimates from the 1995 National Household Survey on Drug Abuse

15 ibid.

16 J. M. McGinnis and W. H. Foege, 'Actual Causes of Death in the United States', *Journal of the American Medical Association*, Vol. 270, No. 18, (Chicago, Ill.: 1993), 2207–12

17 University of California, Los Angeles (UCLA) Higher Education Research Institute, (12 January 1998)

18 Substance Abuse and Mental Health Services Administration US 1997

19 *Washington Post* (12 November 1996)

20 NCJR US Government data

21 *Economist* (19 April 1997)

22 Office of National Drug control Policy, *Pulse Check, National Trends in Drug Abuse* (Washington, DC: Executive Office of the President, Spring 1996)

23 Substance Abuse and Mental Health Administration, Preliminary Estimates from the 1995 National Household Survey on Drug Abuse

24 Lloyd Johnston, *Monitoring the Future Study – 1996*, press release

25 Office on Smoking and Health, *Preventing Tobacco Use Among Young People, A Report of the Surgeon General* (Rockville, Md.: Centre for Disease Control and Prevention, US Department of Health and Human Services, July 1994)

26 American Cancer Society, *Facts About Children and Tobacco Use* (Atlanta, Ga.: American Cancer Society, 1997)

27 Survey of 7,666 teenagers with church affiliation Drug and Alcohol Dependence 46 (1997), 9–17

28 Lloyd Johnston, *Monitoring the Future Study – 1996*, press release

29 Substance Abuse and Mental Health Services Administration, Preliminary Estimates from the 1995 National Household Survey on Drug Abuse

30 J. C. Merrill, K. Fox, S. R. Lewis, and G. E. Pulver, *Cigarettes, Alcohol, Marijuana: Gateways to Illicit Drug Use*

31 Centre for Substance Abuse Prevention (CSAP), Teen Drinking Prevention Programme

32 Health Education Reports (27 November 1997)

33 NCJR US Government data

34 Substance Abuse and Mental Health Services Administration, Preliminary Estimates from the 1995 National Household Survey on Drug Abuse

35 NCJR US Government data

36 PRIDE survey of 141,077 students (28 October 1997)

37 ibid.

38 Lloyd Johnston, *Monitoring the Future Study – 1996*, press release

39 ibid.

40 Substance Abuse and Mental Health Services US 1993

41 Lloyd Johnston, *Monitoring the Future Study – 1996*, press release

42 ibid.

43 Substance Abuse and Mental Health Services Administration, Preliminary Estimates from the 1995 National Household Survey on Drug Abuse

44 Lloyd Johnston, *Monitoring the Future Study – 1996*, press release

45 US Department of Health and social Services (20 December 1997)

46 National Drug Control Policy Group press release (20 December 1997)

47 PRIDE survey of 129,560 students in 1995–96

48 British Crime Survey 1996

49 *The Times* (14 April 1998)

50 *Guardian* (15 April 1998)

51 *Four City Study 1992* (Home Office 1993); *British Crime Survey*

1992 and 1994 (Home Office 1994 and 1996); *Drug Realities* (Health Education Authority 1996); *School Studies Series* by John Balding (Exeter University published 1997) and *Drug Futures* by Parker et al (ISDD 1995). Also *Guardian* (6 February 1998) quoting latest British Crime Survey

52 *Hansard* (13 November 1984)

53 Office of Population Censuses and Statistics (1983)

54 Royal College of Physicians report (1983)

55 This five to one ratio of registered to actual users of controlled drugs is confirmed by the comprehensive studies carried out by Hartnoll et al in 1985, following a detailed study of heroin use in Camden and Islington. See *Trends in the UK Illicit Drug Markets* (Home Office Research Study No. 95)

56 *Scottish Daily Record* describing street life in Aberdeen (13 March 1998)

57 Personal communication (4 April 1998)

58 Institute for the Study of Developmental Disabilities (ISDD), 1988

59 *Independent* (2 October 1997)

60 Action on Smoking and Health (ASH) figures 1998

61 *Guardian* (9 March 1998)

62 *Columbus-Ledger Enquirer* (8 February 1997)

63 American Council for Drug Education (ACDE) figures 1997 (Phoenix House affiliate)

64 US Department of Labor 1997 – survey of cocaine users calling a national Helpline

65 National Institute on Drug Abuse, *Research on Drugs and the Workplace: NIDA Capsule 24* (Rockville, Md.: US Department of Health and Human Services, 1990)

66 US Department of Labor 1997

67 *Columbus-Ledger Enquirer* (8 February 1997)

68 US Department of Labor

69 Alcohol Concern figures 1995

70 *Scotsman* (29 November 1997) quoting Andre Cubie, former chairman of the Scottish branch of the Confederation of British Industry

71 Royal College of General Practitioners report: *Alcohol - a balanced view* (1986) *British Medical Journal*

72 P. Anderson, 'Managing alcohol problems in general practice', *BMJ* (1985; 290, 1873–5)

73 P. Caviston and A. Paton, 'Doctors, alcohol and society', *Irish Medical Journal* (1986; 79, 205–6)

74 L. Bissel and R. W. Jones, 'The alcoholic physician: a survey', *American Journal of Psychiatry* (1976; 133, 1142–6)

75 E. J. Menl et al, 'Success of re-entry onto anaesthesiology training programs by residents with a history of substance abuse', *Journal of the American Medical Association* (1990; 263, 3060–2)

76 'The misuse of alcohol and other drugs' *BMA* (January 1998)

77 *BMA* News Review July 1996

Chapter 2 The True Cost of Addiction

1 UNDCP figures

2 *Independent on Sunday* (8 February 1998) and *Guardian* (15 April 1998)

3 UNDCP figures

4 Foreign and Commonwealth Office (FCO) Information Department Report 1995

5 ISDD 1998

6 UK Government figure 1997

7 Substance Abuse and Mental Health Services Administration 1997

8 Dorothy P. Rice, Sander Kelman, Leonard S. Miller, and Sarah Dunmeyer, *The Economic Costs of Alcohol and Drug Abuse and Mental Illness: 1985*, report submitted to the Office of financing and coverage Policy of the Alcohol, Drug Abuse, and Mental Health Administration (San Francisco, Calif.: Institute for Health & Ageing, University of California, US Department of Health and Human Services, 1990)

9 Substance Abuse and Mental Health Services Administration 1997

10 'Behind bars: substance abuse and America's prison population' (Centre on Addition and Substance Abuse (CASA) Columbia University 8 January 1998)

11 Centre for Substance Abuse Prevention (CSAP), *Teen Drinking Prevention Program* (Rockville, Md., US Department of Health and Human Services, 1996)

12 National Highway Traffic Safety Administration, *Fatal Accident Reporting System* (Washington, D. C.: US Department of Transportation, July 1996)

13 'Crash characteristics and injuries of victims impaired by alcohol versus illicit drugs', *Accident Analysis and Prevention*, Vol. 29, No. 6 (1997)

14 US National Centre for Health Statistics, 'Alcohol and Drugs: Advance Report of final Mortality Statics, 1989', *Monthly Vital Statistics Report*, Vol. 40, No. 8, Supplement 2 (Hyattsville, Md.: US Department of Health and Human Services, 1992)

15 Centres for Disease Control and Prevention, *Monthly Vital Statistics Report, Advance Report of Final Mortality Statistics*, (1994, Vol. 45, No. 3., Supplement) (Hyattsville, Md.: US Department of Health and Human Services, 30 September 1996)

16 Centres of Disease Control and Prevention, *HIV and AIDS Trends, Progress in Prevention* (Hyattsville, Md.: National Centre for Health Statistics, 1996)

17 Substance Abuse and Mental Health Services Administration, *Preliminary Estimates from the Drug Abuse Warning Network, 1995 Preliminary Estimates of Drug-Related Emergency Department Episodes, Advance Report Number 17* (Rockville, Md.: US Department of Health and Human Services, August 1996)

18 ibid.

19 National Institute on Drug Abuse (NIDA), 1992–3 National Pregnancy & Health Survey: *Drug Use Among Women Delivering Livebirths* (Rockville, Md.: US Department of Health and Human Services, 1996)

20 ibid.

21 L. Schrager, J. Joyce, and L. Cawthon, *Substance Abuse, Treatment,*

and Birth Outcomes for Pregnant and Postpartum Women in Washington State (Olympia, Wash.: Washington State Department of Social and Health Services, 1995)

22 'Behind bars: substance abuse and America's prison population' (Centre on Addiction and Substance Abuse (CASA) Columbia University, 8 January 1998)

23 Substance Abuse and Mental Health Services Administration 1997

24 Bureau of Justice Statistics, *Comparing Federal and State Prison Inmates, 1991* (Washington D. C.: US Department of Justice, September 1994)

25 B. Spunt, P. Goldstein, H. Brownstein and M. Fendrich, 'The role of marijuana in homicide', *International Journal Addiction*, 29(2), 195–213 (January 1994)

26 Reuters (13 January 1998)

27 'Behind bars: substance abuse and America's prison population' (Centre on Addiction and Substance Abuse (CASA) Columbia University, 8 January 1998)

28 Federal Bureau of Investigation, *Crime in the United States*; Uniform Crime Reports 1995

29 Internal Revenue Service, unpublished data – NCJRS website

30 Government Actuary figures (18 November 1997)

31 Alcohol figures from various sources 1998

32 Figures from Alcohol Concern 1998

33 J. Shepherd et al, *British Medical Journal* (31 January 1997)

34 Figures from Alcohol Concern 1998

35 ibid.

36 J. Shepherd et al, *British Medical Journal* (31 January 1998)

37 *Economist* (24 May 1997)

38 *Yorkshire Post* (1 August 1997)

39 Home Office figures for year ending in June 1997

40 Home Office figures 1996/7

41 These and other figures are from ISDD http://www.isdd.co.uk

42 Hospital Episode Statistics 1994–5 vol. 1

43 T. Waller et al, 'Prevalence of hepatitis C in drug injectors', *Druglink* 1995 (10, (5) 8–11)
44 *Lancet* (31 January 1998), 351–545
45 Alcohol Concern 1998
46 FCO UK Report 1996
47 *Daily Telegraph* (1 August 1997)
48 Reuters News Service (20 August 1997)

Chapter 3 Addicted to Pleasure

1   General Household Survey UK Government 1995
2   Findings of EU Commission 1996
3   *Chronicle of the Twentieth Century* (JL International Publishing, 1992)
4   *Encyclopaedia Britannica* (1979)
5   1 Timothy 5:23
6   http://www.isdd.co.uk/trends/problems.html
7   See http://home1.gte.net/sdg/sfaddic.htm for examples
8   Adapted from *Prevention Works* (Centre for Abuse Prevention 1997)
9   'Homogeneity of cigarette smoking within peer groups: influence or selection?', *Health Education and Behaviour* (December 1997)
10 Derbyshire S, *BMJ,* (12 April 1977, 314, 7087)
11 *In the Blood* by Stephen Jones (HarperCollins 1996)
12 Patrick Dixon, *Futurewise – the six faces of global change* (HarperCollins 1998)
13 General Household Survey UK Government 1994
14 American Cancer Society *PR Newswire* (31 July 1997)
15 *BMJ* (18 October 1997, 973–80 and 980–8)
16 UK Independent Scientific Committee on Smoking and Health Report 1988
17 Report of the US Surgeon General 1986
18 Office of Environmental Health Hazard Assessment Report by State of California (ASH 1998)

19 *Los Angeles Times* (10 August 1997)
20 *Daily Telegraph* (6 August 1997)
21 *Economist* (19 April 1997)
22 *Economist* (30 August 1997)
23 *Los Angeles Times* (10 August 1997)
24 *Business Line* (17 August 1997)
25 *Economist* (19 April 1997)
26 Reuters News Service (19 August 1997)
28 *Economist* (19 April 1997)
28 Reuters News Service (22 August 1997)

Chapter 4 Caffeine, Alcohol and Tobacco

1   R. Ford et al, *British Medical Journal*, (27 January 1998)
2   A. Nehlig and G. Debry, 'Potential teratogenic and neuro-developmental consequences of coffee and caffeine exposure: a review on human and animal data', *Neurotoxicol Teratol*, 16 (6): 1994 Nov–Dec, 531–43

Chapter 5 Cannabis

1   ISDD figures 1997
2   National Institute on Drug Abuse (NIDA) 1997
3   NIDA US 1997
4   ibid.
5   N. D. Volkow, H. Gillespie, N. Mullani, L. Tancredi, C. Grant, A. Valentine, and L. Hollister, 'Brain glucose metabolism in chronic marijuana users at baseline and during marijuana intoxication' *Psychiatry Res*, 67 (1) 31 May 1996, 29–38
6   D. J. Castle and F. R. Ames, 'Cannabis and the brain', *Australia and New Zealand Journal of Psychiatry* 30 (April 1996) 179–83
7   H. G. Pope Jr, A. J. Gruber and D. Yurgelun-Todd, 'The residual neuropsychological effects of cannabis: the current status of research', *Drug Alcohol Dependency* 38 (1): (April 1995) 25–34
8   ibid.

9   N. Solowij, B. F. Grenyer, G. Chesher and J. Lewis, 'Biopsycho-
    social changes associated with cessation of cannabis use: a single
    case study of acute and chronic cognitive changes', *Life Science*,
    37 (23–24) (1995) 2127–34
10 H. G. Pope Jr, D. Yurgelun-Todd, 'The residual cognitive effects
    of heavy marijuana use in college students', *JAMA*, 275 (7) (21
    February 1996) 521–7
11 NIDA US 1997
12 ibid.
13 N. Solowij, 'Do cognitive impairments recover following
    cessation of cannabis use?', *Life Science*, 56 (23-24 1995) 2119–
    26
14 NIDA US 1997
15 ibid.
16 J. C. Merrill, K. Fox, S. R. Lewis and G. E. Pulver, *Cigarettes,
    Alcohol, Marijuana: Gateways to Illicit Drug Use* (New York, N. Y.:
    Centre on Addiction and Substance Abuse at Columbia
    University, 1994)
17 ibid.
18 *Daily Telegraph* (7 August 1997)
19 *Daily Telegraph* (20 November 1997)

Chapter 6 Cocaine, Crack and Heroin

1   ISDD data 1998
2   *Independent on Sunday* (8 February 1998)

Chapter 7 Amphetamines, LSD, Ecstasy and the Rest

1   ISDD figures 1998
2   http://www.drugdetection.com – quoting *US Today*
3   *Canada Newswire* (12 February 1998)
4   http://area51.upsu.plym.ac.uk/infoserv/drugs/graphical/
    sterhist.htm
5   NIDA Report 1996

6   Eternity Magazine survey November 1995
7   *Independent on Sunday* (8 February 1998)
8   ibid.

Chapter 8 Why Governments are Scared of Prevention

1   *Independent on Sunday* (8 February 1998)
2   Home Office figures 1996
3   Home Office figures 1997
4   *Independent* (2 January 1998)
5   Hartnell and Lewis figures per user 1984, quoted in *Home Office Research and Planning Unit Study No. 95*
6   *Advertiser* (Adelaide) (23 March 1998)
7   Substance Abuse and Mental Health Services Administration 1997
8   ibid.
9   ibid.
10 *Los Angeles Times* (15 February 1998)
11 National Drug Control Policy Group press release (20 December 1997)
12 NCJR web-site – US Federal Government
13 Personal anecdote from pupil
14 'Sex-related alcohol expectancies as moderators of the relationship between alcohol use and risky behaviour in adolescents', *Journal of Studies on Alcohol* (January 1998)
15 'Young male drivers and impaired driving intervention: telephone survey', *Accident Analysis and Prevention*, Vol. 29, No. 6 (1997)
16 Anne Johnson et al, *Sexual Attitudes and Lifestyles*, (Blackwell Scientific Publications 1994)
17 M. Shiner and T. Newburn, *Independent Evaluation by Drugs Prevention Initiative*, Paper 19
18 PRIDE survey of 141,077 students (28 October 1997)
19 *Crain's Chicago Business* (9 March 1998)
20 Drug Detection Report (20 March 1997)

21 Substance Abuse and Mental Health Services Administration, *Drug Use Among US Workers: Prevalence and Trends by Occupation and Industry Categories* (Rockville, Md.: US Department of Health and Human Services, May 1996)

22 American Management Association, 1996, *American Management Survey on Workplace Drug Testing and Drug Abuse Policies: summary of Key Findings* (New York, N. Y.: American Management Association, 1996)

23 *Crain's Chicago Business* (9 March 1998)

24 IAC Trade and Industry Database (1 March 1997)

25 ibid.

26 US Journal of Commerce (25 September 1997)

27 *Daily Telegraph* (10 October 1997)

28 *Sunday Times* (15 June 1997)

29 *Scotsman* (19 December 1997)

30 *Sunday Mail* (30 March 1997)

31 http://www.isdd.co.uk/trends/activities2/htm

32 Grampian's Chief Constable Dr Ian Oliver quoted in *The People* (22 June 1997)

33 *Yorkshire Post* (23 June 1997) Channel 5 survey

34 *Business Worlds* (22 July 1997)

35 *Bangkok Post* (18 January 1988) and *Advertiser* (Adelaide) (23 March 1998)

36 *The Lawyer* (22 July 1997)

37 *Salt Lake Tribune*, Utah (18 January 1998)

38 *Toronto Globe and Mail* (9 April 1998)

39 *Crain's Cleveland Business* (7 April 1997)

40 *Columbus-Ledger Enquirer* (8 February 1997) and *PR Newswire* SmithKline Beecham data (30 January 1997)

41 Substance Abuse and Mental Health Services Administration, *Drug Use Among US Workers: Prevalence and Trends by Occupation and Industry Categories* (Rockville, Md.: US Department of Health and Human Services, May 1996)

42 *Journal of Clinical Epidemiology* (6 February 1998) quoted in *Daily Telegraph*

43 *PR Newswire* SmithKline Beecham press release (8 April 1998)
44 *Miami Herald* (8 April 1988)
45 *Scotsman* (12 March 1998)
46 UK Government press release (25 March 1998) – actual positive tests fell 2.8 per cent for cannabis and 1.4 per cent for opiates from 1993 to 1997
47 *Salt Lake Tribune*, Utah (18 January 1998)
48 *PR Presswire,* Substance Abuse Technologies (26 March 1997)
49 *Transport and the Regions,* Department of the Environment press release (11 February 1998)
50 *Sunday Mail* (Adelaide) (8 February 1998)
51 *Crain's Chicago Business* (9 March 1998)
52 Ibid.

Chapter 9 Treatment Works

1 NCJR web-site – US Federal Government
2 Substance Abuse and Mental Health Services Administration, *The Need for Delivery of Drug Abuse Services* (Rockville, Md.: US Department of Health and Human Services, 1995)
3 *Modelling the Demand for Cocaine* (Rand Corporation)
4 NDATUS survey 1996
5 ibid.
6 National Treatment Improvement Evaluation Study (NTIES) of 4,411 clients in US 1996
7 D. R. Gerstein, R. A. Johnson, H. J. Harwood, D. Fountain, N. Suter and K. Malloy, *Evaluating Recovery Services: The California Drug and Alcohol Treatment Assessment* (CALDATA) (Sacramento, Calif.: California Department of Alcohol and Drug Programs, 1994)
8 Centre for Substance Abuse Treatment, *The National Treatment Improvement Evaluation Study, Preliminary Report: The Persistent Effects of Substance Abuse Treatment – One Year Later* (Rockville, Md.: US Department of Health and Human Services, September 1996)

9   *Economist* (24 May 1997)
10 American Correctional Association 1994
11 Secular Organisations for Sobriety (SOS)
12 'Efforts to quit smoking among persons with a history of alcohol problems – 1995–6', *Morbidity and Mortality Weekly Report* (5 December 1997)
13 My visit took place before the recent change in attitudes with drug testing
14 Personal communication
15 *Socio-economic Evaluations of Addictions Treatment* (Washington, DC: President's Commission on Model State Drug Laws, December 1993)
16 J. A. Inciardi, *A Corrections-Based Continuum of Effective Drug Abuse Treatment* (Washington, D. C.: US Department of Justice, June 1996)
17 *The Times* (12 March 1998)
18 *Sunday Times* (8 March 1998)

Chapter 10 Legislation and Decriminalisation – The Arguments over Cannabis

1   UCLA Higher Education Research Institute (12 January 1998)
2   Brewers' Society Statistical Handbook 1993
3   Home Office figures 1996
4   ibid.
5   *Daily Telegraph* (1 May 1997)

Conclusions

1   Times Mirror Company (21 January 1998)
2   *Independent on Sunday* quoting findings of Peter Walker, member of Home Office Advisory Council for Misuse of Drugs (29 March 1998)
3   *Daily Telegraph* (17 September 1997)

4   Department of Environment, Transport and the Regions press release (11 February 1998)

5   ibid.

6   *Herald Sun* (19 February 1998)

7   PRIDE survey of 141,077 students 18 October 1997

8   ibid.

9   ibid. Similar links between strong Christian faith and lower drug taking was found in the UK – *Drug and Alcohol Dependency* 46 (1997), 9–17

10   ACDE, affiliate of Phoenix House

11   Anne Johnson et al., *Sexual Attitudes and Lifestyles* (Blackwell Scientific Publications 1994)

Index